THE APOCALYPSE IN ENGLAND

STUDIES IN LITERATURE AND RELIGION

General Editor: David Jasper, Director of the Centre for the Study of
Literature and Theology, University of Glasgow

Studies in Literature and Religion is a series of interdisciplinary titles, both
monographs and essays, concerned with matters of literature, art and
textuality within religious traditions founded upon texts and textual
study. In a variety of ways they are concerned with the fundamental
issues of the imagination, literary perceptions and theory, and an
understanding of poetics for theology and religious studies.

Published titles include:

David Scott Arnold
LIMINAL READINGS
Forms of Otherness in Melville, Joyce and Murdoch

John D. Barbour
THE CONSCIENCE OF THE AUTOBIOGRAPHER
Ethical and Religious Dimensions of Autobiography

Tibor Fabiny
THE LION AND THE LAMB
Figuralism and Fulfilment in the Bible, Art and Literature

Max Harris
THEATRE AND INCARNATION

David Jasper (*editor*)
POSTMODERNISM, LITERATURE AND THE FUTURE OF THEOLOGY
TRANSLATING RELIGIOUS TEXTS
READINGS IN THE CANON OF SCRIPTURE
Written for Our Learning

Ann Loades and Michael McLain (*editors*)
HERMENEUTICS, THE BIBLE AND LITERARY CRITICISM

Irena S. M. Makarushka
RELIGIOUS IMAGINATION AND
LANGUAGE IN EMERSON AND NIETZSCHE

Kevin Mills
JUSTIFYING LANGUAGE
Paul and Contemporary Literary Theory

Linda Munk
THE TRIVIAL SUBLIME

George Pattison
KIERKEGAARD: THE AESTHETIC AND THE RELIGIOUS

The Apocalypse in England

Revelation Unravelling, 1700–1834

Christopher Burdon

First published in Great Britain 1997 by
MACMILLAN PRESS LTD
Houndmills, Basingstoke, Hampshire RG21 6XS and London
Companies and representatives throughout the world

A catalogue record for this book is available from the British Library.

ISBN 0–333–65946–5

First published in the United States of America 1997 by
ST. MARTIN'S PRESS, INC.,
Scholarly and Reference Division,
175 Fifth Avenue, New York, N.Y. 10010

ISBN 0–312–16542–0

Library of Congress Cataloging-in-Publication Data
Burdon, Christopher.
The Apocalypse in England : Revelation unravelling, 1700–1834 /
Christopher Burdon.
p.   cm. — (Studies in literature and religion)
Includes bibliographical references (p.   ) and index.
ISBN 0–312–16542–0 (cloth)
1. Bible. N.T. Revelation—Criticism, interpretation, etc.–
–England—History—18th century.   2. Bible. N.T. Revelation–
–Criticism, interpretation, etc.—England—History—19th century.
3. Bible. N.T. Revelation—In literature.   4. Bible. N.T.
Revelation—Influence.   5. English poetry—18th century.   6. English
poetry—19th century.   I. Title.   II. Series.
BS2825.2.B86   1997
228'.06'0942—dc20   96–34795
                                                              CIP

This book is printed on paper suitable for recycling and made from fully managed and sustained forest sources.

10   9   8   7   6   5   4   3   2   1
06   05   04   03   02   01   00   99   98   97

Printed and bound in Great Britain by
Antony Rowe Ltd, Chippenham, Wiltshire

For Rosemary

Contents

List of Illustrations   ix
Preface   xi
List of Abbreviations   xiii

Introduction   1

1 A Book Resisting Interpretation   5
   Apocalypse, Prophecy, Allegory and Midrash   8
   Telling, Seeing, Hearing and Writing   16

2 Apocalypse and Reason   31
   Providence   39
   Chronology   48
   'Usefulness'   54
   Purity   60

3 Prophecy and Poetry   67
   'The Uncertain Continuance of Reason'   67
   The Reasons of the Heart   74
   The Language of the Spirit   80

4 Revelation and Revolution   90
   Proof by Apocalypse   96
   The Dawning Millennium   105
   The Rhetoric of Patmos   119
   The Collapse of Interpretation   128

5 Coleridge and the Limits of Interpretation   134
   Wordsworth and the Displacement of Apocalypse   136
   Eichhorn and Prophetic History   143
   Irving and the Religion of Ideas   152
   The Spirituality of Hades   160
   Prometheus Bound   168

Contents

6 Rewriting Apocalypse: Shelley and Blake   **174**
     Prometheus and the Death of God   175
     Prophecy and State Religion   180
     Revelation Reversed   193
     The Books of Fire   200

7 The Half-Unravelled Web   **209**

Notes and References   219
Select Bibliography   237
Index   245

List of Illustrations

1   William Blake, 'The Angel of Revelation'

2   Blake, *America*, plate 8

3   Blake, *America*, plate 10

4   Blake, *Europe*, plate 1

5   Blake, *Europe*, plate 15

6   Blake, *Jerusalem*, plate 22

7   Blake, *The Book of Urizen*, plate 1

8   Dürer, *The Woman and the Dragon*

9   Dürer, *The Battle with the Dragon*

10 Joseph Mede's synchronisms (from *Clavis Apocalyptica*, 1833 edition)

11 William Whiston's chart of apocalyptic history (*Essay on Revelation*, 1706)

Preface

Though this book follows a mainly historical outline, the impetus for it is more a theological or philosophical one. I have long wanted to test whether religious language can have 'meaning', that is, whether hermeneutics is still possible. Choosing the extreme case of the Apocalypse may seem something of a self-punishment, involving the risk of my joining the abnormally large number of interpreters of Revelation who are recorded as becoming deranged.

I am indebted to my supervisors at Glasgow, David Jasper and Stephen Prickett, for preserving me from such derangement and for their generosity of time and persistent questioning. I also discussed earlier drafts of parts of the book with Thomas Altizer, Richard Bauckham and Joel Marcus, all of whose comments have been helpful. Parts of Chapter 6 were presented at the 'William Blake 1794–1994' conference at Twickenham and parts of the last two chapters at the 'Dissent and Marginality' conference on literature and religion in Glasgow, both in 1994; subsequent discussion in each case helped me clarify several points. So did diverse conversations with Robert Carroll, Michael Ferber, Anne Marie Perkins, Brent Plate, Catherine Raine, Sheila Spector and Kiyoshi Tsuchiya.

The award of a Glasgow University postgraduate scholarship has been a valuable support. I am grateful also to the staff of the libraries that have coped with obscure requests: the British Library, Cambridge University Library, Dr Williams's Library, Essex County Library, Glasgow University Library, King's College Library Cambridge, and the National Library of Scotland. The hospitality of Alison Chapman and Andrew Lynn has been much appreciated, as has the kindness of many at Holy Cross Episcopal Church, Knightswood. Above all, I thank Rosemary, Sara, Eleanor and Jessica for their patience with my frequent absences of body and mind.

The bibliography lists all writings from the period 1700–1834 that I have consulted, together with some of the more important ones from other periods. Quotations from the Bible are normally from the New Revised Standard Version. Quotations from Blake are from David Erdman's edition, references to the engraved books being to plate and line number. Translations from Latin, French and German are my own, unless otherwise indicated.

CHRISTOPHER BURDON

List of Abbreviations

A	Blake, *America: A Prophecy*.
AERTL	*The Apocalypse in English Renaissance Thought and Literature*, ed. C. A. Patrides and J. Wittreich (Manchester 1984).
ANCL	*Ante-Nicene Christian Library* (Edinburgh 1868–70).
AR	Coleridge, *Aids to Reflection* (in CC 9).
BCE	*Before Christian era.*
BE	*The Complete Poetry and Prose of William Blake*, ed. David V. Erdman, rev. edn (New York 1988).
BJRL	*Bulletin of the John Rylands Library.*
BL	Coleridge, *Biographia Literaria* (in CC 7).
BU	Blake, *The Book of Urizen*.
BVFD	*Blake's Visionary Forms Dramatic*, ed. David V. Erdman and J. E. Grant (Princeton, NJ 1970).
C&S	Coleridge, *On the Constitution of the Church and State* (in CC 10).
CBQ	*Catholic Biblical Quarterly.*
CC	*Collected Works of Samuel Taylor Coleridge*, Bollingen Series LXXV (Princeton, NJ 1971–).
CE	*Christian era.*
CIS	Coleridge, *Confessions of an Inquiring Spirit*, ed. H. St J. Hart (London 1956).
CL	*Collected Letters of Samuel Taylor Coleridge*, ed. E. L. Griggs, 6 vols (Oxford 1956–71).
CM	Coleridge, *Marginalia* (in CC 12).
CN	*Collected Notebooks of Samuel Taylor Coleridge*, ed. Kathleen Coburn, 4 vols (London 1957–): references are to volume and note numbers.
CP	Coleridge, *Poems*, ed. John Beer (London 1986).
DNB	*Dictionary of National Biography.*
E	Blake, *Europe: A Prophecy*.
E&D	*Enlightenment and Dissent.*
ET	*English translation.*

Exp T	*Expository Times.*
FR	Blake, *The French Revolution.*
FZ	Blake, *Vala or the Four Zoas.*
H.E.	Eusebius of Caesarea, *Ecclesiastical History.*
Int.	*Interpretation.*
J	Blake, *Jerusalem.*
JBL	*Journal of Biblical Literature.*
JHI	*Journal of the History of Ideas.*
JSOT	*Journal for the Study of the Old Testament.*
L&T	*Literature and Theology.*
LPR	Coleridge, *Lectures on Politics and Religion* (in CC 1).
LS	Coleridge, *Lay Sermons* (in CC 6).
M	Blake, *Milton.*
MHH	Blake, *The Marriage of Heaven and Hell.*
NB	Coleridge, Notebooks (British Library Add. MSS 47,528–47,550).
Nov T	*Novum Testamentum.*
NTS	*New Testament Studies.*
PU	Shelley, *Prometheus Unbound* (in *SPP*, pp. 136–210).
RER	*Revolution and English Romanticism,* ed. K. Hanley and R. Selden (Hemel Hempstead 1990).
RIW	*Revolution in Writing: British Literary Responses to the French Revolution,* ed. Kelvin Everest (Milton Keynes 1991).
SE	Blake, *Songs of Experience.*
SEL	*Studies in English Literature.*
S in R	*Studies in Romanticism.*
SPP	*Shelley's Poetry and Prose,* ed. Donald H. Reiman and Sharon B. Powers (New York 1977).
TT	Coleridge, *Table Talk* (in CC 14).
Vig. Chr.	*Vigiliae Christianae.*
WBK	*William Blake: Essays in Honour of Sir Geoffrey Keynes,* ed. Morton D. Paley and Michael Phillips (Oxford 1973).
YES	*Yearbook of English Studies.*

Introduction

In 1816 there appeared – 'as a psychological curiosity' – a poetic fragment that claimed to preserve an interrupted visionary experience from nineteen years earlier. 'Kubla Khan, Or, A Vision in a Dream' is fraught with the loss of vision as much as with vision's reality; it is concerned with distancing as much as with proclamation. Whatever the actual origins of the fragment, Coleridge's nostalgic but still zestful 'Could I revive within me' epitomises a crisis not just of poetic creation but of religious authority. For the biblical and Christian tradition of which Coleridge was setting himself up as apologist rested and still rests more than most rational believers would wish on visions and on dreams.

It was not long after the publication of *Kubla Khan* that Keats began to recast his own unfinished epic of Hyperion as 'A Dream', opening it with both an affirmation of human visionary powers and a suspicion of their veracity and effects:

> Fanatics have their dreams, wherewith they weave
> A paradise for a sect, the savage too
> From forth the loftiest fashion of his sleep
> Guesses at Heaven ...
> ... Poesy alone can tell her dreams,
> With the fine spell of words alone can save
> Imagination from the sable charm
> And dumb enchantment. Who alive can say,
> 'Thou art no Poet – mayst not tell thy dreams'?
> ... Whether the dream now purposed to rehearse
> Be Poet's or Fanatic's will be known
> When this warm scribe my hand is in the grave.[1]

There can be dispute over the status, poetical or fanatical, not only of the dreams but also of their interpreters. In unravelling the fine spell of words are the poets and interpreters hijacking the undoubted power of dream for their fanatical or ideological purposes,

1

or are they revealing a visionary core? Or again, does the unravelling lead to a realisation that there is *no* core and no purpose, and
could this not instigate an even more dangerous form of madness
than the fanatic weaving his paradise for a sect?

Perhaps the key question raised by and about the persistence of
religion is that of apocalypse: if the veil cast by ordinary vision
could only be removed, could humanity then discover an ultimate
reality? The possibility of some such discovery underlies the claims
perennially made in religious experience and literature to *extraordinary* vision. In otherwise diverse traditions, visions that open
up other worlds or at least new perspectives on the familiar world
are presented as unveilings or 'apocalypses'. The Bible, for instance,
is full of visions and dreams – Isaiah and Daniel, Jacob and Peter,
the two Josephs – and the Christian canon is brought to a close by
the most vivid series of visions making the most extreme claims to
authority. Can such vision and authority, such claims to unveiling,
be tolerated by the mind or religious tradition that tries to think
critically and theologically? Can a reader genuinely expose herself
to such a text without finding her logical faculties distorted, or was
Robert South right long ago in quipping that the Book of Revelation
'either finds a man mad or makes him so'?

In its unfinished attempt to unravel that series of visions the
Christian tradition has exemplified the religious tension between
apocalypse and reason, or between two different senses of 'light'.
The search for rational purity associated with the 'Enlightenment'
would seem to exclude the concern for inspiration and inward
vision associated with 'Romanticism'. Yet there is a conjunction of
the two movements – a conjunction not just in historical contin-
gency, nor, say, in the thought of Coleridge or Kant, but more
tangibly in the French Revolution, which was both a fruit of
Enlightenment and a catalyst of Romanticism. The account that
follows is centred on that historical episode in the belief that
English readings of and responses to Revelation then may have
something to say at the end of this millennium, when the tension
of apocalypse and reason is as strong and as urgent as at any time
in between.

There have been several broad surveys of the history of the
book's interpretation, such as those in the older commentaries by
Moses Stuart, E. B. Elliott, Willhelm Bousset, I. T. Beckwith and
R. H. Charles; bibliographies are also provided by Otto Böcher (of
works on the Apocalypse since 1700) and by C. A. Patrides and

Joseph Wittreich (focusing mainly on works written in England since the Renaissance).[2] More recently, Frederick van der Meer has provided an enthusiastic treatment of the book's interpretation in visual art up to the seventeenth century, and Arthur Wainwright has conducted a wide-ranging thematic investigation of scholarly, theological, political and artistic responses to the book over 1800 years.[3] With regard to specifically British interpretation, detailed expositions of earlier periods have been made by Richard Bauckham and Katharine Firth, while David Brady has made a very thorough study of one particular area of exegesis (that of the number of the Beast).[4] The place of the seemingly irrational Apocalypse in the self-understanding, theology of providence and philosophy of history of English Christians of the eighteenth century has not gone unnoticed, as can be seen from the researches of Clarke Garrett and J. F. C. Harrison into both popular and more elitist 'prophetic' movements of the period.[5] There have also been fascinating glimpses of its place in the history of ideas in books by E. L. Tuveson, Elinor Shaffer and W. H. Oliver, focusing respectively on the contribution of 'prophetic' English exegesis and biblical teleology to progressivist thought, on the relationship between 'higher criticism' of the Bible, Romantic poetry and the figure of John of Patmos, and on the persistence of millenarianism in the early nineteenth century.[6] Nor have scholars neglected the influence of the Bible and the claims to continuing apocalypse in English Romantic poetry.[7]

Yet none of these studies covering the period after 1700 concentrates specifically on the Book of Revelation, nor does any of them relate the reading and rewriting of the Apocalypse in the time of the French Revolution and Romantic movement to the apocalyptic imagination and the crisis of interpretation of the twentieth century. This is what I attempt in the survey contained in the following chapters, covering the period from the beginning of the eighteenth century to the death of Coleridge. I have concentrated the focus on England, with occasional forays into Scotland, Ireland, Wales and Germany. There are also some omissions: for instance I say little about popular millenarianism, very little about Keats or Gothic novels, and less than I would have wished about Shelley. Some of these omissions are because the subjects have already received close study and some because I wanted to concentrate on readings of *the* Apocalypse rather than on broader trends that might be termed 'apocalyptic'.

In looking at the book's extraordinary resilience to its use – first in the service of reason and enlightenment (Chapter 2), then in that of poetry and evangelism (Chapter 3) and then in that of politics both radical and conservative (Chapter 4) – I hope to amplify the thesis of the first chapter that this is a text that both demands and resists interpretation. My contention is that the main subjects of my fifth and sixth chapters, Coleridge and Blake, were both aware of this, though they responded differently – Coleridge reaching the limits of interpretation and Blake overleaping them. The seventh chapter supplies rather less of a climax or conclusion than does the seventh trumpet of the Apocalypse, but I hope it clarifies both the subversive and the conservative effects of that book and establishes that what Jacques Derrida calls the 'apocalyptic tone' is a crucial element of religious rhetoric.

1
A Book Resisting Interpretation

The Book of Revelation was seen by D. H. Lawrence – to his disgust – as the most influential of the whole Bible. Haunted by memories of its vengeful and bloody images propagated in the grim chapels of his boyhood, not long before his death he tried to exorcise what he saw as its baleful grip on the psyche of the Christian world by writing *Apocalypse*. Here is Lawrence at his most pagan and Nietzschean, the author of *The Plumed Serpent*, writing with anti-Semitic and misogynist undercurrents about this 'book of thwarted power-worship'. He sees its last-minute entry into the New Testament – and hence its hold over the Western world and particularly over 'the masses' – as that of a Judas: with its treacherous kiss, this literary incarnation of the vulgar, weak, envious, collective, democratic spirit slinks back to overturn the aristocratic individualism of Jesus. 'Revelation had to be included in the New Testament, to give the death kiss to the Gospels.'[1]

If there is any basis in Lawrence's polemic, then this is a strange destiny for a book that almost certainly began as a witness against Empire. From the birth of 'Christendom' after the conversion of Constantine the once subversive text becomes a sacred writing of the new religio-political power and with its strong mythical appeal can easily form the dominant symbolic universe, being converted into 'totalitarian kitsch'.[2] Biblical scholars since patristic times have often resisted such popular or imperial developments; but what force has clerkly scepticism against the lurid images and prophecies of apocalypse? Indeed it is a modern representative of clerkly scepticism, Frank Kermode, who sees a *trahison des clercs* arising from the connection between apocalypse and fascism. Referring to Yeats, to the declared fascists Pound and Wyndham Lewis, and to Eliot the 'poet of apocalypse', he notes that 'the fictions of modernist literature were revolutionary, new', yet clearly 'related to others, which helped to shape the disastrous history of our time. Fictions,

5

notably the fiction of apocalypse, turn easily into myths; people will live by that which was designed only to know by.'[3] And much more prominent than literary modernism is a social appropriation of apocalypse that has long flourished: the fringe of Christian culture that Lawrence hated in the chapels of the Midlands and Norman Cohn vividly outlined in his study of medieval messianism.[4] The best-selling American book of non-fiction in the 1970s – with 28 million copies in print in 15 years – was Hal Lindsey's *The Late Great Planet Earth*, with its scenario of ten-nation conspiracies and Roman dictators based on a literal interpretation of Daniel and Revelation; and it was this mentality that enthralled Ronald Reagan.[5]

One may have some sympathy for the orthodox Christian interpreter trying to steer a course between this fanatical irrationalism and the other fringe of pagan or psychoanalytic deconstruction. And a more ancient threat hangs over all who try to interpret the Apocalypse:

> I warn everyone who hears the words of the prophecy of this book: if anyone adds to them, God will add to that person the plagues described in this book; if anyone takes away from the words of the book of this prophecy, God will take away that person's share in the tree of life and in the holy city, which are described in this book (Rev 22:18f.)

What interpretation can avoid sifting and judging, adding and taking away? Is it fanciful to see the way that 'the book of this prophecy' both demands and confounds interpretation as the operation of its closing anathema? Jesus is identified as 'the Word of God' and is most typically seen in this book as 'the Lamb', in the closest possible proximity to the One seated on the throne; as in the fourth gospel, his presence and his words are the perfect representation of the divine. Therefore, whether his name in the title is read as a subjective or an objective genitive ('revelation of Jesus Christ' or 'revelation given by Jesus Christ'), the book that follows assumes the highest imaginable authority, finality and comprehensiveness. Its author – or better, scribe – has seen the ultimate and vouches for the truth of his vision, with blessings pronounced on those who read and hear and guard his book, which is, as it were, an entire scripture in itself. All that came before, even in the words of the prophets to which John constantly alludes, was veiled; now comes the unveiling.

This unveiling is not merely intellectual or aesthetic. It unleashes action. The Apocalypse is a book whose various readings, from Münster to Waco, have caused violence and madness. From the mouth of its Christ comes a sharp two-edged sword, and there have been times when that sword has been not just figurative. The words of blessing and curse, coming as they do at the very end of the Christian Bible, can be and often have been taken as applying to all that precedes them in the holy mock-leather book, reinforcing the notion of Scripture as infallible Command and handing it over to politicians civil or ecclesiastical as divine validation of their authority. So that, far from being a subversive Judas, the Apocalypse would seem to be the ultimate weapon in shoring up the structures of power and orthodoxy and in scattering its ammunition over the whole of the canon. This means that its interpretation is not just a matter of theological or aesthetic curiosity but of ethical urgency. The only responsible way, while this Judas remains in the canon, is to brave the curse and risk one's sanity by attempting to unveil the unveiling.

The Apocalypse is a text that is hard to steer towards the production of systematic doctrine or morality. So it is not surprising that some famous interpreters of the Bible have avoided the book. Luther, with his cavalier attitude towards the canon, omitted it altogether from the first edition of his German Bible, claiming in the 1522 Preface that it was 'neither apostolic nor prophetic ... Christ is neither taught nor known in it' – though he did change his mind in 1530, identifying the Turks with Gog and the Pope with Magog, and translating the book in his 1530 Bible with a much more positive introduction.[6] The Swiss Reformer Zwingli declared it to be 'not a biblical book', while the other two most influential Protestant exegetes, Calvin and Schleiermacher, both wrote extensively on the whole of the New Testament – except the Apocalypse, which they deliberately avoided.[7] In the twentieth century, Bultmann's extensive exegesis and theology of the New Testament practically ignored the book, which he saw as 'a weakly Christianized Judaism'.[8] And in England, during the period I shall be examining more closely, at least four learned commentaries on the New Testament were published that simply stopped (in three cases without explanation) when they reached the end of the Letter of Jude.[9]

It could be that these men refrained from interpretation because they just dismissed the book: perhaps its abuse by political and religious enthusiasts or its irrational claim to visionary experience meant that Revelation had become extra-canonical for them in practical terms. Or did they prefer not to risk the subversion of their theological or ethical systems by exposure to the rhetoric of unveiling? Could it be that they subconsciously feared that the naked divinity that was unveiled on Patmos was mundanely *veiled* in the more manageable propositions of Paul and narratives of the gospels – that they, the expert interpreters, would be found wanting in the face of direct vision? But one could construe their silence more generously and conjecture that they had neither dismissed nor feared the book but rather had tried to interpret it and failed. Daniel Whitby in 1700 admitted as much, when after the Letter of Jude he ended his formal commentary on the New Testament but added 'A Treatise of the True Millennium', which he prefaced by saying,

> Scaliger was pleased to say,… 'Calvin was wise, because he did not write upon the Revelations'. I confess, I do it not for want of Wisdom; that is, because I neither have sufficient Reading, nor Judgment, to discern the Intendment of the Prophecies contained in that Book.[10]

It was, one could suggest, their very possession of 'wisdom' that made the Apocalypse so intractable for Whitby, for Calvin, Schleiermacher and Bultmann, and for numerous interpreters to the present day. For whereas the enthusiastic reader will leap at images in the text and readily give them 'meaning' by transferring them to elements of his own experience, the wise or critical reader tries to compare the text with others, to sift and judge, to add and take away. And so the curse comes into operation: *this* text seems not to fit and actively to disperse whatever categories and expectations the critical reader brings to it. I shall attempt to show that whatever genre one tries to place the book in (even that of 'apocalypse' to which it gives its name) and whatever hermeneutical strategy one tries to adopt, the text persists in destabilising the alert reader.

APOCALYPSE, PROPHECY, ALLEGORY AND MIDRASH

The title of John's book, *apokalypsis Iēsou Christou*, has given its name to a literary genre. But this did not happen until the early nineteenth century, when the distinction between prophecy and apocalyptic was first made and when many early 'apocalypses' were rediscovered. The existence of 'apocalypse' within as well as outwith the biblical canon has been a matter of embarrassment to some Christian scholars, while for those who like precise generic definitions the term (meaning 'unveiling' or 'revelation') has not always been helpful.[11] A working definition of an apocalypse has been agreed by the Society for Biblical Literature (it is 'a genre of revelatory literature with a narrative framework, in which a revelation is mediated by an otherworldly being to a human recipient, disclosing a transcendent reality which is both temporal, insofar as it envisages eschatological salvation, and spatial, insofar as it involves another, supernatural world').[12] Much work has also been done – without reaching any consensus – on the socio-historical origins of apocalypses.[13] But according to Christopher Rowland the essence of Jewish apocalyptic literature lies not in eschatology but in the claim to direct revelation. The nature of such revelation distinguishes the visionary's productions from the more rational world of Wisdom or the more anthropocentric world of prophecy: it is the disclosure of *hidden knowledge*.[14] This knowledge, though usually mediated by an angel to a seer, derives from the Creator himself, and the visionary – like Isaiah in the divine council or Ezekiel seeing the chariot – is being admitted to the thoughts of God. But the knowledge is fragmentary and the books are sealed, awaiting (in their fictional world) the perfect reader who will possess the divine wisdom required to share the vision.

Does the *un*sealed Book of Revelation suggest the same aim or respond to the same kind of reading? Is it best approached as fragments of hidden knowledge? F. D. Mazzaferri makes a thorough case against reading *the* Apocalypse as *an* apocalypse: its eschatology, he says, is transformed by the Christ-event in the past, there is no pseudonymity, and the writer's message is 'conditional, not deterministic'.[15] In other words John is consciously writing as a prophet, modelling his writing in particular on Ezekiel's. Mazzaferri's painstaking argument is vitiated by an insistence on extremely precise divisons between discrete 'genres', but the differences he describes are real ones and demand a different kind of reading and different kinds of expectations from those with which one might approach the hidden knowledge of other apocalypses. The richness of the book's imagery and the dynamism of its visionary–narrative cycles invite rereading and reinterpretation, each one uncovering more layers of meaning and reference without dissolving the whole in extratextual meaning. So the web of allusions that Austin Farrer partly unravelled in *A Rebirth of Images* is probably much more complex than even he could expound.[16] There are fragments, loose ends, riddles, as in other apocalypses; but here they are woven into the whole. Hence the effects that Lawrence deplored and that for others convey the assurance of joy and salvation; hence the powerful sense of closure that has made the book so dangerous – for in the end heaven and earth flee away, all is destined either for destruction or for indwelling by God, and there are no intermediate levels of vision to distance this absolute proclamation. Unlike any other New Testament writing, this is a self-consciously 'scriptural' text conveying divine speech; it is (in David Lawton's words) 'by far the most pretentious book in the Bible, and the most authoritarian'.[17]

The irony is, however, that this authority and impetus to closure occur in a book that, more than any other apocalypse, is open. At the end the scribe or seer is told, 'Do not seal up the words of the prophecy of this book' (Rev 22:10 – a deliberate contrast to Dan 12:4 and similar texts). The simultaneous openness and closure of the book, its combination of riddles, gaps and external reference with the impression of structural and symbolic coherence and of authoritarianism, can be seen as the consequence of the first two 'non-apocalyptic' features that Mazzaferri indicates. The Apocalypse is, first, inescapably Christocentric: the mediator of revelation who is also the object of universal worship is the catalyst of the actions seen in vision, and all derive from an actual event in recent history. Past, present and future are bound together through the exaltation of him who is 'the Alpha and the Omega, the first and the last, the beginning and the end' (22:13); heaven and earth likewise, inviting from the reader (or attempting to coerce from her) submission to the revelation and to the authority of the quasi-divine Revealer.[18] Secondly, and unlike all previous apocalypses, Revelation is not pseudonymous. The seer names himself as one known to his readers, and he dates his revelation (1:9f.). John is presented not as a sage ancient or modern but as a *prophet*, and his book is defined as 'prophecy'.[19] Prophecy is open address; it invites hearing not as an offer of total knowledge but as a call to repentance and right living. And the 'spirit of prophecy' (Rev 19:10) means that, for all its driving to closure and attempts to express total vision, the book is open and strangely vulnerable to the prophetic – or historical or rhetorical – situations in which it is read.

Approaching the book as prophecy rather than as apocalypse or vision in no way lessens its potential authority or authoritarianism. The visionary claims to write what he sees, the prophet what he hears; and the prophet–seer of Revelation saturates his writing with allusions to the classical prophets, whose successor he believes himself to be.[20] John's self-designation as a 'prophet', coupled with the evident pastoral and political references in his book, also mean that the interpreter cannot evade its historical origin as an anti-imperial statement and call to repentance. But although Revelation has been read from the beginning as 'prophecy', that term has covered a wide range of hermeneutical styles. The same 'prophetic' text can be read first as exhortation, secondly as prediction, thirdly as allegory (and sometimes as a mixture of two or more of these elements). What distinguishes any such reading from approach to the text as apocalypse or simply as narrative is that the words or symbols are held to have clear *reference* to a world outside the text: in the first case to the actions urged by the prophetic word, in the second to future events, in the third to historical or spiritual or noetic realities.

This veering between literal, moral and allegorical styles of 'prophetic' interpretation can be seen in the first four Christian centuries. For the second-century writers Justin, Irenaeus and Tertullian, the Apocalypse contains literal prediction of a future millennium, which entails the end of the Empire and provides ammunition against the spiritualising religion of the gnostics.[21] In contrast, for the third-century Origen – the early Church's most prolific and versatile interpreter – the ultimate subjects of the Bible and therefore the ultimate realities are not historical or eschatological events but God, the Logos and the soul. So when he writes on Revelation, as on the apocalyptic passages of the gospels, the eschatological conflict becomes an intellectual one: the white horse of Rev 19, whose rider is called 'the Word of God', is an allegory of the voices that communicate the revelation of the Logos, the war he wages is a war against unreason, the rider's eyes like flames of fire uncover and destroy material thoughts.[22] Origen's disciple, Dionysius of Alexandria, equally resisting literal interpretation, is agnostic about the authorship and authority of a book with such 'barbarous idioms' and 'solecisms'.[23] But an Origenistic forsaking of futuristic eschatology need not mean that the images of Revelation and the prophets apply only to spiritual or noetic realities: they can also be released to attach themselves to events in the history of the

church and the world, as in Eusebius's sermon for the dedication of
the basilica at Tyre, where he sees Old Testament typology pointing
not just towards Christ but to the triumph and piety of Constantine,
to the building he is preaching in and to Bishop Paulinus, a new
Zerubbabel in 'a new and far goodlier Jerusalem'.[24]

Something similar happens in the interpretation of the Donatist
exegete Tyconius (died c. 390), who had considerable influence on
Augustine. Tyconius's commentary on Revelation survives only in
fragments, but it is clear that (in Paula Fredriksen's words)
'Tyconius's reading of Scripture ... emphasized the historical realization of prophecy while denying the sort of social and temporal
transparency to the text which would allow for a millenarian interpretation'.[25] The sixth chapter of his surviving *Liber Regularum (De
recapitulatione)* includes the judgement that Jesus' warning about
the desolating sacrilege (Mt 24:15f.) 'is happening now in Africa',
presumably in conjunction with the hostility between Donatists
and Catholics.[26] Yet this statement is made in the context of a thorough assessment of the correct way to apply the allegorical statements of the Bible (which for Tyconius is almost its entire text) – an
attempt to bring some order and method to Origenistic allegorising.
Allegory enables a synchronic reading of the Bible, but it need not –
as it practically did for Origen – destroy the sense of history. The
same is true for Augustine, who continued to use the allegorical
method in exegesis yet in his later writings (especially in *The City of
God*, books 15–20) sees the biblical types as forming a huge historical drama of salvation. The binding of the devil and the Millennium
are the present era of the Church, the first resurrection (a resurrection of the soul) has already taken place; yet Augustine avoids a
simplistic Eusebian triumphalism by applying these figures to the
invisible Church of the elect, and the future reference still remains
in his much more literal interpretation of the second resurrection
and final judgement.[27]

For almost all the Fathers, Scripture is oracular in nature: it is
divine speech, with no redundancy. Moreover, all its books in both
Testaments form a unity: there is in fact only one book, one word of
God (which Origen identifies with the sealed book of Rev 5, the
writing on the outside symbolising the literal sense, that on the
inside the spiritual).[28] And thirdly, the images and narratives of
scripture are referential: the reference is to a reality, whether material or spiritual, outside the text. Not only prophecy and apocalyptic
but all the Bible is filled with darkness, says Origen, asking 'who,

on reading the revelations made to John, could fail to be amazed at
the deep obscurity of the unspeakable mysteries contained therein,
which are evident even to him who does not understand what is
written?'[29] For enlightenment, the 'key of knowledge' of Luke 11:52
is needed, he says; and Origen is fairly confident that he possesses
that key. The same images of keys and light occur in the introduction to the 'book of rules' for interpretation by Origen's more
systematic follower Tyconius:

> I considered it necessary to write a book of rules (*libellum regu-
> larum*) and so to fashion keys and lamps, as it were, to the secrets
> of the law (*secretorum legis veluti claves et luminaria fabricare*). For
> there are certain mystic rules which obtain in the inner recesses
> of the entire law and keep the rich treasures of the truth hidden
> from some people. But if the sense of these rules is accepted
> without ill will, as we impart it, whatever is closed will be
> opened and whatever is dark will be illuminated; and anyone who
> walks the vast forest of prophecy (*prophetiae immensam silvam
> perambulans*) guided by these rules, as by pathways of light, will
> be kept from straying into error.[30]

But use of Tyconius's *regulae mysticae* need not lead to a wooden
use of allegory any more than Origen's looser method does; rather,
allegory enables alluring glimpses through the vast intertextual
forest and into the open space of noumenal reality beyond it.

Allegory as used by the Fathers is usually much more versatile
than is implied by the Romantic distinction between allegory and
symbol or by the modern theological distinction between allegory
and typology. It is a way – for many of them the only way – of
combining close attention to both the detail and the totality of the
biblical text with an imaginative freedom of response and an involvement with the concerns of the interpreter and his community;
a way also of finding in texts that did not lend themselves to a typo-
logical or diachronic meaning a lively, practical and self-renewing
way into religious and ethical living, whether in the context of the
life of the soul or in response to the fall of Empire. So allegory can be
seen, with Gerald Bruns, as 'a function of spiritual life rather than a
technique of reading: it is a type of contemplation that is practised in
front of or in the light of a traditional text'.[31]

Here, though, is precisely the problem. The allegoriser's spiritual
yearning and his stance 'in front of' rather than within the text

drive him to identify what Augustine called the *res* and Origen the *pragma* of the text as something only obliquely related to it. There is, in Jon Whitman's words, 'a subversive element in the very technique of allegory, a tendency to disrupt philosophic and rhetorical norms that finally turns allegory even against itself'.[32] This wandering movement may be highly productive of meaning as of desire. What it does not do is root its object in the text or divine speech with the directness and immediacy that the prophet claims to convey. Just as literal prophetic meaning is dispersed by the failure of events to correspond to their predictions, allegorical prophetic meaning is dispersed by the constant slippage of reference. A part of the Bible like Revelation, with its already rich pattern of allusions and its creation of a new symbolic world, may seem to invite such interpretation. In fact, however, it is precisely the structural complexity and closure of the book that the method cannot cope with: elements are moved from their narrative and scriptural context to correspond to or hint at other levels of signification, whether metaphysical or psychological, in a process of endless concatenation (Origen's *heirmos tōn pneumatikōn*). In the end the text becomes simply pre-text, the prophecy swallowed up by its supposed fulfilments or references; the chain has neither beginning nor end, and the coherence sought through prophetic verbal association is as elusive as that sought through apocalyptic vision.

Concatenation as a method of reading is not confined to allegory. Origen's *heirmos* is related to the midrashic *harijah* or stringing together of canonical texts developed by the rabbis – indeed he deliberately studied their hermeneutical method. *Midrash* is, however, to be distinguished from the allegorical method, both in the aims it espouses and in the kind of reading it facilitates. For midrashic interpretation, according to Daniel Boyarin,

> the correspondences are not between things seen and their hidden or inner meanings, but between texts and the historical contexts in which they were produced or to which they apply, or texts and other texts; between signifiers and signifiers, not between signifiers and signified.[33]

Here is a way of reading that combines the freedom of prophetic allegory with constant return to the text: the rabbis' joy is in inhabiting the scriptural world without recourse to metaphysical grounding. It is natural to ask whether it is appropriate to read the

Apocalypse midrashically, or indeed to read it as being itself midrash on the Old Testament, taking up suggestions from Austin Farrer, who asserted in his commentary that 'the Seer meditated the scriptural matter into life', treating it 'rather as quarries than as models': 'like the rabbinic preacher of his time, he seeks new inspiration by drawing old texts into fresh combinations'.[34]

Midrash is not a literary genre but a way of relating readers or hearers to a canonical text. It attempts to 'unlock' the often obscure words of the Bible, but to do so not out of curiosity or aesthetic appreciation but to enable right living in the present, working on the assumption that the Torah (written and oral) is the address of Yahweh himself.[35] In unlocking it the rabbis are sometimes described as 'playing' with the text, though it must be stressed that this is serious, holy play. So, for instance, a fragment of midrash on Exodus 15:1 (*Exodus Rabba* XXIII.7) weaves around the text 'Then sang Moses' echoes of the psalms and prophets, close textual analysis, comments by rabbis, and parables. One could compare the passage to Revelation 15, where the allusions to Exodus are pervasive: as well as the sea and the song of Moses, there are the mentions of plagues, conquest, smoke (as on Sinai) and the tabernacle, with echoes too from Deuteronomy 32, Psalms 111 and 86, Jeremiah 10 and 16 and Ezekiel 9. Like the midrash, this is consciously and deliberately intertextual, inviting the reader to saturate her mind with images from other parts of the Bible. But even if the scriptural allusions actually constitute the material of this chapter and of most of the Apocalypse, they are still not citations and they are not presented as the subject of exegesis. Indeed, although the Apocalypse is more drenched in the Hebrew Bible than any other book of the New Testament, it nowhere actually quotes it. The references in *Exodus Rabba* are actual quotations, and, whatever other homiletic aims the writers may have had, the purpose of the whole passage is exegesis of Exodus 15:1 through the medium of Psalm 68; whatever meanderings the 'stringing together' of midrash pursues, it remains true that 'the central feature of a midrashic comment is its *explicit* relationship to the Bible'.[36] From that fixed and authoritative point the midrash branches out with all kinds of loose ends, stories, arguments and discursive comment. The commentary is gentle and often homely, not overwhelming the reader but letting her wander in and out of the discussion and the texts it treats, even making it impossible for her mind *not* to wander. The authoritative text, written in Torah, lies over against the discussion. *Aggada* and *meshalim* are certainly seen as vehicles of divine speech too, as contributing to 'oral Torah', but they do not become part of the discrete scriptural macronarrative.

The Book of Revelation, for all its evident intertextuality, does not assist such gentle, exploratory reading. Its scriptural material is more subtly inwoven, while its structure is more explicit. Above all, unlike any midrash, it forms a macronarrative, and seems even – like Mark's Gospel, perhaps – to be moulding a new scripture out of the old. With this come the claims to vision (over which the rabbis were consistently sceptical) and the urging to climax and closure that are conspicuously absent in midrash. It is not so much a writing of midrash as a writing of scripture intended to be read midrashically. But now the reader is pushed into submission or resistance. However agile the dancing flames of scriptural concatenation, they are being fanned to press him towards one meaning, one choice, one course of action.[37] There is in the Apocalypse an insistent linearity and an insistent God-centredness. Yet ironically none of the traditional religious ways of reading seems to be able to engage fruitfully with this strange text.

TELLING, SEEING, HEARING AND WRITING

The Book of Revelation clearly tells a story or stories. Reading it simply as *narrative* or *myth* would mean refraining from seeking its meaning in elements outside its own text, as is done in different ways by all the 'religious' readings outlined above. Rather, narrative is its own meaning, asking its readers or listeners simply to attend to the story and to let it work subliminally in their mental and social worlds. If translated into reference or moralising, even in such an indirect way as that of midrash, it ceases to be read as narrative.

Can this be true of the Apocalypse? Certainly, both artists and ordinary Christian believers have responded to it as a thrilling story without always attempting to point to its 'meaning'. And professional exegetes too have often spoken of its powerful narrative thrust. In this century, for instance, Ernst Lohmeyer wrote of its 'great epic movement' and Farrer of its 'steady building of climax'.[38] Yet both Lohmeyer and Farrer explore extensively the worlds of scriptural and mythical allusion that form the stuff of this narrative, and it can be asked whether without familiarity with these worlds the undeniable narrative thrust is going to be aimless for the reader. It may be true that all writing is intertextual and all narrative partakes of a deep structure. But for John both intertextuality and structure are deliberate and blatant, suggesting that reading his text is a matter of following clues as well as participating in the dynamics of story: the scriptural allusions and the surface structure are invitations to an *intellectual* unravelling of the narrative.

For instance even a casual reading of the first half of the book will bring awareness of the sevenfold pattern of letters, seals and trumpets, and of the building up towards climax (if not at this stage towards meaning) that this achieves. But as the climax seems to be arriving, the next series is quashed: the seven thunders are to be 'sealed up' (10:4). After interruptions (the eating of the scroll and the episode of the two witnesses) the seventh trumpet finally sounds (11:15), but the shouts of triumph are superseded by a new series of visions whose sequence is incoherent, and the sevenfold pattern is not resumed until chapter 16. The linear narrative is thus a kind of deliberate delusion and the moods of anticipation or fear that it creates are liable to destabilisation by intervening events or references that invite a more investigative interpretation. Again, the juxtaposition of episodes is often puzzling rather than enlightening or encouraging; and the interruption of them, as of the apparent linear narrative, by references to the world outside the text (especially in chapters 2, 3, 13 and 17) pushes the reader into an examination of the text more intellectual and more literary, that is, in a sphere outside the timebound world of oral narration.[39] It may seem more appropriate to the digressive kind of reading that the book encourages to see it as a vision or series of visions that use fragments of narrative just as they use fragments of the Bible. Each fragment of narrative gets dissolved as the book proceeds, until finally the purported macronarrative itself is dissolved in the vision of the new Jerusalem where there is in fact no more story, for nothing happens except worship.

Thus there is a tension at work throughout the book, urging the reader out of the narrative into the story of his or her own life and that of the world and the churches. It is a rhetorical rather than a narrative strategy, a kind of *Verfremdungseffekt*, urging a conscious decision in the 'real' world rather than an enjoyment of the story-world. Since what narration there is is that of a vision, many of the normal ingredients of narrative and myth are absent from the book. There are no actual characters, human, bestial, angelic or divine, only symbols and caricatures; there is a minimum of dialogue; no trace of humour. Something of the darkness and flexibility of narrative is expelled by the authoritative claims to vision and infallibility. In reading it one cannot evade the issue of authorial intention, for here is an author who imposes himself, even if the exact nature of his intention is unclear, even if one may be highly suspicious of it. He writes not a narrative that authenticates itself in the act of reading, but a letter with paranaetic aims.

This letter claims to be more than a communication between one human being and groups of others. For it is introduced as 'revelation of Jesus Christ, which God gave him to show...'; a book whose perplexing 'narrative' begins after the words 'Write what you *see*...' (1:1,11). No fewer than 36 times in his 22 chapters, John writes *kai eidon* ('and I saw'). What he sees is a series of *visions* – visions bizarre, vivid and memorable, from the first sight of the 'one like the Son of Man' to the conclusion in the new Jerusalem. The temporal or narrative axis is disjointed, but the spatial or visual one seems constant: within it the action moves between heaven, earth and the abyss, with the seer receiving revelations focused on each plane, whether he himself is depicted as standing on earth or penetrating the 'open door' into heaven. The visions, filled with colours, jewels, shapes and measurings, are less like a moving picture than 'stills', as Farrer puts it – juxtaposed rather than leading into one another within a coherent narrative. Yet visual motifs run through the book as a whole, associating the various visions: the four creatures, horses, swords, sun and moon, scrolls, and so on. So the book is sometimes described as 'kaleidoscopic', making a powerful religious impression through ceaseless visual impact on the reader, who may be seen using the words as in a dream, with eyes closed, translating them into non-verbal scenarios of the imagination. Can this even be a reason for the eccentric and often ungrammatical Greek in which the Apocalypse is written, that the words are there only to point away from themselves, from the darkness and ambiguity of language into the incontrovertible light of vision, where seeing is believing? Are the artists then the real interpreters of the book, should the reading of the text be simply a way into sharing its visions?

These questions raise the further ones of how far the visions, for all their vividness, actually are coherent, and how far a 'vision' that is recounted (rather than viewed in the way that a picture is) can actually convey the same images or 'meaning' to different readers.

The coherence of the visions becomes less convincing the more one tries to dwell on them visually. In an interesting comment on the Rider on the white horse in Rev 19, Lohmeyer noticed the aporias and non-sequiturs of the text but put his trust in a symbiosis of visual and reflective reading:

> The Rider's robe is white, but dipped in blood; yet no battle has taken place. He is clothed in white, but his name is seen on his thigh; he rides his horse while treading the winepress; nobody knows his name, yet his name is visible everywhere. Each feature seems to contradict the next, yet they are indissolubly joined to each other; for throughout the book, what is seen in the image is bound up with what is believed non-graphically. The image (*Bild*) is given, generally as fulfilment of an Old Testament meaning (*Sinn*), and the seer's interpretation dwells in both together. If this be called allegory, it must be objected that image and meaning are not sharply separated: the former is not the object of seeing alone, the latter not the product of believing alone – rather, the image is viewed as meaning, the meaning as image.[40]

But if this is to be true for reader as well as writer, it can be so only through great familiarity with the Hebrew Bible and at the end of a long process of reflection, at many stages of which it will seem that the bond between image and meaning is far from indissoluble. For with writing that is scriptural as well as visionary, a reading that attempts to dwell visually on the images actually constitutes a distraction – distraction from the multiple correspondences with the Old Testament that rely on verbal echoes, and distraction from the new canonical structure that John is trying to create.

The *appearance* of the colour red, of the cuboid shape of the city, or of the beast rising from the sea, is not what matters. Many of the visions, if examined in detail, are in any case grotesque or unimaginable, as representations of them in figurative art show. For instance Dürer's faithful attempts in his woodcuts to portray the Son of Man seated on a rainbow and holding seven stars, with eyes flaming and sword proceeding from his mouth, or the Lamb in heaven with seven eyes and seven horns, actually produce images evoking curiosity, perhaps ribaldry, but not awe (*see plates 8 and 9*). Literally unimaginable without absurdity are the creatures and elders falling down before the Lamb while still managing to hold on to their harps and bowls of incense (5:8) or the beast with many heads but one mouth (13:2–5). The details are verbal codes, not graphic illustration; if they operate according to any logic it is (in John Sweet's words) one 'more auditory than visual'.[41]

It might be thought that one of the most impossible scenes to represent visually would be that of the fifth trumpet (Rev 9:1), when a star falls from heaven to earth and is given the key to the shaft of the bottomless pit, which the star then opens. Interestingly, a page in the ninth-century Cambrai Apocalypse depicts precisely this, combining it with the preceding scene of the eagle flying in midheaven crying 'Woe, woe, woe!' The eagle is at the top of the picture, placed with the sun in a heaven separated by a sharp line from all that is below. On the next storey down are the seven angels, one blowing his trumpet; and through this storey streams the wake of the falling star, which lies holding its key at the mouth of the pit on the lowest level. The pit's bottomlessness is represented by a flight of steps leading towards the viewer, and beside it are the emerging locusts and the seer himself. The fact that the writer is included in the picture (as he usually is in medieval Apocalypses) is a clear sign that the artist is not attempting to reproduce what John saw but to interpret what he wrote, just as the ordering of the universe on three or four distinct levels shows that this is not a depiction of what might appear before the human eye. The picture has an intellectual rather than a figurative structure. It is literally an adjunct to the text, as is shown even more clearly in the fourteenth-century Hamburg Apocalypse, where the text is intertwined with the illustrations. In other words the medieval representations are emblematic, in strong contrast to Dürer's illusionism. The latter's very skills in perspective, draughtsmanship and composition tempt him to realistic representations of the visions of Revelation, in which the seer is omitted unless he is a participant in the action and in which all the elements are combined in a carefully structured whole without the artifice of different levels of reality. Dürer's Apocalypse woodcuts are impressively original in their 'subjectivity' and 'emancipation from the text', as Karl Schellenberg pointed out.[42] But the result of such originality when put to work on a text so stubbornly and vitally verbal as that of Revelation is in fact doubly wooden. 'Vision' conveyed through earthly perspective is converted into grotesqueness.

A similar contrast between illusionist and emblematic treatments of the Apocalypse can be seen in Romantic visual art, again suggesting that it is the stylised interpretation that is more faithful to the text than the realistic. For instance Benjamin West – using naturalistic colouring and perspective in works such as 'The Destruction of the Old Beast and False Prophet', 'The Son of Man in the midst of Seven Golden Candlesticks' and 'The Beast Riseth Out of the Sea' – preserves the oddity of John's visions, but without the scriptural symbolic universe that provides the hints to their meaning or any new symbolic world that the visions can inhabit. Yet the Revelation pictures of his contemporary William Blake have 'a flat, emblematic composition, all the more convincing for its lack of naturalistic elements'.[43] (*See plate 1*) A similar contrast occurs a generation later, when John Martin comes to produce his massive, literalistic canvases from Revelation, a curiously static kind of academic kitsch when set beside the visionary space of Turner's 'The Angel standing in the Sun'.[44]

This is not just a contrast between plodding artists like West and Martin and innovative ones like Blake and Turner. The first two, both of whom saw their art as a kind of Christian evangelism, read the text of Revelation, it seems, in a lurid and literal way and tried to reproduce its visions in the midst of the known world, asking the viewers of their pictures to imagine the power of God invading it. The religions of the last two were less explicit and doctrinal; but both, in their very different ways, were men who thought and grappled with the symbolic text and scriptural context of Revelation and who realised that it could be expressed visually only by transposition into a style that attacks the viewer rhetorically, asking her to imagine instead a new world. And it is the latter method, attempting to go beyond the visual and emotional response while sitting looser to the details of the text, that does greater justice to the complex rhetorical strategy of the Apocalypse itself. John's text certainly creates visual images; but if they are, so to speak, framed as compositions in the mind (like the pictures of Dürer, West and Martin) they are deprived of their dynamism and intertextuality. Instead – as with the figures in the Hamburg Apocalypse, literally straying outside the frame and mingling with the text within it, or with the extraordinary sharp visions of the right-hand panel of Memling's 'Mystic Marriage of St Catherine' – the images can be used not to invite the reader to admire or feel but to address her intellectually, referring back to other parts of the book, other parts of the Bible and events and fields of decision outside the text.

The ultimate dispersal of vision by text should not in fact surprise, since the revelation begins not with seeing but with *hearing*. In an echo of Ezekiel 3:12 the seer says, 'I was in the spirit on the Lord's day, and I heard behind me a loud voice like a trumpet, saying, "Write in a book what you see..."' (1:10f.) First is the hearing, then the command to write, and only then, after an act of turning round, the seeing. This priority of hearing over seeing is in the tradition of the Hebrew prophets. It may also suggest that the book is seeking, like the prophets, a more interior kind of address to its readers.[45] If such an address is possible, then, after the process of contextualising in scripture and in the world around them, the readers might reach a point of integration or conversion or 'second naïveté', which the 'dispersed' text would then reassemble to support. This raises the possibility of interpreting the Apocalypse as a sort of music, working with the world of scriptural and historical reference but straining beyond it to an interior, non-verbal but still auditory field of communication – or possibly to the related but non-auditory and abstract 'language' of mathematics.

Although the visual symbols are most prominent, there is no lack in the Apocalypse of aural and musical ones. There are the trumpets and the hymns, the harps, thunders and winds, the silence of chapter 8 and the repeated *phōnē megalē* ('great voice'). The structuring, as has often been observed, is at least partly numerological, and could suggest parallels between mathematical and musical form, while the patterns of place and event have led to speculation that these are aids to mnemonic techniques stemming from the book's origin as 'oral enactment'.[46] Do this symbolism and structuring invite a sort of shifting away of all the apocalyptic scenery and textual reference to adumbrate a non-referential, apophatic language, the realm of pure listening or apprehension hinted at in Flaubert's famous simile of human language as 'a cracked kettle on which we beat out tunes for bears to dance to, when all the time we are longing to move the stars to pity', or in John Banville's description of the young Copernicus's 'few notions he had managed to put into words, gross ungainly travesties of the inexpressibly elegant concepts blazing in his brain'?[47] If this is the case, then transcendent meaning could be said to lie not so much in as behind the words or sounds of the text. It is such a deep mathematical simplicity that the late Coleridge feels towards in his reading of the Apocalypse; and interestingly he speaks in the last year of his life of a sense of kinship with Mozart or Beethoven 'when I am at once waiting for, watching, and organically constructing and inwardly constructed by, the *Ideas* – the living Truths, that may be re-excited but cannot be expressed by Words'.[48] Again, George Steiner's argument for the possibility of presence, meaning and transcendence expressed in art hinges above all (if inevitably obliquely) on the experience of music, which is, he claims, 'brimful of meanings which will not translate into logical structures or verbal expression.... Music brings to our daily lives an immediate encounter with a logic of sense other than that of reason'.[49] Is it possible, then, for a verbal text, for the text of the Apocalypse, to be the gateway to this purportedly deeper or more theological level of 'meaning'?

It is natural to look for musical or mathematical analogies in the structure of the book and to see in them a clue to such a reading. Yet the analogies are very hard to sustain. The notoriously complex symbolic-numerological structure that Austin Farrer outlined in *A Rebirth of Images* has not convinced many other people – indeed Farrer himself was agnostic about much of it in his later commentary – and fails to show how its putative pattern would actually work on the psyche without extensive recourse to scriptural texts and calculations. George Caird, also responding to the recapitulative element of the text, spoke of its unity as being 'neither chronological nor arithmetical, but artistic, like that of a musical theme with variations, each variation adding something new to the significance of the whole composition'.[50] But it is very unclear what the 'theme' of the book is according to such an analogy, and unclear too that the structure is as linear and progressive as that musical form suggests. It might be more appropriate to compare the book to a fugue, that is, to a cyclical form where the composer gives the impression of music that is self-generated and self-enclosed, except that Revelation still seems to contain so many loose ends and external references that are hard to fold in fugally; or to the more dialectical sonata form, where one theme succeeds and contends with another, except that the whole development of the book leads to conquest, not synthesis.

If quasi-narrative texts can bear any analogy with musical forms, then it seems that classical and baroque ones are unhelpful in the case of the Apocalypse, which is perhaps attempting to use language in a less formal and more elemental or Romantic way.[51] A pentecostal way, perhaps, straining beyond the reason-bound structures of grammar, rather as music like Beethoven's late quartets or the end of Mahler's *Das Lied von der Erde* strain beyond the

time-bound patterns of rhythm towards the transcendence of time
and of discursive reason. So the narrative of Revelation urges the
reader forward with its cycles of seven, each unable to resolve itself
with a cadence; and interrupting the tidal surge are strange delays,
interludes and hymns (such as the sealing in chapter 7, the seven
thunders of 10:3f., and the eagle's cry of 8:13), while the refrain that
'the time is near' foreshadows the climaxes of chapters 19 and 20
that seem actually to lead to the dissolution of time in the defined
space of the holy city. This straining within *chronos* for the overcoming of *chronos* is what Ernst Bloch, in *Das Prinzip Hoffnung* and in
his 1925 essay 'On the mathematical and dialectical character in
music', described as the 'utopian' power in music, its 'apocalyptic
momentum', a deep but still human yearning for the Other.[52]

Yet for all its surging to cadence and closure, the Apocalypse
considered as an attempt at supraverbal 'music' bears too many
textual and historical scars to lift the reader or listener out of the
world of *chronos*, however much that world is questioned by it. The
text resists its spiritualisation into some ethereal 'grammar' or
'geometry' and insists on returning its reader into the rhetoric and
conflict of the material world. Insofar as it provides Bloch's 'flash of
eternity' or 'ontology of music', this comes as promise, not
fulfilment, as an alternative structuring of reality that destabilises
but does not yet destroy the present world of time and history.[53] If
music itself cannot ultimately escape time, *a fortiori* words cannot –
and in the case of the Apocalypse are not designed to.

The failed attempt to read the book as straining towards a kind of
music could be seen as providing evidence that the book cannot ultimately be treated in a formalist way as self-enclosed or fugal, a
work that is its own meaning; or, to put it another way, that it is
inescapably rhetorical. Rhetoric, as Paul de Man expressed it in a
sentence that describes the Apocalypse very neatly, 'radically sus-
pends logic and opens up vertiginous possibilities of referential
aberration'.[54] It may even be that the chaotic grammar of John's
Greek is a pointer away from univocal or spiritual meaning – the
illusion of logic that tidy grammar achieves – and back to the
untidy political and religious world of the reader, where ethical
decisions must be made and where the referential aberrations
within and outside the text may serve as tools for decision-making.

In the end it is not possible to evade tackling the Book of
Revelation simply as *writing*, as a collection of words ordered consciously or unconsciously according to rhetorical patterns; and

words inescapably have reference, however much poets may use them to try to create a purely musical or expressive or transcendent language. No fewer than twelve times John is ordered 'Write' (*grapson*), and the result is a book. Yet a book or scroll is inert until it is read – or eaten? or enacted? It is in its oral performance and 'digestion' that the reader or hearer becomes conscious of its underlying dynamic, one that Lawrence saw as refreshingly 'pagan' and Amos Wilder, less polemically, as 'precultural ... a kind of archetypal idiom'.[55] Because of the way such language is performed, and because of the claims made for it as writing, the reader who opens herself to such language risks madness but also risks entering a kind of sacred space of conversion.

For this is a book, it must be repeated, conscious of its own authority, a book written as 'scripture' and with a high view of the place of writing. As well as the frequent commands to write, the book's framework emphasises the blessings attached to its reading (1:3; 22:7). But it is the text itself that is ostensibly privileged, not the writer: John presents himself as a scribe and brother to his readers rather than an heroic otherworldly explorer like Enoch. The 'narrator' simply looks through the door in heaven and writes, and apart from 'I saw...' and 'I heard...' and the occasional dialogue with angelic interpreters he does not emerge as a person. It is what he writes and how he writes that count. (This contrasts with the position of the narrator in that other highly influential apocalyptic poem, *The Divine Comedy*. For Dante presents himself as a person involved in action and experience and dialogue rather than just writing what he hears and sees; as a person moreover who is engaged in a quest for love that runs parallel with the theological illumination of his poem. By effacing himself, on the other hand, John of Patmos privileges his writing while depriving it of the Dantean possibilities of irony and humour.)

But there is also a book – or two books or three books? – within the book. A book gradually unsealed is the spring of the actions of judgement and promises of salvation in chapters 5–8. A book eaten by the seer in chapter 10 is the source of further prophesying and writing (10:11; 11:1). And it is on the basis of what is written in books that the dead are judged (20:12; 21:27). In a sense all these books have one author – the primordial pronouncement of God – and the suggestion is made in chapter 22 and through the imagery of eating in chapter 10 that they are also one with John's book, which finally lies unsealed before the reader (22:10).[56] If in some sense the book John writes is held to be a digestion or transcription of this heavenly book, then it is presented as far more than a record of visions or a prophetic exhortation or an exegetical meditation, though it does incorporate all three. It is laid before the reader as *the* revelation of (or from) Jesus Christ, that is, as the word of God (19:13).

The reading or enactment of such authoritative writing is normally undertaken in a *liturgical* setting. This has clearly been true of the Apocalypse, and it is necessary finally to ask whether reading it liturgically or reading it as a liturgy can be the clue to its interpretation. As a letter or letters it was originally not distributed to interested parties to study but almost certainly read aloud in the liturgical context of the Asian churches' Eucharists.[57] In a more piecemeal way it has formed part of the Christian liturgy of almost all traditions – in the use of its hymns, in the adaptation of its imagery of worship, and above all in the notion of worship as participation in the heavenly liturgy. So it is not surprising that scholars have sensed and tried to prove that the book not only uses liturgical language and depicts a heavenly liturgy but is actually structured on liturgical principles and therefore invites reading as a kind of worship. It has been variously interpreted as a prophecy closely modelled on the paschal liturgy of the primitive church; as a theological commentary on the Eucharist; as 'celestial liturgy performed by Christ and the angels'; and as visions that derive from the reading of Ezekiel in a liturgical lectionary or from the use of responsory dialogue.[58]

What, though, can be the purpose of such 'liturgical' writing, what can be the effect of such reading? The Apocalypse is not literally a liturgy, its 'performance' cannot have the ostensibly direct orientation to God as adoration, praise, thanksgiving, confession or petition that Jewish or Christian worship expresses. Can it be used, however, as a medium to enable such an attitude of whole-hearted attention to and worship of God to the exclusion of any rival – the Beast/Empire or its various avatars? Its reception could then be seen in sacramental terms as a kind of transubstantiation of the traditional symbols it employs, effecting in turn a transformation of the lives, values and intentions of its readers. The 'lion' is really a lamb; the tyrannous Empire is really a monster; the eternal city is really a whore; the downtrodden readers are really victorious rulers. So John Hurtgen uses Michael Halliday's concept of 'anti-language' to see the Apocalypse 'relexicalizing' the world and thus affirming 'the ability of persons, as "homo loquens", to resist, endure, and ultimately prevail linguistically in the midst of adverse social conditions'.[59] Elisabeth Schüssler Fiorenza goes further, seeing John using cultic symbols to create a new 'symbolic universe' and so taking the threatened community of his readers on a 'dramatic-cathartic journey': through the transformation of symbols 'the empirical community is transported to a cosmic plane and made majestically independent of the vicissitudes of individual existence'.[60] David Barr is even more confident of the text's transforming power. Speculating that the book is 'a mimesis of liturgy (a liturgical fiction?)', he too uses the language of catharsis to claim that its transformation of symbols actually 'transforms reality' for its readers, in the way that Lévi-Strauss saw myth doing:

> The liturgical recital of the Apocalypse becomes a real experience of the Kingdom of God.... This is no ephemeral experience. The hearers are decisively changed. They now live in another world. Persecution does not shock them back to reality. They live in a new reality in which lambs conquer and suffering rules.[61]

This language of realised eschatology has frequently been applied to Christian liturgy and sacraments but its claims need to be met with some suspicion, whether they are applied to first-century or to twentieth-century worshippers. And its applicability to the Apocalypse is also uncertain. For while the reading of the book in a community of faith undoubtedly raises such hopes of the transformation of reality – it was to the success of such reading that Lawrence objected – the text can also jolt those hopes. It deconstructs its own meticulous construction of sacred time and space in two opposite ways. First, the liturgical revelation, which begins 'in the spirit on the Lord's day' and leads to the opening of the temple in heaven and then to the tabernacling of God with mortals, actually ends in the new Jerusalem where there is no temple, where space is unimaginable and time abolished with the disappearance of sun and moon. After all the careful measurements and liturgical construction, the transcendent reality dissolves the liturgy; and to claim that the readers can actually inhabit the new Jerusalem in the present is taking realised eschatology to a degree of absurdity. Conversely the liturgical construction is also ruptured *in via*, in the course of the 'cathartic journey', by the various interjections and glosses within the text. Some of these (as in chapters 7 and 11) are themselves liturgical interludes, like the singing of an anthem in modern liturgy; but others (as in chapters 13, 14 and 17) are definite breaks out of the structure, slippages into another level of discourse – more like a churchwarden giving out notices, or even the congregation going off to a pub for a discussion. While the book is certainly aiming for a transformation of symbols, this cannot without some form of hidden censorship operate sacramentally on the readers in quite the holistic way that Barr and Schüssler Fiorenza envisage. From the flight into celestial liturgy the book keeps falling back explicitly if obscurely to the socio-political reality its readers inhabit and to the decisions they must make. And it suggests that those decisions are to be made not by some elemental cathartic transformation but by the more *indirect* use of the celestial liturgy's alternative time and space to inform and empower ethical and religious thought on the mundane level.

A sophisticated examination of the liturgical time and space of the Apocalypse is made by Jacques Sys, who stresses the slippage of time, space and reference in a text operating on different planes and with a fragile structure. Christ is the theological 'centre' of the action, and the 'rhetorical centre' of the text is the conflict of the woman and the dragon, he says; but these 'centres' are subject to *une règle de décentrement*, to repeated subversion by the restless activity of the narrative. The effect of this oscillation between *monde impossible, espace intermédiaire* and *monde possible* is to lead the readers to a place of conversion or *metanoia* that is, he implies, for each of them to build for herself out of the text:

> Space in this narrative is the place of a conversion, an overturning or subversion of terrestrial space and time. From this collapse the narrative can generate the possibility of a new orientation – whether in a radically new time and space, or in the vista of a possible world whose newness is yet inchoate.[62]

The 'liturgy' of the Apocalypse, then – indeed any liturgy – is inescapably rhetorical as well as theological. It operates in the *aptum* between writer or institution, readers or worshippers, and the 'text' of symbols, words or actions and their referents.[63] If the readers of the book objectify it by submitting completely to its authority and supposed symbolic universe, as the author seems to require, then rhetoric is made into tyranny. If, on the other hand, its readers do not submit or participate at all but objectify the text by purely historical investigation, then rhetoric is denied and reading becomes detached and solipsistic. Either way the 'place of conversion' – that is, the dialogical and ethical engagements between text and reader and between 'reality' and 'possibility' – is avoided. Liturgy as it is sometimes claimed to be, a direct participation in the divine, may be a dangerous model for reading the Apocalypse, and liturgy as an academic study only mildly helpful. But ironically, liturgy as it is actually experienced by most participants, with its jumble of enlightenment and mystification, of beauty and banality, of rapture and thinking, may be a very apt one.

* * *

The difficulty of finding a satisfactory way of reading and interpreting the Apocalypse, whether using traditional religious categories or more literary ones, has at least two consequences. Many readers dismiss the book as literally unreadable or morally repugnant, including many Christian readers who question its place in the biblical canon. On the other hand, the many who do read it (and perhaps more than any other New Testament book it appeals to those outside the church) emerge with a bewildering variety of interpretations. By its authoritative claims, by its place in the canon, above all by the power of its imagery and narrative, the book attracts and often dominates readers. By its obscurity and riddles it demands interpretation and generates impatience in its interpreters. And by that impatience and by its own opacity it confounds their interpretations. Hence the history of disconfirmations of its 'meaning', and hence also what Frank Kermode calls the 'extraordinary resilience' of the book.[64] It may be true that there is no such thing as *the* meaning of any text; that, as Harold Bloom maintains, all interpretations are 'mis-readings'. But in this case the misreadings are wilder than those generated by most books, often more bizarre even than the original, often destructive and amoral; and the book itself is part of scripture. The need therefore for reading that is both responsible and responsive is all the greater.

As a work that seems to offer total vision and structural wholeness but that actually dissolves into fragments in reading, Revelation perhaps receives such responsive reading only in fragments and particularly at historical periods when political events and the sense of judgement (*crisis*) bear some analogy to those of the first century: in the thirteenth century, say, or in Puritan

England, in the period of the French Revolution, the nuclear age, the Confessing Church of Nazi Germany, times when there is what Schüssler Fiorenza calls a 'fitting' rhetorical situation.[65] But such readings – in millenarianism or revolutionary politics or Romantic poetry – often appear to be less interpretation of the book than rewriting of it. The more eager and responsive the reading, the less likely, it seems, it is to be responsible. For one of the effects of the Apocalypse's persistent destabilising of its readers' responses is the frantic search for extrinsic reference for the text's images.

Such lust for explanation can frequently be seen in interpretations of the book by English scholars, poets, preachers and politicians in the century or so surrounding the French Revolution. But as well as calling for hermeneutical vigilance in the modern reader, such interpretations also provide evidence of the power of John's narrative and symbolism in generating rewritings of 'vision' that often urge religious, cultural or political change. The chapters that follow will compare those misreadings and rewritings of the Apocalypse in a culture that craved total vision in a variety of modes yet had to come to terms with the fragmentation or illusoriness of its visions. In that comparison I hope to show how the book both inspired and confounded its interpreters and to suggest that the same is true today.

2

Apocalypse and Reason

Luther, Calvin and Schleiermacher were not the only biblical scholars to avoid the last book of the Bible. Nor was their neglect of it simply an instance of protestant aberration, for to this day the Apocalypse is largely ignored by most eastern churches, where it was not fully recognised as canonical until the eighth century, and largely avoided in the catechesis and lectionary of the Roman Catholic Church. After the charismatic excesses of Montanism, most early Christian interpreters were suspicious of Revelation's wild and often vengeful language; and after the establishment of Christianity as the imperial religion its thinly veiled attacks on the Roman Empire could be seen as subversive. So it is not surprising that for the next thousand years in the West it was the spiritualising interpretation of Tyconius and Augustine that held sway when attention was paid to the book at all. Above all, what part could it play in the Christianity of the eighteenth century, which prided itself on being ordered, rational and calming?

Yet there were not lacking in seventeenth- and eighteenth-century England men who were convinced that their reading and judgement – in contrast to Daniel Whitby's – were adequate 'to discern the Intendment of the Prophecies contained in that Book'.[1] Unlike Germany, where chiliasm was anathematised by the Augsburg Confession, England produced a long line of biblical scholars who were prepared to make a huge outlay of philological, exegetical and mathematical labour in applying the 'prophecies' to the history of the church and the world and discovering in them confirmation of the scientific order they saw as the work of God's providence. Among them were highly respected and influential scientific thinkers like Isaac Newton, David Hartley and Joseph Priestley.

The tradition can be traced back through the Reformation and Foxe's *Acts and Monuments of the Christian Church* to Joachim of Fiore in the twelfth century and the Franciscans of the late Middle Ages.[2] In *The Image of bothe Churches*, which appeared between 1541

and 1547, John Bale drew on Joachim, on the traditional Augustinian interpretations and on the work of contintental Reformers, to
relate the text of Revelation to the pattern of history, including that
of his own time. Bale does not posit a univocal correspondence
between events in the visionary text and those in subsequent
history and is cautious of any forays into future history. The central
theme of the Apocalypse he sees (like Tyconius) as the 'two
churches' of God and Satan, and although he was convinced that
the Reformation of his own day was (in Richard Bauckham's
words) 'an eschatological event' it was only 'a specific instance of
the age-long conflict of the two churches'.[3] John Foxe's use of the
Apocalypse in his very widely read *Acts and Monuments* (1563, with
further editions in 1570, 1576 and 1583) was also fairly general. But
in his late, uncompleted commentary *Eicasmi seu meditationes in
sacram Apocalypsin* (1587) Foxe abandoned 'the pattern of particular
and universal fulfilments ... in favour of finding a single historical
counterpart for every item in the prophetic symbolism'.[4] Luther's
identification of the Beast and Antichrist with the Pope is now
taken for granted, and in Foxe's full survey of world and church
history up to the 'events' of Rev 17 there is a special role for
England as for other European nations in the providence of God
revealed to John. Foxe, unlike Bale, was also keen to use numerological and chronological calculations in the deciphering of the
pattern of history from the apocalyptic text.

So from the reign of Elizabeth I most of the features of the
English 'prophetic' historiography were present. But the scholarly
industry of English apocalyptic interpretation really begins with
Thomas Brightman, whose 1609 commentary on Revelation went
through many editions and brought together the Joachimist pattern
of world history, an emphasis on the English nation, belief in the
conversion and return of the Jews, and millennial optimism. He
perceives in John's writing (no doubt correctly) a highly elaborate
sevenfold structure, upon which he erects with his 'indefatigable
love of invention' a 'grand and convoluted superstructure'.[5] The
obscure symbols of John are refined into a continuous prophecy of
the history of the church, which becomes more and more detailed
as the millennium approaches. For instance the seventh unsealing
is the Council of Nicaea, the seventh trumpet the English
Reformation, and the pouring of the third bowl of wrath the
destruction of the Jesuits by William Cecil. Such deductions soon
became commonplace. As Katharine Firth comments,

By the end of the first decade of the seventeenth century, the apocalyptic tradition had not only been firmly absorbed into British Protestantism, but had also become the subject of quite sophisticated study. The mysteries of divine prophecy could be probed successfully only by those skilled in the arts of philology, chronology and history. ... In the apocalyptic tradition sacred and universal history were inextricably bound together; the exposition of Scripture and prophecy was the exposition of history as God had eternally ordered and judged it.[6]

These claims for the privileges of scholars in the exegesis of scripture and history redound through the next two centuries. Yet they do so against the background of Luther's hymning of the *bibelfester Laier* and of the English Reformation's own insistence on access to the Bible as an open book. The openness of the Bible was to lead – as earlier in Germany – to proletarian attempts to seize the course of history in the name of God; and once commentaries like Brightman's were translated into the vernacular they played their part as much in the fomenting of revolution as in assuring the scholarly élite of God's calm control of past, present and future. Christopher Hill has demonstrated the important part played by interpretation of the Apocalypse, as well as of the Old Testament, in English radical politics of the mid-seventeenth century.[7] But the 1650s saw growing disillusionment with extreme millennial hopes, and this became institutionalised with the Stuart restoration of 1660, after which the embers of the great theological and political debates of the revolution barely smouldered. Millenarianism went underground, most Dissenters acquiesced in political marginalisation, and intellectual scepticism grew – fertilised, as Hill shows, by the very debates about the Bible that assumed its universal authority.

Yet it is an exaggeration to say with Hill that these developments led rapidly to 'the Bible dethroned', that it 'became a historical document, to be interpreted like any other', or that it 'was revealed as the greatest idol of all'.[8] Certainly it was not so after the restoration for Bunyan, in whose *Pilgrim's Progress* the Bible generates a doctrinal and narrative vivacity of extraordinary power. Nor was it for Milton – though clearly both *Paradise Lost* and *Of Christian Doctrine* steer a very independent course in biblical interpretation – and Milton's poetic authority remained immense throughout the next 150 years. Nor did the decline in popular millenarianism involve any decline in the scholarly reputation of Milton's tutor at Cambridge, Joseph Mede (1586–1638).

Mede, an Anglican and royalist, undertook substantial refinements of Brightman's interpretation, which he published in 1627 as *Clavis Apocalyptica* and which were translated into English by order of the Long Parliament in 1643. Mede's system of chronological calculations, charts and 'synchronisms' gave authority to a millennial exegesis that in most other protestant and all Catholic countries would have been seen as heretical. After his death in 1638 he was, in Firth's words, 'transformed from scholar to prophet'.[9] It is almost impossible to read an English commentator of the next two centuries who does not refer to Mede, usually with respect and often with awe; as late as 1833 R. B. Cooper wrote his *Commentary on the Revelation of St John ... by an Humble Follower of the Pious and Profoundly Learned Joseph Mede B.D.*, providing with it a new English translation of Mede's *Clavis*. Although Mede's historical and anti-papal interpretation of prophetic history did not differ substantially from Brightman's, he contributes a spirit of optimism, a new elegance and a close attention to the text that bear fruit in his influential system of 'synchronisms'. The diachronic events in history to which the symbols refer are subsumed within the 'synchronic' pattern of symbols. One of the keys is the word 'again' at Rev 10:11, showing, for Mede, that the previous prophecy of seals and trumpets begins and ends at the same points in external history as does 'the other prophecy ... of the open book, which, commencing from the same beginning of apocalyptical time, retraces the times of the former prophecies'.[10] So the visions of the two-horned beast, the ten-horned beast, the woman in the wilderness, the lamentation of the witnesses, the harlot and the company of the sealed 'all synchronize with each other' (p. 3).

There are two connected features of Mede's methodology that lend him his unique authority. First is his sense of finding a 'key' within the text itself that will give an authoritative means of interpreting this mysterious and potentially explosive book. His synchronisms are in fact presented as a theorem proven by close examination of the text before there is any attempt to discover its reference; so Mede frequently uses 'Q.E.D.' and speaks of being able to 'put an end to the matter by clear and irrefragable demonstration'. But that mathematical sense depends upon a second, a more religious or aesthetic sense of affinity between the interpreter's ingenuity and the author's – the interpreter being Mede, the author the Holy Spirit. For instance Mede remarks that in Rev 11 (the vision of the witnesses)

> the all-wise Spirit runs through the whole period of the sealed prophecy, as a warp through a woof, and connects the same with the seventh trumpet as with a sort of clasp, for the sake of directing the time to the series of the seals. But for what purpose, except that to the first vision thus fixed and compared with the seals, the remaining prophecies of the little book which succeed, being connected also by their own characters, the whole system of the renewed prophecy with the seals might be dexterously accommodated? (p. 27)

Mede's diagrammatic 'Scheme of the Synchronic Periods comprised in the Apocalypse' epitomises what I have termed the mathematical, religious and aesthetic senses of his hermeneutical principles (*see plate 10*). So too does the imagery of his eloquent subtitle to the *Clavis Apocalyptica*:

> The Apocalyptical Key; or, The synchronism and order of the Apocalyptical Prophecies, according to the things transacted, on no hypothetical interpretation, nor preconjecture about the events; but firmly demonstrated from the very characters of the visions themselves, purposely inserted by the Holy Spirit, and offered to examination according to a self-evident scheme: so that it may prove, as it were, a Thesean clew to those who are involved in this sacred labyrinth, and a Lydian stone to discover the true, and to refute every erroneous interpretation.[11]

Clearly the authority of Mede's system depends on the assumption that the Holy Spirit *was* the 'author' of the Apocalypse. Its application rests also on the assumption that the symbols refer to historical events after the time of the visions – an assumption that does not compel an antipapal historiography but that fits it very neatly.

I have dwelt at some length on these seventeenth-century exegetes because nearly all English commentaries of the two centuries between Mede's Latin 'key' and Cooper's translation of it did in fact share those two assumptions and adhered to some version of Brightman's and Mede's so-called 'church–historical' scheme of interpretation, identifying the Beast with the papacy. The same mathematical ingenuity and the same anti-Roman ideology can be seen in the elaborate exegeses of Revelation undertaken by Isaac Newton early in the eighteenth century and by G. S. Faber early in the nineteenth. By less ambitious interpreters they are usually taken for granted – though, as I hope to show, the cultural and political contexts in which the text is interpreted vary widely and greatly influence the interpreters' rhetoric as well as some of their detailed identifications of prophetic fulfilment. The language becomes calmer, the political controversy more remote in the eighteenth century; but there is little real evidence for the thesis presented in different ways by Christopher Hill, P. J. Korshin and M. H. Abrams that millennial thought and 'prophetic' interpretation became secularised, marginalised or 'internalised'.[12] While Hill may be right to say that after 1660 'the name of Antichrist ... could now be dismissed as unsuitable for polite drawing-room conversation', the adjective 'antichristian' nevertheless retains a strong polemical meaning well into the nineteenth century, while the noun 'beast' still retains the pejorative associations that became attached to it in the seventeenth century as a result of reading Revelation.

There are some dissenters from what had become by the middle of the seventeenth century this general English position: Roman Catholic scholars like Bishop Walmesley, and among protestants most notably the Presbyterian Daniel Mace, whose new version of the New Testament with extensive and impressive textual notes was published anonymously in 1729. Mace follows the Dutch theologian Hugo Grotius (1583–1645) in relating the visions of Revelation to first-century history only (the 'preterist' interpretation, eventually made general by nineteenth-century historical criticism). He actually went further to hint that the whole book could be an 'imposture' or 'fraud', quoting at length the reservations of Dionysius of Alexandria.[13] But Mace was admired more on the continent than in Britain, where, as David Brady remarks,

> those who argued for the preterist interpretation of the Book of Revelation, and for that matter the futurist interpretation also, were playing to empty galleries, until at least the fourth decade of the nineteenth century. Their views were anything but popular and those who followed them could soon find themselves branded with the infamous mark of the papal beast.[14]

The tradition reached a *ne plus ultra* (though even today it has not reached complete burn-out) in the 2300 pages of E. B. Elliott's immensely learned *Horae Apocalypticae*, which went through five editions between 1844 and 1852 and was to provide the sole comfort to the dying Mrs Gosse in 1857.[15] Throughout this period, then, even in the self-consciously 'rational' eighteenth century, we are dealing with people for whom apocalyptic imagery was as familiar as it had been in the thirteenth, when Pope Gregory IX condemned Frederick II as the Beast and the Emperor responded by calling Gregory the Dragon.

* * *

There is of course a huge social and cultural gap between Mede or Elliott in their clerical libraries and the millenarian prophets of the English Revolution or the Napoleonic period, though the gap in terms of the two groups' underlying religious sensibility may be less than historians have maintained.[16] At any rate, most 'millennialists' – as the first group is generally called to distinguish them from 'millenarians', though the distinction is hardly an absolute one – are as keen as anybody in the eighteenth century to deny that they are 'enthusiasts'. Their religion is scientific, not mystical; they are not prophets but interpreters of prophecy. Sir Isaac Newton, who wrote far more about prophecy than he ever did about mathematics and physics, was a famously cool and private person, and his insistence that an interpreter of prophecy is not making prognostications but confirming the veracity of scripture *post eventu* is repeated by many subsequent commentators: 'The folly of Interpreters has been, to foretel times and things by this Prophecy, as if God had designed to make them Prophets', he writes; but God gave revelations not in order to gratify people's curiosity about the future, 'but that after they were fulfilled they might be interpreted by the event, and his own Providence, not the Interpreters, be then manifested to the world'.[17] Prophecy fulfilled is evidence of the providence of God and the inspiration of the Bible: the argument occurs repeatedly in the disputes between churchmen and Deists in the first half of the eighteenth century. And where it appears that the prophecy has not yet been fulfilled, a commentator will usually refrain from interpretation. So Newton's disciple and successor to his chair at Cambridge, William Whiston, simply prints the text of Revelation chapters 16 and 18–22 without comment. Similarly Moses Lowman, a Presbyterian minister and authority on Jewish antiquities, concludes his *Paraphrase and Notes on the Revelation of*

St John (1737) with a pious evocation of the new Jerusalem and the
words,

> It is with great Advantage, this Encouragement is given the
> church in such a Prophecy. An Observation of the faithful and
> punctual Accomplishment of the former Parts of this Prophecy,
> in Times past, for several Hundreds of Years, serves much to
> confirm our Faith and Hope, in as faithful and punctual
> Performance of what remains.[18]

This congratulation of the Lord on his reliable timekeeping has
clear echoes of Newton's concern for chronology and of the
popular eighteenth-century image of God as watchmaker. It was in
Lowman's time that the British Admiralty prize for the first
chronometer to be accurate to one minute per year was claimed. As
well as laying the foundation for naval victories over the next
hundred years, the achievement provided rich poetic, philosophical
and theological imagery. The One seated on the throne in the Book
of Revelation is now cast as a judicious technocrat. And, in
Tuveson's words, 'the Apocalypse ... became, with the assistance of
a new scientific philosophy of universal law, and encouraged by
the great advances in knowledge of nature, the very guarantee and
assurance of progress'.[19]

Similarly, a generation after Lowman, Richard Hurd's Warburton Lecture on prophecy (1772) includes the caution that the
prophetic system

> pretends, not to give immediate conviction, but to lay in, before-
> hand, the *means* of conviction to such as shall be in a condition to
> compare, in due time, the prediction with the event. Till then,
> prophecy serves only to raise a general expectation of the event
> predicted ... the *declared* end of prophecy is, not that we may be
> enabled by it to foresee things before they come to pass; but *when*
> they come to pass, that we may acknowledge the divine author
> of the prophecy.[20]

As is common in religious apologetics, claims are made for the
writers' complete objectivity. Newton, Whiston, Lowman and
Hurd each promise to 'take my Scheme of the Prophecy entirely
from the Book [of Revelation] itself'.[21] To question that the book
was one of 'prophecy' and that prophecy meant 'prediction' seems

not to have been possible for them, despite the doubts raised by biblical scholars such as Whiston's adversary Anthony Collins and going back to the time of Spinoza.

The battering that this 'objective' science has received – from the political revolution in France, the Romantic revolution in consciousness and the historical revolution in biblical hermeneutics – has been at least as great as that received by Newtonian physics from the twentieth-century revolution in science. Today, in fact, Newton's biblical work seems far more remote than his physics. Yet in both there is an elegance and coherence, the heady sense that the Bible and the 'Book of Nature' are in harmony and that a systematic presentation of both can be made in lucid prose. And could it be that this is not just an example of Enlightenment intellectual complacency but – as for Mede – a genuine if tangential response to the elegance and coherence of the Apocalypse itself?

It is hard, however, not to reflect that Calvin *was* wise in avoiding commentary on Revelation; even that those who did so had actually a better incipient notion of what 'prophecy' was than those who drew up their charts and diagrams of its fulfilment. Perhaps the former kept their tongues silent and their pens idle neither because of lack of knowledge nor because of political conservatism, but out of the religious sense that whatever mysteries are contained in the book's symbols and structures can *not* be represented diagramatically, discursively or historically. Examining the way the book was or was not interpreted under the impact first of the Enlightenment then (in subsequent chapters) of the upheavals in political and poetic consciousness and in biblical criticism at the end of the eighteenth century may help to determine whether there can be *any* appropriate exegetical criteria for the Apocalypse, or whether the biblical scholars would be better handing the book over to artists, poets, liturgists and (possibly) preachers. In the rest of this chapter I shall examine how the Apocalypse supported much of eighteenth-century England's faith: first, faith in providence, then in an ordered chronology, in moral 'usefulness', and in a pure and rational religion.

PROVIDENCE

Whoever reads the Scriptures, with seriousness and attention, and with a tolerable degree of understanding, will observe the

great and uniform Design running through the whole, to be the
promotion of Virtue, and true Piety, for the Happiness of
mankind, and the rooting out of Idolatry, Vice and Superstition,
with all their natural and consequent Evils. ... [The Apocalypse]
is what closes up, and completes the volume of all other
Prophecies; without this they are dark and imperfect; but with it
they are lightsome, and truly comfortable.[22]

These words from Thomas Pyle's preface to his commentary on
Revelation (1735) can serve as an epigraph to eighteenth-century
English interpretation of the book. The belief in a providential
order sustaining the physical world, the words of the Bible and a
moralistic religion, with more or less veiled hints at the contrary
darkness of popery and an assertion of what Pyle calls the 'usefulness' of Revelation, these are features that one encounters again
and again. Part of the usefulness derives from the evident sense of
comfort given by the reading and study of the book. Trying to steer
between the dogmatism of Roman Catholics and Calvinists and the
scepticism of Deists and infidels, the 'rational' Christians of the first
half of the century were keen to discover 'evidences' of the truth of
a basic Christian belief and to incorporate those evidences into a
clear system that avoided any taint of mysticism or 'enthusiasm'.
They were keen to believe in a providence that was not only
general but particular, yet with the particularities not arbitrary
divine interventions but suitably rational and well-timed miracles,
like comets and earthquakes. History is the fulfilment of prophecy,
nature the reflection of divine order: together they stand at the head
of the 'evidence' for the truth of the Christian revelation.

Thomas Newton, who was Bishop of Bristol from 1761 until his
death in 1782, remarked that whereas in earlier times miracles were
'the great proofs of revelation', in the new age prophecies had
taken priority. Prophecies, or rather their fulfilment, were indeed 'a
growing evidence': for long the prophetic parts of scripture had
seemed 'obscure', but 'the more they are fulfilled, the better they
are understood. In this respect as the world groweth older, it
groweth wiser ... the perfect accomplishment will produce a
perfect knowledge of all the prophecies'.[23] In his 26 widely read
Dissertations on the Prophecies (1754–8), Newton investigated the
fulfilment of almost every prophetic passage in the Old and New
Testaments from Noah to Paul, with learned footnotes, coming in
his two longest dissertations (24 and 25) to 'An Analysis of the

Revelation'. Warning against both neglect and overhasty interpretation of the book, he quotes Isaac Newton to stress the sobriety of
his interpretation and Mede on many of the details of fulfilments.
The seals visions are fulfilled in the time of the pagan Roman
Empire, the trumpet visions in the time of the Christian Roman
Empire (1754 is still in the time of the sixth trumpet), while the
fulfilment of the bowls and the millennium are still to come. The
first beast is the Pope, and the history, geography and characteristics of popery – including features like celibacy, fasting and the
denial of the chalice to the laity – are all foretold in Revelation,
together with the assurance of deliverance for true Christians. He
even claims (or admits) that 'this is proving our religion in some
measure by ocular demonstration'.[24]

It is necessary to take this apologetic background into account if
we are to make any sense of the place of Revelation's wild and subversive images in such a bourgeois and etiolated religion. But it is
impossible also to ignore the fact that the apologists failed and that
their harmony of biblical revelation and the religion of nature and
reason could not be sustained. And this in turn raises the question
whether it was actually possible to draw the sting of those wild
images; whether they do not bite back against the attempt to make
them 'lightsome and truly comfortable' and instead shed darkness
(if perhaps a religious darkness) on the tottering system. Perhaps
much of the stability and ease of bourgeois protestant England
actually depended on the belief in a dark and mercifully distant
demonic presence in the prophetic text and in the Vatican.

While its tottering clearly gathered pace in the second half of the
century, there are signs of darkness already in the religious system
of the first half that is epitomised in Pyle's complacent words. (This
division of the religious thought of the century into two halves is
based on the still convincing thesis of Mark Pattison's essay of 1860,
'Tendencies of Religious thought in England, 1688–1750' [published
in *Essays and Reviews*]: Pattison saw a change taking place about the
year 1750, when the endeavour to prove the truth of Christianity
moved, under the impact of the growing historical consciousness,
from the concentration on internal to that on external evidence.)
Looking first at the earlier period and the place in it of 'prophecy'
and the Apocalypse, it is important to appreciate the sense of
confidence that the political, scientific and philosophical advances
of the late seventeenth century gave. This was not just an intellectual ease, the sense sometimes expressed in England that since the

'Glorious Revolution' of 1688 and the discoveries of Isaac Newton there was little more progress to be made. There was also a sense of intellectual excitement, the faith that all knowledge could be comprehended in a system ultimately very simple and that, since the world was God's creation, this knowledge was the knowledge of God previously sought in such roundabout and uncertain ways by mystics and theologians.

For all their differences, the systems of Descartes, Spinoza, Leibniz, Locke and Newton exemplify this aim of simplicity and comprehensiveness – and interestingly there is an element in all five men that could be called contemplative. It is easy now to detect the seeds of dissolution carried in each system; easy to see the vulnerability of those systems to later changes in historical and psychological outlooks. But until about 1750 the authority in England of Locke and Newton in particular was massive, and whether religious thinkers adopted their empiricism or the more *a priori* continental methods there is found in nearly all of them the same confidence that a clear system of universal knowledge can be perceived and communicated, if not to the masses at least to the educated few.[25] For all the bad temper of the theological and political disputes between Deists and 'orthodox' Christians, it is remarkable how far they actually shared the same rationalist assumptions, the same faith in clarity.

The assumptions can be seen already in the commonsense approach of that devout Christian rationalist John Locke. The argument of *The Reasonableness of Christianity, as delivered in the Scriptures* (1695) is full of appeals like 'as is clear' and 'all men will agree': for instance, when raising the vexed question as to the salvation of those who died before the time of Christ, Locke says that 'the answer is so obvious and natural, that one would wonder how any reasonable man should think it worth the urging'.[26] The truths of religion, if not self-evident, must be clear to the mind of the 'reasonable man', and any dogma that goes beyond reason is dangerous mystification – it is noteworthy that Locke's long array of proof-texts are nearly all from the apparently straightforward Gospels and Acts, not from the more puzzling lucubrations of St Paul. Leslie Stephen commented of this rather repetitive book that Locke, 'a rationalist to the core,... does not even contemplate as possible an appeal to any authority but that of ordinary reason. ... It was simply a question of evidence'.[27] From his rational vantage point Locke is even able to congratulate Jesus on 'the admirable wariness of his carriage, and an extraordinary wisdom', and to speak of 'the admirable contrivance of the divine wisdom' (VII.86, 84). Revelation concurs entirely with reason, he argues – though it is nevertheless necessary, since most people lack the education or leisure to discover the truth for themselves and need plain teaching and commandments (VII.133–40).

Here is the beginning of the theologically debilitating antinomy of revelation and reason that dominated the religious debate of the next half-century and resurged in the twentieth century. And clearly Locke's position is a tenuous one. Only a year after the publication of *The Reasonableness of Christianity*, Locke's embarrassing disciple John Toland exhibited the consequences of his master's argument in *Christianity not Mysterious*, the aim of which is to expel all hypothesis and 'mystery' from pure rational religion. Claims to 'revelation' that do not concur with empirical reasoning are simply nonsense. So Mary is commended for not believing the angel Gabriel until her objection was answered; she no doubt held with Toland that

> as 'tis by *Reason* we arrive at the Certainty of God's own Existence, so we cannot otherwise discern his *Revelations* but by their Conformity with our natural Notices of him, which is in so many words, to agree with our common Notions.[28]

For Toland, reason is the logical faculty of assessing evidence, and 'since PROBABILITY is not KNOWLEDG, I banish all HYPOTHESES from my PHILOSOPHY' (p. 15). But God is no mere hypothesis, so Toland can confidently assert that 'neither GOD himself, nor any of his Attributes, are *Mysteries* to us for want of an adequate Idea: No, nor *Eternity*' (p. 80); he can call not only the Fathers but also the 'Reasoning' of Abraham to witness that, far from being supernatural or suprarational, faith is 'entirely built upon *Ratiocination*', an act of 'perswasion' consisting of 'Knowledg' and 'Assent' (pp. 127–32). The extreme intellectualism of a man like Toland, combining doggedly empirical reasoning with an easy assumption of traditional metaphysical categories like the attributes of God, could hardly survive in the face of the growing knowledge of history and attention to 'external' evidence, which Pattison saw as the mark of the second half of the eighteenth century. For Toland, 'Religion is always the same, like God its Author, *with whom there is no Variableness, nor Shadow of changing*' (p. xii f.)

The same ahistoricism and trust in the self-evident clarity of rational religion are exuded by the thorough logic of Samuel Clarke's much admired Boyle Lectures of 1704–5. Clarke, an ardent follower of Newton, was seen as a powerful defender of orthodoxy against Deism and atheism, though his basic premises are hard to distinguish from the Deists'. Against the 'atheists' Hobbes and Spinoza he uses Newtonian physics and the theory of the necessity of a vaccuum to prove the necessity of a self-existent being, coupling this with a Newtonian argument from design – the planets could have gone in other ways, like comets, so their direction 'is an evident proof that these things are solely the Effect of Wisdom and Choice ... the larger the Improvements and Discoveries are, which are daily made in Astronomy and Natural Philosophy; the more clearly is this Question continually determined, to the Shame and Confusion of Atheists'.[29] For Clarke, faith is rational assent to self-evident religious and moral truths, equivalent to assent to mathematical theorems. But he devotes his fifteen propositions and many hours of speaking in the 1705 lectures to proving that revelation too is necessary and that the Christian revelation agrees in every point with reason (the only two other possible claimants, Judaism and Islam, are peremptorily dismissed in half a page). Even parts of it that could not be discovered by purely logical thought, like the sacraments, are shown to be eminently rational, 'a wise and excellent Institution of *practical* Religion; highly conducive to the Happiness of Mankind; and worthy to be established by a Revelation from God'.[30]

As Matthew Tindal pointed out some years later, Clarke was really a 'Christian Deist' like himself, but one who retained traditional orthodox narrowness in talking of the need for atonement and revelation, which according to his logic should be redundant. Certainly one suspects in Clarke's elaborate arguments a conservative desire to fit the main elements of protestant Christianity into his mathematical system without a deeply felt sense of what one might call their spiritual coherence: thus the doctrines of Christ and of the Holy Spirit occupy just half a page, and while he is eloquent on moral duty he can say little about original sin.

Tindal, on the other hand, takes Clarke's rationalism and desire for perspicuity to their logical conclusion. The title of his book, published in 1730, gives a clear summary of its conclusion: *Christianity as old as the Creation, or, The Gospel a Republication of the Religion of Nature*. It consists of thirteen propositions cogently argued, followed by a critique of Clarke's Boyle Lectures. Again, the wording of the propositions is admirably clear: 'That the Religion of Nature is an absolutely perfect Religion; and that external Revelation can neither add to, nor take from its perfection. ... That Natural and Reveal'd Religion having the same End, their Precepts must be the same. ... That they, who, to magnify Revelation, weaken the force of the Religion of Reason and Nature, strike at all Religion: and that there can't be two independent Rules for the government of human actions'.[31] The culprits, for Tindal as for most of the Deists, are the Christian clergy, who, like pagan priests, have been keen since early in the present era to shroud the originally pure natural religion of Christianity in mystery as a way of increasing their authority and wealth. But, he says, 'Whatever is confus'd and perplex'd, can never come from the clear fountain of all knowledge, nor that which is obscure from the Father of inexhaustible Light'.[32]

Outside the rather arid debate between Deists and Christian apologists, this combination of moral optimism, of trust in rational clarity and of unhistorical belief in a pure original religion, can be traced in diverse forms in the England of the early part of the eighteenth century. It emerges in the popular 'physico-theology' of the distinguished biologist John Ray, in the attractive ethical system of Shaftesbury, in the growth industry of landscape gardening.[33] It flourishes in a remarkable way in that astute observer of the fashions of his age, James Thomson. Thomson's long poem *The Seasons* went through numerous editions between 1726 and his death in 1748, each one incorporating more of his heady brew of modern science and British patriotism filtered through close observation of the natural world. Controlling this fermentation is a genuine if not especially profound belief in the immanence of the Creator in the natural, moral and scientific world, though Thomson often moves towards an identification of God and Nature:

> O Nature! all-sufficient! over all
> Enrich me with the knowledge of thy works;
> Snatch me to heaven; thy rolling wonders there,
> World beyond world, in infinite extent
> Profusely scattered o'er the blue immense,
> Show me; their motions, periods, and their laws
> Give me to scan[34]

Thomson does not shirk the violence of the natural world. But this is a cause not for terror but for awe, at any rate for those with understanding: 'the rushing comet ... with awful train projected o'er the heavens' may make 'the guilty nations tremble', but

> ... above
> Those superstitious horrors that enslave
> The fond sequacious herd, to mystic faith
> And blind amazement prone, the enlightened few,
> Whose godlike minds philosophy exalts,
> The glorious stranger hail.
>
> ('Summer', 1708–16)

As inspired British guides to these enlightened few, Thomson rhetorically hails Bacon, Shaftesbury, Boyle, Locke ('Who made the whole internal world his own') and Newton ('pure intelligence, whom God/To mortals lent to trace his boundless works/From laws sublimely simple').[35] This natural and moral religion is expressed in the spatial exploration of the natural order, both at the astronomical and at the microscopic level; but the exploration has an important temporal dimension too. In Thomson's poem this dimension is rather confused; it is, however, a confusion that mirrors the difficulty facing more profound thinkers of the period, one of which they were largely unaware, namely that of reconciling the rational scientific order of universal regularity discovered in nature and morality with the more teleological and prophetic biblical order that was still embedded in their minds. So Thomson's 'Hymn on the Seasons' celebrates the annual round – 'These, as they change, Almighty Father! these/Are but the varied God. The rolling year/Is full of thee' – but ends by moving out of the seasonal cycle to 'wing my flight to future worlds. ... In infinite progression' (1–3, 108–16). And his longer cycle ends (at the conclusion of 'Winter') not with a return to the beginning but with progression to 'one unbounded Spring':

> 'Tis come, the glorious morn! the second birth
> Of heaven and earth! awakening Nature hears
> The new-creating word, and starts to life
> In every heightened form, from pain and death
> For ever free.
>
> ('Winter', 1042–46)

Though it is appropriate to see Thomson as an eloquent representative of the natural religion of educated Englishmen of the period, he himself would be the first to give deference to Isaac Newton, even to see Newton's scientific achievement as part of that religion. What Pope concisely proclaimed in the couplet,

> Nature and Nature's laws lay hid in night:
> God said, *Let Newton be!* and all was light!

Thomson expressed more periphrastically in his 'Poem Sacred to the Memory of Sir Isaac Newton', written soon after 'the great soul of NEWTON quit this earth,/to mingle with his stars' in 1727. Here is praise of the intuition and the labour of the

> All piercing sage! who sat not down and dream'd
> Romantic schemes, defended by the din
> Of specious words, and tyranny of names;
> But, bidding his amazing mind attend,
> And with heroic patience years on years
> Deep searching, saw at last the SYSTEM dawn,
> And shine, of all his race, on him alone.
>
> (23–9)

Thomson's praises are echoed more soberly by Samuel Clarke and by most of the intelligentsia of Europe at the time – indeed, according to F. E. Manuel, Newton himself sensed that he was a means of revelation to the world.[36] The pictures of Newton variously given later by the hostile Blake (in 'Europe' and 'Newton') and the admiring Wordsworth (in *The Prelude*, Book III) are acute ones: here is the 'ethereal self', 'voyaging through strange seas of Thought, alone', and dispassionately measuring time and space in his 'soul-shuddering vaccuum'. But few other than the secretive sage himself realised how thorough were his researches into the measuring of *time* and how extensively these were based on biblical prophecy; indeed many of his writings in this field have still not been published (and are now unfortunately scattered over three continents). Newton did not see himself as a prophet – for according to him the age of prophecy was over – but as the supreme interpreter of prophecy, as of nature. And while Scripture as a whole had authority for him, Daniel and Revelation formed the canon within the Canon. Given the right key, they are no more obscure than the movements of the planets: both are the incontrovertibly clear revelation of the great Designer of space and time.

CHRONOLOGY

What then was Newton's key? Thousands of words went into the construction of a dictionary of 'prophetic hieroglyphs', where the meaning of each biblical symbol had to be exactly consistent wherever it occurred in scripture – for if it were otherwise God would be irrational. Newton's rules for interpretation largely follow those of 'the judiciously learned and conscientious Mr Mede': it is necessary, he says, to

> observe diligently the consent of Scriptures and analogy of the prophetique stile ... to assigne but one meaning to one place of scripture ... to keep as close as may be to the same sense of words especially in the same vision [and] to chose those interpretations which are most according to the litterall meaning of the scriptures unles where the tenour and circumstances of the place plainly require an Allegory.[37]

In seeking this divine harmony the interpreter must 'reduce things to the greatest simplicity. ... It is the perfection of God's works that they are all done with the greatest simplicity. He is the God of order and not of confusion'. And it is taken for granted that the 'prophecies' of Daniel and Revelation predict the subsequent course of history, particularly that of the church, so that the interpreter must 'proportion the most notable parts of Prophesy to the most notable parts of history, and the breaches made in a continued series of Prophesy [as between the sixth and seventh unsealings and the sixth and seventh trumpets] to the changes made in history'.[38] All this labour, far from being abstruse speculation, is intensely practical, leading to the knowledge of God's authority and hence to pure living, to eternal salvation and to the purging of hypocrites from God's church: just as a properly constructed engine or grammatical sentence makes its fitness clear, so, Newton writes,

> a man ought with equal reason to acquiesce in that construction of these Prophecies when he sees their parts set in order according to their suitableness and the characters imprinted in them for that purpose ... God who knew how to frame [the Apocalypse] without ambiguity intended it for a rule of faith.[39]

Newton's 'First Book Concerning the Language of the Prophets' (Keynes MS 5) runs to about 50 000 words, beginning with 'A Synopsis of the Prophetic Figures', where natural and political analogies are used to assign precise meanings to each symbol, whether appearing in John, Daniel, Isaiah or any other 'prophet': the sun is kings, winds are war, dens and rocks are temples, the hairs and feathers of beasts are people, a forest is a kingdom, and so on.[40] The book proceeds with a meticulous application of these principles to the narrative of Revelation, with extensive corroboration from Newton's research into Jewish liturgy, and with precise descriptions of the order of the visions. For instance, after the treading of the wine-press (Rev 14:20), Newton notes that 'John has hitherto prophesied out of the first six leaves and the first page of the seventh leaf of the eaten book & now proceeds to prophesy out of the second page of the seventh leaf' (fol. 23). And since water represents people and a stream of water a body 'ecclesiastick' or 'politick', the water from the Dragon's mouth in Rev 12 is identical with the Beast and so with 'a western kingdom', while the waters on which the Woman sits are 'the peoples nations multitudes & tongues over whom the Woman reigneth' and her flying upon the two-winged eagle 'the division of the Church catholic into two parts' (fol. 44). Newton was far from working *de novo*. In the previous generation Benjamin Keach had undertaken the classification of biblical 'types' and Henry More had clarified the 'keys' that were to decode the language of scripture; Egyptian hieroglyphics remained undeciphered until the discovery of the Rosetta stone in 1822, but already provided a vivid picture of the nature of sacred language as a mystery that challenged scholars to unveil it.[41]

In a way this concern with the measurement of time and space is not inappropriate in interpretation of the Apocalypse, for John too ascribes great importance to it (for example Rev 8:1; 11:1–3; 12:6,14; 13:5; 14:20; 20:6; 21:15). The measurements of the temple and city are precise, as are the intervals in time between the visions. Since the rise in historical consciousness that came later in the eighteenth century and its huge eventual impact on biblical interpretation, it might seem self-explanatory that these measurements are the creation of an alternative symbolic time and space, set explicitly in 'heaven'. For an earlier age, however, it was more natural to see the 'measuring rod of gold' as not really different in kind from Newton's scientific instruments and to imagine the counting of apocalyptic time being undertaken by a grand version of a naval chronometer. It is interesting to note in the elaborate and elegant charts of the structure of Revelation drawn up by both Mede and Whiston the straight horizontal line that cuts through the ellipses of seals, trumpets and bowls: it is the line of terrestrial chronology, which in Whiston's diagram is calibrated like a ruler with the years of the Christian era (*see plate 11*). The charts express both the aesthetic completeness of the Apocalypse and the sense that without ostensive reference to measurable time the symbols remain dumb.

Newton's interest in chronology went back to his early days at Cambridge, though it was only at the end of his life that a breach of copyright forced him to prepare his great chronological scheme for publication. It eventually appeared after his death as *The Chronology of Ancient Kingdoms Amended*, a book many times more tedious than its title. The core of the amendments may not seem revolutionary, being a redating of the voyage of the Argonauts to 936 BC; the work's interest now can lie only in its scientific principles. His labour, said Newton, would 'make Chronology suit with the Course of Nature, with Astronomy, with Sacred History, with *Herodotus* the Father of History, and with it self'.[42] He did not limit his studies to ancient or biblical history: for instance in his Latin manuscript *Tuba quarta* he records detailed research into the movements of Goths and Vandals in the sixth century, in order to clarify the interpretation of the fourth trumpet of the Apocalypse.[43] Both the entire course of history and its every detail were the direct work of the Creator; so when Leibniz mocked Newton's talk of divine intervention, Newton (in F. E. Manuel's words)

> glorified those very interventions as the supreme acts of God's providential will. ... The whole creation and all of history were interventions. For Newton intervention did not imply physical or historical chaos. There were underlying operational designs in the world that could be defined as the history of the motions of the planets, which displayed a marvellous orderliness, and the history of the revolutions of empires and churches, which had a similarly simple pattern – one so simple that it could be contained in two small books, Daniel and the Apocalypse, that were really repetitions of each other.[44]

The empirical study of chronology and history cannot extend from present into future; yet, Newton assumed, the inspired Daniel and John have given prophecies (if not precise indications) of what is to be, so that there need never be any fear of descent out of providence into chaos. Other interpreters were less cautious than Newton about the future, and did not hesitate to predict dates for fulfilments on the basis of apocalyptic measurement. Thus Whiston's first edition of his commentary announced 'the commencement of our Saviour's Kingdom' for ten years on in 1716 – a date that naturally had to be revised several times, as Whiston lived to 1752.[45] The most elaborate of all calculations, involving the use of four-figure fractions, came not from an Englishman but from the German pietist and distinguished textual scholar Johann Albert Bengel (1687–1752), who uniquely predicted two millennia, the first commencing in 1836 (thirty years before the date Whiston finally settled on), the second lasting from 2836 to 3836. Though there is little sign of British scholars following Bengel on this point, his influence in England was considerable, since Bengel's German commentary on Revelation was translated into English at John Wesley's request in 1757. Wesley made extensive use of the *Gnomon Novi Testamenti* of 'that great Light of the Christian World' in preparing his *Explanatory Notes on the New Testament* (1755), and prefaces his notes on Revelation with the confession that he had for years neglected 'the intermediate Parts' of the book,

> as utterly despairing of understanding them, after the fruitless Attempts of so many wise and good Men; and perhaps I should have lived and died in this Sentiment, had I not seen the Works of the great *Bengelius*. But these revived my hopes of understanding even the Prophecies of this Book. ... The following Notes are mostly those of that excellent Man.[46]

Wesley simply laid Bengel's interpretation before his readers without elaboration or comment, but another early Methodist, James Kershaw, shared both his pietism and his mathematical interests. After working with Wesley for a time as an itinerant preacher, Kershaw settled in about 1770 in Gainsborough, Lincolnshire, where he wrote sermons, verse and a number of leisurely dialogues, including *An Essay on the Principal Parts of the Book of the Revelations; in a Series of Dialogues between Didascalos and Phylotheos*. Didascalos makes the usual historical identifications of seals and trumpets, quoting Pyle and Isaac Newton as well as Bengel, but his conversation with the admiring Phylotheos often

wanders far from the biblical text in describing papal 'superstition',
with forays into both rhyming couplets and arithmetical calculations. In 577 pages of dialogue they get only as far as Rev 13, but
the 'usefulness' of the Apocalypse is sufficiently established to elicit
from Phylotheos the keen response, 'My dear Didascalos, my
prayer is, and ever shall be, from Popery, Slavery and Arbitrary
Power both in Church and State, good Lord deliver us. Amen, and
Amen'.[47]

Bolder than the Methodists both in his antipapalism and in his
chronology of the future was the Taunton dissenter Thomas
Reader, author of *An Inquiry whether Popery is a proper Subject of
Toleration in Protestant States* (to which the answer was a firm No).
In 1778 Reader published his *Remarks on the Prophetic Part of the
Revelation of St John; especially the Three Last Trumpets*. Its prognostications are a complex mixture of the dating of the apocalyptic 1260
years from 606 CE (when Phocas declared the Bishop of Rome to be
universal Bishop) and of the progress of millennial 'weeks', requiring precise computations of the exact moment of Jesus' resurrection
(three hours' difference in this meaning a difference of 125 years in
the date of future fulfilments).[48] The Book of Revelation shows, he
says, that in 1816 the conversion of the Jews is to begin and in 1862
the two witnesses are to be slain, before the 1260 years end with
the seventh trumpet in 1866; at its sound the Jews will return to
their land, the Muslims will become papists and the Roman beast
will become a dragon and later ally with the Grand Turk. Further
on in the nineteenth century the true Church is to flee to the
American 'wilderness' (Rev 12:6), and in 1936 the Temple is to be
rebuilt at Jerusalem (Rev 15:8) in time for the outpouring of the
seven bowls and the Millennium beginning in 2016. The details of
the subsequent judgement (lasting from 3125 to 3351) were elaborated in a later pamphlet *Of the Time of the General Judgment,* and
Reader's mathematical exposition of the Apocalypse was completed in 1785 by his *Remarks on the Three First Chapters of the
Revelation*: this used conjectural Greek etymology of the names of
some of the seven churches to allocate each to a period of history
and added further evidence from the square and square root of 666
to show, should any of his readers still doubt it, that the beast was
the Pope.

Concern for past and future chronology was shown also, as we
have seen, by Newton's successor as Professor of Mathematics at
Cambridge. William Whiston was an Arian like Newton, though

unlike him he was so openly and lost his chair as a result, spending the rest of his life in scientific research, freelance lecturing and a campaign to abolish the Athanasian Creed. But driving his diverse and engaging energies and driving his interpretation of Revelation is the Newtonian faith in and search for order. With a logic emulating Samuel Clarke's, he prefaces his lengthy *Essay on the Revelation of St John* (1706) with a series of 18 'propositions', stressing the historical reference of all the book's symbols and their mathematical coherence, which is more graphically demonstrated in his diagram. When it comes to detailed exposition, he generally follows Mede. So the first unsealing represents the spread of the Gospel in the Roman Empire; the second the persecution of the Jews by Trajan and Hadrian; the third seal takes the reader to Septimus Severus, the fourth to Maximinus, the fifth to Diocletian, the sixth to Constantine and the seventh to the corruptions afflicting the post-Constantinian church. All these interpretations are supported by historical 'evidence' and corresponding details from the text. The first trumpet then sounds, bringing hail from the north, which represents the invasion of the Empire from the north by Goths. But the providence of God, confirmed by the prophecy of Scripture with its mention at this trumpet of 'earth' and not sea, ensures that the Goths got no further than inland Europe:

> So exactly did the Providence of God confine the Instruments of this Trumpet to the Object therein specify'd: and whenever, during the space particularly allotted to this Trumpet, they ventured beyond their bounds, they were still Discourag'd, Repuls'd, and Beaten, and so oblig'd to content themselves with the Proportion allotted to them (p. 161).

When he gets to the sixth trumpet or second woe (Rev 9:13–21), which he says is 'a most lively Description of the *Turks*, and of the Miseries they have brought upon *Europe*', Whiston's researches lead to elaborate confirmations of the movements of particular sultans in the Euphrates area, with an eight-page argument to prove that the 'hour and day and month and year' (in hieroglyphics 396 years, 106 days) exactly corresponds to the interval between the Ottoman institution of public prayers on 19 May 1301 and Prince Eugene's victory over the Turks on 1 September 1697.[49] Whiston's later memoirs show how far this hunger for signs with unequivocal prophetic meaning went, for he lists 99 'predictions' or 'completions' in 'An

Account of the fulfilling of those Signals whose Times are already past', ranging from the Turkish wars, meteors, eclipses and earth-quakes, to the increase of learning since the time of Mede, improved navigation, and the death of a million people from drinking gin.[50]

If the symbols in the biblical text were not also 'signals', if prophecy were not univocal, then for Whiston it would suggest that providence was failing. To avoid such a possibility he is prepared to go to great lengths in rationalising the canon of scripture. For instance his horror of both sexual immorality and allegorical inter-pretation lead him to speak of 'the fatal introduction of the impure book of *Canticles* into the canon of the Old Testament'.[51] And believ-ing that the proof of Jesus' messiahship from Old Testament prophecy required literal fulfilment of the text, but realising also that this was hard to demonstrate, he went to great lengths to show that the current Hebrew text was faulty and that the first century had access to the correct one, from which the New Testament proof-texts were drawn. This original was reconstructed with a mixture of erudition and wild fancy in his *Essay Towards Restoring the True Text of the Old Testament* (1722), which led inadvertently to one of the pioneering works of biblical criticism of the eighteenth century. For Anthony Collins, the Deist already known as an *esprit fort* from his *Discourse of Free-Thinking* (1713), was as sure as Whiston that it was intolerable for texts to carry a multiplicity of meanings. But he had little difficulty in mocking the *Essay*'s speculations. With a lightness of touch that eluded the erudite and ingenuous Whiston, he showed that the interpretation of scripture by St Paul and other New Testament writers was firmly 'rabbinical' and allegorical rather than literal. Collins has already established that the truth of Christianity depends on its fulfilment of Old Testament prophecy: how, he asks implicitly, can such eccentric interpretation prove any such thing? So – although Collins does not make the conclusion explicit at this stage in his polemical career – the whole 'argument from prophecy' is exploded and the notion of Christianity as a religion that can be demonstrated is undermined.[52] Such was the logical outcome of the dual assumption that 'prophecy' meant prediction and that texts could bear one meaning only.

'USEFULNESS'

Another exegete of the Apocalypse to cross swords with Collins was Moses Lowman. His *Argument from Prophecy that Jesus is the*

*Messiah vindicated, in some considerations of the Old Testament as
grounds and reasons of the Christian Religion* appeared in 1733, and
was followed four years later by his *Paraphrase and Notes on the
Revelation of St John.* Lowman lacks Whiston's eclecticism, but is
equally confident in assigning precise meanings to the text. His
demonstration of the 'exact Conformity between the Prophetick
Description and the real State of the World and Christianity, for a
series of many Hundred Years' will, he hopes, 'greatly confirm the
Evidence of the Christian Religion'.[53] Like Whiston, Lowman prefaces his commentary with an historical chart, aligning the stages of
the narrative with their fulfilments in the history of the church. But
Lowman's tone is gentler than Whiston's, and his outline ends (at
Rev 22:6) by claiming that

> THE CONCLUSION confirms the Truth and Certainty of these
> Prophecies, warns against corrupting them, exhorts to hope the
> Accomplishment of them; an useful Spirit and Temper, to give
> good Men Consolation in all their present Afflictions, and to pre-
> serve them from the Corruptions of Religion, how prevailing
> soever in their own Times; which is, The useful Moral, and prin-
> cipal Doctrine of all these Prophecies (p. xxxiv).

For Lowman is a master at using the violent apocalyptic symbols
to soothe his readership and protect them from any political or
religious extremism:

> The Lake of Fire and Brimstone, and the Terrors of the second
> Death, the Portion of the Fearful and Unbelieving, the Glory and
> Happiness of the holy *Jerusalem*, and a Right to the Tree of Life ...
> are represented in so strong and lively Images, as are fit to fix the
> Attention, and make way to the Heart and Affections, and
> engage them with Zeal to follow the wise Directions of
> Understanding and Judgment (p. xxiv).

His paraphrase of the wild anti-imperial missive from Patmos is
filled with flowing and moralistic periphrases designed to appeal
to the 'Persons in Eminent Stations' that he refers to in his preface,
with the note that if they act wisely and piously 'we are directed
by these Prophecies to consider them, as raised by GOD' (p. v). For
instance 'Jesus Christ, who is the faithful witness, and the first
begotten of the dead' (Rev 1:5) becomes 'whom God rais'd from
the Dead ... and thereby gave us full Evidence, and reasonable

Assurance of our own Resurrection'; the smoke from the bottomless pit (Rev 9:2) is 'a very proper Representation of great Errors,
darkening the Understanding, obscuring the Truth, and attended
with Violence and Destruction'; the cry of the angel of the waters,
'Thou art righteous, O Lord' (Rev 16:5) becomes 'How does thy
Righteousness appear in thy Ways of Providence, O God, who art
unchangeable in thy Perfections, and constant in thy righteous
Administration of Government'.[54] Lowman recognises that many
believers avoid the book of Revelation for fear of 'enthusiasm', its
becoming 'an Occasion of great Disorders in the World, which I
am sure it is Wisdom carefully to watch against'; yet, he continues,

> sure I am, there is no Encouragement to [Enthusiasm] in any Part
> of the Christian Religion...; except the Wisdom and Prudence of
> their own Conduct, which is the Duty of all Men at all times, and
> is the furthest thing in the World from Enthusiasm, either in Life
> or Religion, the Church has no other Directions in these Pro-
> phecies, but to *stand still, and see the Salvation of God* (p. xxvi f.)

Far from being an encouragement to enthusiasm, the Apocalypse is
'a wise Preservative against it'.

The fanatics of the seventeenth century are firmly put in their
place by this calmly reasonable exegesis, as they are later by the
Practical Observations on the Revelation of St John of Elizabeth Stuart
Bowdler (mother of the notorious editor of Shakespeare). Bowdler
calls on Mede and explains the symbols by direct correspondence
to events, though she is unusually gentle on the papacy and indeed
on everybody, converting the visionary landscape into an English
pastoral with moralising comments. Considering the dramatic
events of the sixth seal, for instance – the earthquake, the blackened
sun, falling stars, the sky vanishing and the kings of the earth
cowering among the rocks – she chooses to meditate on the wisdom
of providence in giving 'different conditions. ... for the advantage
of mankind':

> Why should not all be thankful? The Labouring Man, when fol-
> lowing the plough, might be taught to observe the refreshing,
> healthy smell, that rises from the earth, and to acknowledge the
> assistance he receives from the sparrows and crows. ... Why
> should not the Rich Man look up with gratitude, when he tastes
> the simple innocent pleasures of a walk or a ride...?[55]

It is interesting to note how many interpreters of the Bible other than Lowman chose to present their exegesis in the form of 'paraphrases', where the commentary purports to remain close to the text while actually furnishing a translation of it into a rationalistic and moralising language foreign to that of the parables or epistles or apocalypse. Among the paraphrasers are Locke, Samuel Clarke and the influential dissenter Philip Doddridge, as well as Thomas Pyle, whose *Paraphrase ... in the Manner of Dr Clarke* (1735) was quoted above. Pyle's commentary ends with words epitomising the domestic but genuine spirituality seen also in Lowman's work. The new Jerusalem, he says, affords

> the most astonishing and amiable sight to the beholder. By all of which lofty *figures* is signified, that this Christian *church* shall be made up of such *professors* as are of sincere and approved *piety*, of pure and uncorrupt *worship*; every member (or the *generality* at least), living in the practice of virtues bright, and solid, and shining; its *pastors* and *teachers* endowed with *knowledge* truly spiritual, clear, and useful; and leading their people by an *example* of holy conversation, illustrious, charming, and influential (p. 230).

A similar use of the text can be seen in the sermons of the respected Samuel Clarke. Interestingly, of the 173 of his sermons he collected for publication, 11 are on texts from the Apocalypse – more than on texts from Luke or John or Romans. But the apocalyptic appeals are blunted and moralised. The tirade against the apathetic church of Laodicea is turned into a discourse 'Of the Nature of true Christian Zeal' – and 'the Great, the Principal, the Proper Object of Zeal, is the Practice of Virtue and True Righteousness'. The final warning of Rev 22:14 is the text for a sermon with the title 'Religion consists in keeping the Commandments only', while 'He that hath ears to hear, let him hear' leads to an exposition of the 'Good Disposition' giving ears to hear as 'Attentiveness or Consideration ... a Delight in Examining into Truth and Right; a taking pleasure at all times in beholding the Light, and in hearing the Voice of reason ... Moral Probity, Sincerity, and Integrity of Mind'.[56]

The rage for moral and physical order that is evident in the biblical interpretation of this period should not be seen, however, just as a search for religious comfort. The Newtonian physico-theological project, before it was dissolved in a more thoroughgoing secularism, was for many a deeply worshipful response to the creator

God. Indeed God's creation in time and space was seen as so mar-
vellous that its scientific interpretation was the supreme homage to
him: the rational prose in which this homage was often expressed
should not blind us to its religious impulse, seen not only in Ray's
biology and Newton's physics, but also in Whiston's astronomy, in
Locke's epistemology and later in Hartley's psychology. The great
eighteenth-century theological insight, implicit though rarely articu-
lated in the disputes of the time, is that if a doctrine of creation is
taken seriously then natural religion *is* revealed religion.[57] The
rational flight from mysticism and 'enthusiasm' led ironically to the
sense of spirit pervading the whole creation, even (in Joseph
Priestley's case) to the identification of matter and spirit. And for
many the key to this rational spirituality lay in the apparently irrational visions of Daniel and Revelation.

Thus Locke's sober reverence and sincerity is evident in his writings, while of Newton F. E. Manuel can claim (perhaps with some
exaggeration) that his scriptural religion was 'not a dry one; it was
charged with emotion as intense as the effusions of mystics who
seek direct communion with God through spiritual exercises and
illumination'.[58] Yet Newton's religion was scarcely one of immanence or incarnation; there is repeated reference in his religious
writings to God as the *Pantokrator*, that is, the utterly sovereign
ruler of the universe. Addison too shows a strong sense of the
Creator's transcendence, but he goes beyond an 'argument from
design' to a religious rejoicing in design when he proclaims:

> The spacious firmament on high,
> With all the blue ethereal sky,
> And spangled heav'ns, a shining frame,
> Their great Original proclaim....
> What though in solemn silence all
> Move round the dark terrestrial ball;
> What though nor real voice nor sound
> Amid their radiant orbs be found;
> In reason's ear they all rejoice,
> And utter forth a glorious voice,
> For ever singing as they shine,
> 'The hand that made us is divine'.

Thomson's effusions, on the other hand, are directed towards the
immanent Creator as well as towards Nature itself:

Hail, Source of Being! Universal Soul
Of heaven and earth! Essential Presence, hail!
To thee I bend the knee; to thee my thoughts
Continual climb, who with a master-hand
Hast the great whole into perfection touched.

('Spring', 556–60)

Later in 'Spring' Thomson vigorously hymns the breeding of
animals and birds, then exclaims,

What is this mighty breath, ye curious, say,
That in a powerful language, felt, not heard,
Instructs the fowls of heaven, and through their breast
These arts of love diffuses? What, but God?
Inspiring God! who, boundless spirit all
And unremitting energy, pervades,
Adjusts, sustains, and agitates the whole.

('Spring', 849–55)

The depth of Thomson's religious feeling may be hard to gauge,
but his words are carefully chosen and reflect the commonly held
belief that the truly rational Newtonian man – that is, for most of
Thomson's educated contemporaries, the true Christian – is the one
whose mind is raised to a quasi-divine consciousness and perspective of the whole creation.

In this kind of scientific–ethical mysticism, the need for traditional
religious practice – sacrifice, penance, petitionary prayer – withers
away; there is no longer place for a doctrine of the Fall or for any developed Christology, for the believer is able through thought and
moral action to imitate God directly. So the seventeenth-century
deist Charles Blount could write that God is to be worshipped not
through a mediator but 'positively, by an inviolable adherence in
our lives to all things *phusei dikaia*, by an imitation of God in all his
imitable Perfections'.[59] Half a century later Matthew Tindal is using
the same language, seeing it as incontrovertible and 'evident by the
Light of Nature that there is a God' who is perfect and happy and
therefore does not require the worship or faith of humanity but does
inspire imitation. This is far from 'enthusiasm', he says, stressing
(like Clarke) the need to control 'irregular passions' and 'immoderate
desires', but in any other period the language he uses of God would
be called enthusiastic:

From the consideration of these perfections, we cannot but have
the highest veneration, nay the greatest adoration and love for
this supreme Being ... a wonderful and surprizing sense of the
divine Goodness, [to] fill us with admiration, transport and
extasy (of which we daily see among contemplative persons remarkable instances) and not only force us to express a never-
failing gratitude in raptures of the highest praise and
thanksgiving; but make us strive to imitate him in our extensive
love to our Fellow-Creatures.[60]

Such confidence in moral kinship with God may seem far from
Joseph Butler's diffident spirit, but behind his doctrine of conscience too lies a similar devout sense of the wisdom of the Creator
and of the centrality of a moral response to him. For both the Deist
and the bishop, it can be argued, the obsessive avoidance of 'enthusiasm' actually enabled a genuinely rational spirituality.

PURITY

The desire for religious clarity is not of course peculiar to the eighteenth century or to protestantism. Seen through the concern for
chronology and prophecy, however, there is a peculiarly protestant
rationalist form of that spiritual desire. It emerges in the consistent
antipapalism of the various readings of Revelation considered
above, but it goes beyond that familiar English phenomenon into
an urge, even a campaign, to purify Christianity of all corruption.
    In their different ways, Tindal, Pyle and Thomson celebrate the
liberating power of the Revolution of 1688 to complete the task that
had been only begun by the sixteenth-century Reformers.[61] Political
and religious liberty are to depend on a purging not simply of
papal power but of the bulk of the dogmatic structure of Christianity. A pure religion – variously defined as 'natural', 'reasonable',
'primitive' and 'scriptural' – is at last within reach. So for Locke the
messiahship of Jesus is the only essential article of faith, while his
follower Toland attempts in *Nazarenus* to recover a primitive
Ebionite Christianity.[62] The Deists, particularly Collins and Tindal,
write virulently against the corruptions of 'priestcraft', implicating
the easy-going Anglican clergy as much as the more flamboyantly
corrupt papists and pagans in the decay of pure religion. But the
campaign is most evident in the writings of the millennialists Isaac

Newton, Whiston and (later) Priestley. And it may be no coincidence that so many of those drawn to exegesis of the Apocalypse were at one time or other in their lives Arians or Unitarians – Whitby, Newton, Whiston, Clarke, Priestley, Edward Evanson, J. L. Towers and S. T. Coleridge among them. It is not just that there is little place for Jesus in their understanding of prophecy and fulfilment, though that is certainly true – indeed it is remarkable that so Christocentric a book as Revelation can be repeatedly interpreted with only passing reference to Jesus as a Messiah–prophet, and it is arguable that in Newton's world chronology and theology of revelation the place of Jesus is inferior to that of Noah. Nor is it true to say (with Reventlow) that the Newtonians' Arianism 'is an indubitable sign that the view of God held by these people was primarily oriented on "the book of his works"', for that is to underestimate the value they placed on the Bible as direct (if not always inerrant) Word of God.[63] Rather, one can see the various English forms of Arianism, Socinianism and Unitarianism, whether within the established church or in the world of Dissent, as an attempt to form a pure scriptural Christianity, purged not only of the familiar demons of mysticism, popery and enthusiasm, but also of the whole structure of patristic dogma and metaphysics that the Reformation had barely touched. And to achieve that, a simplified biblical hermeneutics of what Hans Frei calls 'ostensive reference' is required.

While Newton's sense of God's transcendence is inescapable, he eschewed all metaphysics, reducing Christianity to belief in an omnipotent Creator, the inspiration of the Bible, the commandments to love God and neighbour, and a very simplified church order.[64] Manuel sums up his religion thus:

> Newton's statement of fundamental religious principles, his interpretation of prophecy, his textual criticism of the historical works of Scripture, his system of world chronology, his cosmological theories and his euhemeristic reduction of pagan mythology all bespeak the same mentality and style of thought. If nature was consonant with itself, so was Isaac Newton's mind. At the height of his powers there was in him a compelling drive to find order and design in what appeared to be chaos, to distil from a vast, inchoate mass of materials a few basic principles that would embrace the whole and define the relationships of its component parts.[65]

The desire for unity and hatred of corruption, whether patristic or papal, is very clear in Newton's extensive researches into early church history, preserved mainly in the Yahuda manuscripts. He writes with animosity of the arch-villain Athanasius, while the various drafts of his 'Irenicum', designed as a common basis for all protestants to unite on, studiously avoid any metaphysical statement beyond the assertion of God's existence and omnipotence.[66] Metaphysics, especially Trinitarianism, was for Newton a denial both of the simple command to worship and obey God alone and of his (Newton's) understanding of the nature of creation and matter. The latter can be seen as a spiritual materialism, a kind of Spinozism with a belief in creation and transcendence awkwardly tacked on. It was taken to its logical conclusion two generations later by Priestley, who campaigned doggedly for the stripping of all dogma from Christianity and for the separation of church and state, yet who – in the milieu of Franklin, Godwin and Paine – remained a determined and passionate Christian minister.

But the combination of materialism with belief in 'prophecy' and with the search for a pure form of Christianity is clearest and most attractive in the life and writings of William Whiston. Whiston's extensive memoirs sparkle with a candour rarely seen in his secretive mentor Isaac Newton, and he is not afraid to attack Newton for concealing his Arianism, as well as for faulty chronology, claiming that after Whiston's dismissal from Cambridge Newton disliked and feared him for his incorruptibility.[67] Among the detailed instructions for those undertaking the republication of his varied writings (editors who have not yet arisen) are scornful recollections of fellow-clergy who, though 'Eusebians' like Whiston, were prepared to subscribe to the 39 Articles in order to gain preferment. It is clear that, for all his mathematical and scientific research and lecturing, the great passions of his life were the interpretation of 'prophecy' and the reconstitution of 'primitive Christianity'. In the final years of his life Whiston associated rather reluctantly with the Baptists, but he remained an Anglican priest with great devotion to the sacraments. Unfortunately, however, the sacrament in the Church of England was marred on certain days of the year by that 'public cursing of Christians', the so-called Athanasian Creed, and Whiston's memoirs delightfully record the development of his conscience as he graduates from simply refusing to join in the words to ostentatiously sitting down during its recitation to the public walking out of church, which he achieved on the Feast of Saints

Simon and Jude in 1746 (though one senses his disappointment on St Andrew's Day of the same year when the priest omitted the prescribed words, so that Whiston 'had no opportunity ... to shew my detestation of that monstrous Creed').[68] A sign of the respect that this sincere eccentric won is in Anthony Collins's attack on Whiston's theory of prophecy. Collins was not shy of polemic and destroys Whiston's essay with bravado, but he feels bound to preface his reply with a long and elegant 'Apology for Mr Whiston's liberty of writing' and to conclude it with a generous sketch of his victim. In this he describes Whiston as 'a great Mathematician, Philosopher and Divine', 'a most Acute Person', 'a good Christian' filled with honesty and integrity and so 'the Reverse of most other Divines', and 'a Zealous Member of the Church of England' despite its persecution of him; but sadly a man 'deficient in judgment', whose 'warmth of temper' and 'preconceived scheme of things' often delude him.[69]

Equal to Whiston in integrity and keener than him in radicalism was a later Anglican priest, Edward Evanson, vicar of Tewkesbury from 1769 to 1778. He resigned his living as a result of his publication in the previous year of *A Letter to the Right Reverend the Lord Bishop of Litchfield and Coventry [Richard Hurd]; wherein the Importance of the Prophecies of the New Testament, and the Nature of the Grand Apostacy predicted in them, are particularly and impartially considered*. It is hard from Evanson's argument to tell how important he really feels the 'prophecies' to be and how far he is using Revelation as a scriptural prop for his advocacy of religious purity – though it could be argued that Bishop Hurd used the text similarly for his virulent attack on papalism. For Evanson this is too narrow a target. While agreeing with Hurd that the fulfilment of prophecy provides increasing evidence of the truth of revelation, he refutes the bishop's theory that a 'prophetic' symbol in the Bible always signifies the same object: that gets apostate non-papists off the hook. For there are, he says, 'many Antichrists', and all established churches – not least that reformed by Henry VIII – have shown signs of the 'man of sin' and of the 'idolatry' bound up with the worship of Christ. The beast's 'blasphemy' depicted in Rev 13 is in fact the doctrine of the Incarnation.[70] And the 1260 years of oppression refer not to papal power but should be dated from the blasphemous decrees of the ecumenical councils – perhaps from Constantinople (381 CE) or Ephesus (431) or Chalcedon (451), since 1260 years after each there is a remarkable sign of progress towards liberty in English history (the last, 1711, being the rather obscure occasion of the failure of the Convocation's prosecution of Whiston). There is in Evanson a spirit of tolerance and universalism that palliates his uncompromising conclusion that

> either those predictions of the Gospel, which ought to have occurred before the present date of the Christian aera, must have really come to pass, or else the Gospel itself is false. The grand object of those prophecies is a Catholic apostacy from the true and rational religion of Jesus Christ to a *mysterious, blasphemous, idolatrous superstition* ... EITHER THE CHRISTIAN REVELATION IS NOT TRUE, OR THE RELIGION OF EVERY ORTHODOX CHURCH IN EUROPE IS FABULOUS AND FALSE (p. 126 f.)

Though he was apparently a popular pastor in Tewkesbury, it was hardly possible for a man with such views to lead the creeds and liturgy of the established Church, which he saw as the second beast of Revelation. He set up a private congregation using Samuel Clarke's expurgated liturgy and later censored the biblical canon too: Revelation was in fact one of the few books left in it from the New Testament, together with Luke, Acts and a handful of Paul's letters.

Evanson could attract few adherents, however, any more than could Whiston's earlier Societies for Promoting Primitive Christianity, which he hoped would convert the Church of England to pure scriptural religion. But Whiston's definition of scripture was even more idiosyncratic than Evanson's. Not only did he hold to an 'original' text of the Old Testament, the source of his dispute with Collins; he also included in the New Testament canon the 'pseudo-Clementine' *Apostolical Constitutions*, which he described as 'the most sacred of the canonical books of the New Testament ... these sacred Christian laws or constitutions were delivered at Jerusalem, or in Mount Sion, by our Saviour to the eleven apostles there assembled after his resurrection'.[71] On the basis of these supposed dominical commands, Whiston rewrote the liturgy of the Church of England. His revisions have some similarity with those of the contemporary Non-jurors (whose integrity Whiston respected); they also anticipate changes that were to come only much later in the wake of the Oxford movement and liturgical movement, and significantly too in the liturgical elaborations of the Catholic Apostolic Church founded by another apocalyptic interpreter,

Edward Irving. It is not surprising that Whiston identifies himself with Milton's Abdiel ('faithful found/Among the faithless; faithful only he'). But his eccentricities cannot hide his zeal for a pure state of obedience to God, whether expressed in a right church order, right morality or right interpretation of prophecy. He also expressed admiration for his fellow-priest and fellow-sacramentalist John Wesley, particularly on account of the latter's revival of primitive practices, though adding 'I hope he will, at last, leave off his athanasian follies, and come intirely into old christianity'.[72]

For Whiston the rationalist Arian, Wesley the high-church Evangelical and William Law the mystical Non-juror all looked ardently to the first century for authoritative deliverance from what they saw as the corruptions of eighteenth-century Christianity. When it comes to the desire for purity and the refusal to countenance opacity or obliqueness in Scripture it seems that Coleridge's 'moonlight' and 'stove' – Socinianism and Methodism – are not so opposed. For whatever their differences over dogma and the place of emotion in religion, Newton, Whiston, Wesley and Priestley are at one in seeking direct instruction from univocal 'prophecy'. The canon may be variously defined by them and their keys for interpretation may be different. But whether that key be a hieroglyphical dictionary, the *Apostolical Constitutions*, a 'heart strangely warmed', the human mind or the study of history, once it is correctly turned the words of Scripture will, they believe, offer clear and incontrovertible direction.

* * *

But it was a belief that could not be sustained. Whiston's ingenious mouldings of the Bible to make it yield the pure and ordered church he dreamed of became increasingly frantic and unconvincing; his reading of a providential scheme of history from the words of Revelation could be achieved only by refusing attention to the actual symbolic worlds those words create and inhabit. For all his attempts at system-building, the very confusion of his thought bears witness to the impact of the biblical world on him and his unconscious rational resistance to its multivalency. Isaac Newton's thought was far more intuitive, and his understanding of the canon far more conventional. Yet when he came to interpret prophecy and scripture his passion for clarity, measurement and univocal meaning ironically drowned the text in a sea of lexical definitions, while the next generation's geological and historical researches and its growth in imaginative historical awareness were to leave his huge scheme of world chronology stranded on a shore that was deserted by all but the most determined fundamentalists. As for the moral lessons and religious comfort that interpreters like Clarke and Lowman tried to draw from the Apocalypse, their distance from the desperate and vengeful world of persecuted Christians in the Roman Empire could hardly be concealed: in this at least, the despised 'enthusiasts' responded much more authentically to the text.

All these interpreters were responding to genuine elements of the Book of Revelation – its concern with history and politics, or its measurements of time and space, or its insistence on pure and whole-hearted witness. But the text of Scripture, and of the Apocalypse in particular, proved too intractable, too chaotic, to fit the keys or to bear the weight of the systems it was required to endorse.

3

Prophecy and Poetry

The Book of Revelation lay before the educated Christians of the Enlightenment, replete with canonical authority and through its mysterious language demanding interpretation. They approached it with their innocent lust for clarity and purity, for firm moral or historical evidence. But as in the past, it confounded the interpretations extracted from it, or rather, laid upon it. There remained obscurity in the text that could not be dispelled by the light of the Newtonian sky. And for all their confidence, there are signs that something of that apocalyptic darkness still lurked in their own experience – a sense that the Reformation and Glorious Revolution, the discoveries of Locke and Newton, had not after all banished the mysteries of Rome and Geneva or ensured a lasting era of reason and prosperity. Pascal's fear of 'the eternal silence of those infinite spaces' was not extinguished, for it came from a level of experience inaccessible to scientific reasoning. And the later words of Dr Johnson's Imlac perhaps spoke for many in a generation that put such faith in clarity and order: 'Of the uncertainties of our present state, the most dreadful and alarming is the uncertain continuance of reason'.[1] The darkness emerges in Newton's furtiveness over his biblical work and in Whiston's concern with sin; it is there in James Thomson's use of the Book of Job and in the incorporation of mystery with order in the great gardens of the period. And it is very consciously present in the work of three of the most original and enduring writers of the age, Jonathan Swift, Joseph Butler and William Law.

Swift was no friend of 'enthusiasm': in *A Tale of a Tub* (written in about 1697) the enthusiastic individualist Jack gets even rougher treatment than the papist Peter. But Swift's satire is directed at system builders of all kinds. Perhaps the most pathetically absurd people his Gulliver encounters are the single-mindedly rational Laputans. When Gulliver moves on to Glubbdubdribb and is able to speak to departed spirits, Aristotle informs him that 'new Systems of Nature were but new Fashions, which would vary in every Age; and even those who pretend to demonstrate them from Mathematical Principles, would flourish but a short Period of Time, and be out of Vogue when that was determined'.[2] The faith in reason and nature and therefore in natural religion and in any system of belief is most severely questioned in the fourth part of *Gulliver's Travels*, where he meets the eminently gentle and reasonable Houyhnhnms and discovers himself to be a despicable Yahoo; so in the devastating conclusion Gulliver finds his wife and family and whole species repulsive and can look for salvation only through communion with horses. The 'nature' of humanity, far from being rational, is savage. Seeing his race reflected in the Yahoos, Gulliver (and Swift with him?) is made to concur with the earlier judgement of the king of Brobdingnag on hearing the description of the British constitution: 'I cannot but conclude the Bulk of your Natives, to be the most pernicious Race of little odious Vermin that Nature ever suffered to crawl upon the Surface of the Earth'.[3] The doctrine of original sin is back in the Age of Reason; and back, it seems, with little hope of redemption, since reason and peace are not even a distant hope of progress or gift of grace, only a nostalgic dream of a lost Houyhnhnm world which the human species cannot enter. The earlier *Tale of a Tub* appears less misanthropic, yet it mocks scientific and literary system building in a more buccaneering way with its luxuriant digressions and the posturing of the 'author'. And it is hard not to see apocalyptic interpretation in the solemn tradition of Brightman and Mede as one of the systems that Swift undermines: his much-interrupted parable of the three brothers can be read as a mirror image of the 'prophetic history of the church' drawn from Revelation, turning the exegetes' systems back to front in a kind of reversion to the apocalyptic tone itself.

A more measured form of satire, at home in yet critical of the fashions of the age, is present in Swift's friend Pope, who as a Roman Catholic could not be expected to sympathise with Mede's historiography. In *Messiah: A Sacred Eclogue* (1712) Pope had attempted a 'prophetic' imitation of both Isaiah and Virgil. But in *The Dunciad* (1728) and particularly its fourth book (1742), he scatters mocking ammunition over a wide variety of targets subsumed under the leadership of Dulness, whose apotheosis is a kind of Augustan apocalypse:

Yet, yet a moment, one dim Ray of Light
Indulge, dread Chaos, and eternal Night! ...
Sick was the Sun, the Owl forsook his bower,
The moon-struck Prophet felt the madding hour:
Then rose the Seed of Chaos, and of Night,
To blot out Order, and extinguish Light,
Of dull and venal a new World to mould,
And bring Saturnian days of Lead and Gold.[4]

The hopes of millennial renovation, focused in science, reason and morality and lent a veneer of biblical language, are relativised by being situated in the overblown theatre of early eighteenth-century London, and at the end of the book the ambitions of civilisation expire in yawns, Chaos returns, 'And universal Darkness buries All'.[5] Pope is careful to say that Religion, unlike Science, Art and Morality, is not extinguished in this anti-apocalypse, merely veiled; but certainly any biblical teleology is abolished, or at any rate deferred beyond the theatre of history.

Something of the same darkness, though none of Swift's or Pope's irony, is found in that most hesitant of apologias for Christian revelation, Bishop Butler's *Analogy of Religion* (1736). After his meandering argument in the first part that 'the constitution and course of nature' provides an analogy for belief in God as moral Governor, Butler turns in the second part to defend the Christian scheme of revelation by the same analogy. He deals with probability, not with proofs; yet as part of the 'evidence for Christianity' he uses the traditional arguments from miracles and prophecy. He is particularly cautious on the subject of miracles, but with prophecy he is more assertive and is prepared to consider not only the fulfilment of Old Testament prophecies in the coming of Christ but also the fulfilment of New Testament prophecies in subsequent history: 'we, or future ages, may possibly have a proof of [Christianity], which [the people of the first century] could not have, from the conformity between the prophetic history, and the state of the world and of Christianity'.[6] But this does not mean that Butler shares the interpretations of contemporaries like Whiston and Lowman. Not only is his approach much more diffident, his whole understanding of prophecy and of biblical language is more subtle. When he speaks of 'the hieroglyphical and figurative language' of prophecy, he is not thinking of a Newtonian lexicon of univocal meanings but, on the contrary, of the slipperiness of all language.

So in the same chapter (II.3) he can say, 'Language is, in its very nature, inadequate, ambiguous, liable to infinite abuse, even from negligence; and so liable to it from design, that every man can deceive and betray by it'. The inspiration of the Bible does not preserve its words from such abuse, nor does it provide them with indisputable 'meaning': unless it is certain that the scriptures are *not* inspired, he says, 'it must in all reason be supposed ... that they may have some further meaning than what the compilers saw or understood' (II.7). And certainly 'the whole scheme of scripture is not yet understood' (II.3), just as in nature 'it is certain, there are innumerable things, in the constitution and government of the universe, which are ... beyond the natural reach of our faculties' (II.2).

This is not a call for thoroughgoing scepticism (though Hume was soon to take Butler's method to its logical outcome), nor is it a call for a reversion to allegorical reading of the Bible. Butler accepts Newton's cosmology and its 'general laws', but he does not draw from them the moral optimism or the faith in the possibility of universal knowledge that were their fashionable consequences and that many of his latitudinarian fellow-bishops preached with an eloquence that eluded him. Rather, with his unusual combination of rationalism and agnosticism, and with what Basil Willey called 'the rather melancholy yet devout spirit which is characteristic of him', Butler is constantly aware of darkness, sin and disorder conflicting with the regularity of the general laws.[7] He is prepared to use this incomprehensibility of the world as a rather dubious argument for believing incomprehensible things in revealed religion – 'the constitution of the world and God's natural government over it, is all mystery, as much as the Christian dispensation', he writes with uncharacteristic conciseness (II.5). But it is far more than an apologetic counter. Behind it lies a deep sense of original, even cosmic, sin:

> Whoever will consider the manifold miseries, and the extreme wickedness of the world; the wrongnesses within themselves, which the best complain of, and endeavour to amend, but that the generality grow more profligate and corrupt with age; that heathen moralists thought the present state to be a state of punishment: to all which might be added, that the earth our habitation has the appearances of being a ruin..., will think he has little reason to object against the scripture account, that mankind is in a state of degradation.[8]

This sounds like the language of Calvinism; yet Butler was no more a Calvinist than any of his Whig colleagues when it came to the means of rescue from degradation. For although he defends the Christian revelation, it is clear that for him 'such frail creatures as we are' are to be saved through the activity of conscience rather than through atonement by Christ and that life on the ruinous earth is a pedagogy or state of 'probation' for that future life which is one of his firmest convictions.

Butler is cautious in using the language of scripture, and *a fortiori* of apocalyptic, to speak of this future. Yet as we have seen he is not averse to speaking of prophecy and fulfilment and is clearly acquainted with and not dismissive of the theories of Mede and Newton, to whom he is probably referring when he writes of the mysterious preservation of the Jewish people and the prophecy of their restoration and the Millennium:

> Such circumstances ... fall in with the prophetic history of things still future, give it some additional credibility, have the appear-ance of being somewhat in order to the full completion of it. Indeed it requires a good degree of knowledge, and great calm-ness and consideration, to be able to judge, thoroughly, of the evidence for the truth of Christianity from that part of the prophetic history which relates to the situation of the kingdoms of the world, and to the state of the church, from the establish-ment of Christianity to the present time. But it appears, from a general view of it, to be very material. And those persons who have thoroughly examined it, and some of them were men of the coolest tempers, greatest capacities, and least liable to imputa-tions of prejudice, insist upon it as determinately conclusive (II.7.ii).

Though the cautious Butler works with probability, not determ-inate conclusivity, he is not a stranger in the world of rationalist biblical interpretation. But by him, as more elliptically by Swift, the darkness that lay behind the rationalist clarity is made explicit. Both men sensed that the darkness was not only in the human heart and 'the constitution and course of nature' but in the language of the Bible and the Christian scheme of revelation itself. And the way in which less cautious interpreters tried – and ultimately failed – to draw from the obscure text of Revelation a clear message in the spirit of the age suggests that that darkness afflicted even them.

The most direct witness to inner darkness and against rationalist optimism in the early eighteenth century was however not a churchman of the Establishment like Swift or Butler but the isolated Jacobite Non-juror William Law, whose *Serious Call to a Devout and Holy Life* exercised such influence over John Wesley and later Evangelicals. *A Serious Call* appeared in 1728, the same year as the first edition of *The Dunciad*, one year after *Gulliver's Travels* (and the death of Isaac Newton) and two years after Butler's reputation was established with the publication of his *Fifteen Sermons*; the following year saw the foundation of the Wesleys' 'Holy Club' at Oxford and so the beginnings of Methodism. Law was later to move away from his orthodox high-church background into absorption in the esoteric doctrines of Jakob Boehme, but his concern remained what it was in the 1720s, namely to insist on a single-minded religion of the heart and of the hand as opposed to the reasonable religion of the head and the respectable religion of custom. Between extravagant charity and complete hardheartedness 'there is no middle way to be taken', he writes, adding later in his characteristic tone that

> This, and this alone, is Christianity, an universal holiness in every part of life, a heavenly wisdom in all our actions, not conforming to the spirit and temper of the world, but turning all worldly enjoyments into means of piety and devotion to God.[9]

Though Law does not countenance 'enthusiasm' and believes that all are called 'to act up to the excellency of their rational nature, and to make reason and order the law of all their designs and actions' (p. 96), he actually uses the rationalist arsenal to attack the comfortable assumptions of rationalist religion. Especially in the eleventh chapter of *A Serious Call*, Enlightenment notions of moderation, happiness and usefulness are neatly reversed with a logic worthy of Samuel Clarke but exercised in a totally different spirit of piety. It is not 'religion moderately practised' but rather 'the strict rules and restraints of an exalted piety' that lead to peace of mind; not the 'inventions of happiness' through clothes, sport, money and so on but the 'strait and narrow way' that is the key to lasting happiness.[10] With a use of analogy less tortuous than Butler's and with a humour more gentle than Swift's, Law depicts in his 'characters' – like Succus the glutton, Negotius the businessman and Feliciana the lady of fashion – the inanity and decadence of all living that is not consciously directed to God:

This is the reason that I have laid before you so many characters of the vanity of a worldly life, to teach you to make a benefit of the corruption of the age, and that you may be made wise, though not by the sight of what piety is, yet by seeing what misery and folly reigns, where piety is not (p. 128).

Again, Law is no Calvinist. What his characters depict is folly rather than depravity, and for all the bleakness of his view of human behaviour there is room for a definite optimism. But it is an optimism founded not on rationalist faith in benign providence, nor primarily on trust in God's saving grace, but on that doctrine that was to have such powerful attraction for the Wesleys, the possibility of 'Christian perfection'. And this possibility is founded in turn on a life of sincere repentance and devotion, fortified if possible by celibacy and voluntary poverty. In other words, Law removes the locus of religion from the design of the universe or the faith of the Church to the inclination of the individual heart. This move is the more explicit in his later 'Behmenist' writing, where – echoing Pascal and anticipating Kant and Coleridge – he makes it clear that the only 'evidence' for Christianity can be internal and intuitive. There is no serious place left for metaphysical or historical reasoning.

Nor is there any place either in Law's earlier or his later writings, so far as one can see, for the argument from prophecy for the truth of Christianity or for the application of the 'prophetic' writings of the New Testament to the course of history. Scripture is used in *A Serious Call* not as proof-texts but as a kind of exemplification, subsidiary to the overriding call to devotion of heart and life and less central to the book than the characters drawn from contemporary life. Law does attach two scriptural epigraphs to his book, one from St Luke ('He that hath ears to hear, let him hear') and one from Revelation ('And behold, I come quickly, and My reward is with Me'); but the chapters that follow make it clear that, just as the hearing is that of the individual believer, so the coming of the Lord is to the individual believer. As by the earlier mystics and the German pietists to whom Law increasingly turned, the apocalypse is internalised. Instead of being the key to calculation about past or future, time for him becomes relative, shifting and almost illusory: 'we are eternal beings' and 'the difference of a few years is as nothing' (p. 141). Though far from being antinomian and insisting very firmly on 'devotion' as a practical and ethical as well as a religious discipline, he sees the mainspring of that devotion in the intention of the heart.

Law's teaching on 'heart-religion' and on Christian perfection might have been restricted to his pious community at King's Cliffe and his small circle of readers had they not been taken up with such energy by his disciple John Wesley. Conversely, while Methodism would hardly have formed a nationwide movement without evangelistic preaching of a kind it is impossible to imagine Law undertaking, its origins nevertheless lie in the 'religious societies' that flourished in the Church of England in the late seventeenth and early eighteenth centuries, including the one in Samuel Wesley's parish of Epworth.[11] It was in the holy cell that a more emotional piety could be nourished, not unlike that of Jansenist Port-Royal where in the previous century Pascal had made his discovery that *le coeur a ses raisons que la raison ne connaît pas;* in such a context that Law's rigorist and world-renouncing spirituality could find their hearing. And from that context, invigorated by George Whitefield's and John Wesley's insistent preaching to 'flee from the wrath to come' and by the latter's organisational skills, grew indirectly the new Methodist societies, which for all their practical concerns were consecrated above all to preparing their members for the life of *heaven.*

THE REASONS OF THE HEART

The stress on the human heart and its heavenly home involves a development in the use of the Bible and in particular of the Apocalypse that can be traced in John Wesley's sermons and in Charles Wesley's hymns. Biblical texts form complex patterns of quotations in the sermons and allusions in the hymns. A fairly literal reading is not abandoned and the Bible is still used for doctrinal argument; yet the use of quotations and allusions characteristically moves in both sermons and hymns away from support for theological or historical information and towards the evangelistic appeal for repentance and the evocation of heavenly rest. For instance in John Wesley's sermon at St Mary's Oxford, given in 1738 a few weeks after he had felt his heart 'strangely warmed', there is an insistence on inwardness and 'heart-religion' beside which the faith of natural religion is 'barely the faith of an

Heathen' and that of mere assent to doctrinal propositions 'the faith of a Devil'; the preacher insists on *saving* faith as championed by Luther and witnessed to by texts from Paul and the prophets, but concludes with a much more rhetorical use of scripture to evoke the progress of the simple believer who will 'march on, under the great Captain of thy Salvation, "conquering and to conquer", until all thine enemies are destroyed, and "death is swallowed up in victory"'.[12] Six years later he preached in the same church on 'Scriptural Christianity', that is, a kind of primitivism that adds to the high-church apostolic and patristic religion an evangelical insistence on individual conviction and being 'filled with the Holy Ghost'. Wesley is not afraid to draw a strong contrast between such inward and scriptural religion and that of the Church of England, particularly the laxity of Oxford dons; but again the sermon ends not with a programme for reform but with an appeal for deliverance from damnation expressed in a web of scriptural allusion:

> Lord, save, or we perish! Take us out of the mire that we sink not! O help us against these enemies! for vain is the help of man. Unto thee all things are possible. According to the greatness of thy power, preserve thou those that are appointed to die.[13]

Judgement is far from being a theme Wesley avoids, and (for instance in his sermon to Bedford Assizes of 1758) he is happy to make fairly literal use of texts from the Old Testament, the gospels and the Apocalypse to describe signs of the end and to speculate on the paradisal 'new earth'. But the judgement is inescapably an individual one – Wesley reckons that the Millennium will actually occupy 'several thousand years' since so many have to be examined so thoroughly – and the final use of the powerful imagery of Revelation and of Matthew 25 is an emotional and individualistic appeal to the assembled judges, magistrates and gentry to ensure their own eternal salvation:

> See! He sitteth upon his throne, clothed with light as with a garment, arrayed with majesty and honour! Behold his eyes are as a flame of fire, his voice as the sound of many waters! How will ye escape? Will ye call to the mountains to fall on you, the rocks to cover you?... He standeth in the midst! Sinner, doth he not now, even now, knock at the door of thy heart?[14]

When he actually preaches on a text from Revelation (on the 'new creation' of Rev 21:5) there is again a scientific and literalistic imagining of the new earth: it will involve the smoothing and taming of nature, so that there will be no rain, no meteors, no wild beasts, no extremes of temperature, no mountains (though gentle hills will probably continue, and 'there will, doubtless, be inequalities on the surface of the earth; which are not blemishes, but beauties'). But the climax and purpose of the whole miracle is in the human heart's experience of 'a deep, an intimate, an uninterrupted union' with the triune God.[15]

As we have seen, Wesley set great store by biblical study and scholarship and made extensive use of the writings of the learned pietist J. A. Bengel as well as classical exegetes like Augustine and Luther. For him as for them, the Bible was a book containing information about God and in particular about God's way of salvation. But study was only a prelude to or a confirmation of a more existential appropriation of the text. It is worth quoting at length from the highly rhetorical but revealing preface that he wrote for his 1771 collection of sermons:

I have thought, I am a creature of a day, passing through life, as an arrow through the air. I am a spirit come from God, and returning to God: just hovering over the great gulf; till a few moments hence, I am no more seen! I drop into an unchangeable eternity! I want to know one thing, the way to heaven: how to land safe on that happy shore. God himself has condescended to teach the way; for this very end he came down from heaven. He hath written it down in a book! O give me that book! At any price, give me the Book of God! I have it: here is knowledge enough for me. Let me be *homo unius libri.* Here then I am, far from the busy ways of men. I sit down alone: only God is here. In his presence I open, I read his book; for this end, to find the way to heaven. Is there a doubt concerning the meaning of what I read? Does any thing appear dark or intricate? I lift up my heart to the Father of Lights ... I then search after and consider parallel passages of Scripture, 'comparing spiritual things with spiritual'. I meditate thereon, with all the attention and earnestness of which my mind is capable. If any doubt still remains, I consult those who are experienced in the things of God; and then the writings whereby, being dead, they yet speak. And what I thus learn, that I teach.[16]

What is interesting here is that while Wesley does not deny the referential sense of scripture he is in practice prepared to dissolve it
in the inspiring, judging and saving power of the Book of God. Like
the Fathers and the Reformers, he is steeped in the text by meditation on it. In contrast to the comforting use of the Bible by a
Lowman or a Pyle, the two stages of moving from text to meaning
and from meaning to use are commonly collapsed by Wesley into
one rhetorical stage moving from text to appeal or evocation. If the
difference between the two hermeneutical strategies can be compared with that between classical and Romantic use of language,
then Wesley is at least a proto-Romantic.

This 'Romantic' and heaven-centred use of the often earthy text
of the Bible is seen still more clearly in the hymns and poems of his
brother Charles. Very many of these move at the end to sing of
heaven or of death (which for the devout Methodist is simply the
gate of heaven) and many have heaven as their whole theme –
section I.ii.5 of the 1876 *Collection of Hymns for the Use of the People
called Methodists* (to the numeration of which most of the following
references are made) is boldly entitled 'Describing Heaven'. The
aspiration to heaven, which clearly made a direct appeal to many in
the crowds addressed by the Wesleys, is consistently spiritualised
and individualised and often transmuted by use of the language of
rapture into an *almost* realised eschatology (for example hymns 143,
205, 207, 333, 519, 807 and 902, and many of the large number on
the themes of Ascension and of the Eucharist). This narrowing of
the gap between earth and heaven is in keeping with the Wesleys'
sacramentalism and high doctrine of the Real Presence and with
their thorough-going incarnationalism, most vividly expressed by
Charles in such 'Patripassian' phrases as 'Th'Immortal dies', 'The
Wounds of God', 'Jehovah crucified' and 'To weep o'er an expiring
God'. So hymn 519 ends,

> CHRIST is now gone up on high,
> (Thither all our wishes fly):
> Sits at GOD's Right-hand above,
> There with Him we reign in Love!

And in the eucharistic hymn 'Jacob's Ladder',

> He calls us to the skies,
> And lo! we spurn the ground,

> Light on the sacred Ladder rise,
> And gain the topmost Round,
> Of Everlasting Life
> The glorious Pledge is given;
> Another Step shall end the Strife,
> And lodge us all in Heaven![17]

Wesley turns naturally and frequently to the Apocalypse in his aspirations to salvation and 'descriptions' of heaven. To take only a few of many examples, number 128 includes the prayer to the 'slaughtered Lamb' 'Wrap me in thy crimson vest'; number 748 ('Come, thou Conqueror of the nations,/Now on thy white horse appear') makes extensive use of the imagery of Revelation 19; number 936 ('Lift your heads, ye friends of Jesus') evokes the darkening of sun and moon, the falling of the stars and the cry to be hidden in the rocks.[18] While these hymns do not dispense with the texts' reference to a future cataclysmic event, their real function is the appeal to the closeness of heaven to the individual believer. As for the 'church-historical' application of Revelation, this is intriguingly altered by Wesley's violent anti-Calvinism, so that the Beast lives not in Rome but in Geneva. It is against Pope Calvin that the prayer of 'The Horrible Decree' is made:

> How long, O God, how long
> Shall Satan's Rage proceed!
> Wilt Thou not soon avenge the Wrong,
> And crush the Serpent's Head!
> Surely Thou shalt at last
> Bruise him beneath our Feet:
> The Devil, and his Doctrine cast
> Into the burning Pit.[19]

Calvin's decree is 'horrible' because it is closing the gates of heaven. This is in fact a further stage of spiritualisation of the text of the Apocalypse. Originally the Beast was identified with the Roman Empire, later (for political as much as religious reasons) with the Roman Church; now it is a doctrinal system. And in place of the radical call of Revelation to 'come *out* of Babylon', Charles Wesley's call centres more on the text from Canticles that he frequently alludes to: 'Arise, my love, my fair one, and come *away*'. There is one final step on the ladder, and the hymns are written with the aim of enabling their singers to live on earth in a state of Christian perfection, as though the step were already made and the reality of heaven were completely manifest.

This yearning for heaven is even more pronounced in the Calvinistic context of Welsh Methodism, where the hymns of Wesley's contemporary Williams Pantycelyn make frequent use of erotic imagery from Canticles and Revelation:

> Jesus, thou mine Heart hast raptured,
> Take my Soul,
> Make it whole,
> In thine Embrace captured....
> Let me in thine Arms untiring
> Make my Nest, happy rest
> In thy Wounds unfailing.[20]

Pantycelyn's use of sensuous religious poetry forms an ironic inversion of Locke's teaching on the primacy of sensation against his teaching on the danger of enthusiasm. He justifies it from the Bible's own use of language. Thus his advice to aspiring hymnwriters is

> Whether or not they can accomplish [a wide reading] let them repeatedly read the Prophets, the Psalms, the Lamentations, the Song of Solomon, Job and the Book of Revelation, which not only abound in flights of poesy, metaphors, invention, ease of diction, lively similes; but can kindle fire, zeal and life in the reader (because they are God's books) far beyond all other books in the world.[21]

Like Wesley's, Pantycelyn's poetry is highly individualistic and Christocentric; but unlike Wesley he wrote a long epic poem, *Golwg ar Deyrnas Crist* ('A View of Christ's Kingdom', 1756 and 1764), which achieves a unique combination of Calvinist theology, modern science and the new experiential religion. 'Christ is everything' is the theme of the poem, forming a refrain in the headings of the six books of the 1764 edition: 'Christ is everything in God's great purpose ... in Creation ... in the Promise of Eden ... in Providence ... in the Bible ... in the Salvation of his Saints'.[22] The eschatological climax in the sixth book is not so much a renewal of the earth as a release of the soul, so that for all the poet's scientific interests and sensual imagery nature is ultimately unimportant, to be swallowed up in the ecstasy of heaven. This is very directly expressed in Pantycelyn's imaginary letter to William Read, where the language of the Apocalypse is the catalyst for the purgation and spiritualisation of both nature and human experience:

> To say that ... the Wall of the City is of *Jasper*, and its pavements of pure Gold, like unto clear Crystal; its Foundations of *Sardonyx*, *Sapphire, Amethyst* and *Emerald*, is but to name the most precious things in this World, which the Holy Spirit hath used to convey the likeness of great things, either on Earth or in Heaven, or both at the same time: But here are none of those things: no Sun or Moon is needed here, GOD and the LAMB provide all the Glory here, material things such as you have are not in use in this strange City. ... Here hath Nature entirely died away, and all the Passions of the Soul which were untamed, inflamed and sinful have become completely extinguished. ... When the Stars of Heaven have been extinguished, when the massive Sun has been totally exhausted of its light-giving power, this heavenly Principle will shine on with enduring Glory; here dwelleth the substance of Love; what you have is but its dross.[23]

'Thus heavenward all things tend', as William Cowper was to conclude his uncharacteristically full rhapsody in *The Task* on the coming of Paradise, replete with the language of Isaiah and Revelation.[24] The use of biblical and apocalyptic language by the poets and preachers of the Evangelical revival, whether in Wales, England or America, evinces a much greater sensitivity to the poetry and metaphor of scripture than is seen in its rationalist interpreters. It is a sensitivity often necessarily in tension with the doctrinal constraints of their systems of salvation. But even with such committed Calvinists as Pantycelyn and John Newton, one senses that in that tension it is the language of the *experience* of salvation and of yearning for the sublime that carries the day.

THE LANGUAGE OF THE SPIRIT

It was not only among evangelicals, however, that a new awareness of the place of poetry and metaphor in the Bible emerged. The popular impact on British culture of the scriptural language of Handel's *Messiah* ever since its first performance in Dublin in 1742 would be hard to exaggerate – and its two most climactic choruses ('Hallelujah' and the final 'Amen') are settings of texts from the Apocalypse. And Robert Lowth's *Lectures on the Sacred Poetry of the Hebrews* (1741–50) evince a close attention to the Old Testament text that is both scholarly and imaginative. Poetry, says Lowth, is naturally and originally religious, and, especially in Israel, it uses passion and spontaneity (which he contrasts with the demands of the 'officious grammarian').[25] The inspiration of the prophets and psalmists is not the dictation of divine information but the much more subtle interplay between the divine and human spirits: 'the natural powers of the mind are in general elevated and refined, they are neither eradicated nor totally obscured' (p. 168). The first task of the interpreter is not to find the extrinsic reference of the prophetic or poetic text but, he says in Lecture V, to respond to its figurative style so as to enter the mind of the writer:

> we must even investigate [this people's] inmost sentiments, the manner and connexion of their thoughts; in one word, we must see all things with their eyes, estimate all things by their opinions; we must endeavour as much as possible to read Hebrew as the Hebrews would have read it (p. 56).

And since the subject of Hebrew poetry is usually such an elevated one, the writers' aim is to instil the sense of the sublime. Whereas Burke (in his *Philosophical Inquiry*, published in 1757, a few years after Lowth's lectures) was to analyse the sublime in terms of Lockean psychology, Lowth is unafraid to use the derided term 'enthusiasm' in a positive sense and to insist (in Lecture XVII) that 'it is the office of poetry to incite, to direct, to temper the passions, and not to extinguish them' (p. 179).

Unfortunately Lowth, who as Bishop of London was a conservative and conscientious churchman, did not extend his innovative criticism into the more contentious field of New Testament 'prophecy', though it is not hard to see how an approach centred on the primacy of poetry and of passion might operate there – indeed within Lowth's lifetime Herder was to adapt his method to interpretation of the Apocalypse. A bishop who did attempt some application of poetical theory to the Book of Revelation was Richard Hurd, whose Warburton Lectures of 1768 were entitled *An Introduction to the Study of the Prophecies Concerning the Christian Church, and, in particular, Concerning the Church of Papal Rome.* Hurd was already known for his *Moral and Political Dialogues* (1759) and *Letters on Chivalry and Romance* (1762), which display some poetical and historical imagination (and some awareness of contemporary fashion) in their elevation of 'Gothicism' over classicism. In the third Dialogue, set at Kenilworth Castle as a conversation between the 'modern', whiggish, sceptical Addison and the 'romantic' and antiquarian Arbuthnot, the latter uses the ruins of the hall, the tilt-yard and the lake to exemplify the virtues of feudalism – its hospitality, gallantry and art respectively – and then moves to a eulogy of the Elizabethan age, when, he maintains, English manners and language reached their apex. This thesis is developed in the *Letters*, which celebrate Shakespeare, Milton, Tasso and in particular Spenser for their 'Gothic' style – that is, a style that is not afraid to be religious or to use magic and the world of faery. Unlike classical or mimetic art (whose propriety Hurd does not deny) this 'more sublime and creative poetry' addresses itself 'solely or principally to the Imagination; a young and credulous faculty, which loves to admire and to be deceived; has no need to observe those cautious rules of credibility so necessary to be followed by him, who would touch the affections and interest the heart'.[26] After Spenser, Hurd suggests, 'the tales of faery' lived a bit longer; but

> reason, in the end,... drove them off the scene, and would endure these *lying wonders*, neither in their own proper shape, nor as masked in figures. ... What we have gotten by this revolution, you will say, is a great deal of good sense. What we have lost, is a world of fine fabling.[27]

One might hardly expect the bishop to describe the Bible as 'a world of fine fabling'; but when he does turn to its interpretation in the Warburton Lectures there are only slight indications that he is prepared to put such 'Gothic' sensibility to work in the reading of its poetry. Certainly, compared with earlier interpreters of Revelation, Hurd has some awareness that 'prophetic' language, being in some sense poetic and 'sublime', may be rather more fragmentary and less consoling than they had supposed. The fulfilment of prophecy may be evidence for Christianity, yet it cannot be univocal or compelling evidence: 'something must be left to quicken our attention, to excite our industry, and to try the natural ingenuity of the human mind'. It is not from piecemeal fulfilments of particular prophecies but from 'all the prophecies taken together, and considered as making one system' that the 'scattered rays' of conviction converge to form a strong light rising into 'a high degree of moral certainty'.[28] Yet Hurd is confident that a dictionary of exact meanings of prophetic symbols can be drawn up – indeed that it has been, in Lancaster's *Symbolical and Alphabetical Dictionary*. Internal biblical comparisons, Egyptian inscriptions, classical poetry and knowledge of 'pagan superstitions' mean that 'there is ... no more difficulty in fixing the import of the prophetic style, than of any other language or technical phraseology whatever' (II.98). And its import is familiar: 'that apostate papal Rome is the very Antichrist foretold', that providence is vindicated, the Reformation upheld and fanaticism dispelled. By allowing so little leeway to his earlier theories of imagination when he came to the anti-imperial symbolism of Revelation, one may suppose that Hurd was able to sleep more easily in the episcopal splendour of Hartlebury Castle.

Two commentaries on Revelation written in the year of the French Revolution exemplify further both Hurd's continuing confidence in the clarity of its language and historical reference and his cautious attempt to apply aesthetic criteria to its interpretation. One was by a Church of Scotland minister, Bryce Johnston, who expressed dissatisfaction with existing commentaries mainly for their lack of consistency in understanding 'prophetic' signification. Johnston claims to have made the 'discovery' – though it is a theory familiar from Isaac Newton as well as Hurd – that all 'prophecies' in the Bible are written in 'symbolical language'. The prophecies supply 'keys' for this language, normally by angelic interpreters such as that of Daniel 10, and 'Every prophet, in whatever country or age he wrote, always used the same hieroglyphic, or the same symbol, to signify the same thing, without a single exception'. Their meaning 'is much more fixed and uniform than that of words is in any alphabetical language', since they are natural rather than arbitrary signs. This symbolical language, like any other, has to be learnt.[29] Its master will see, says Johnston, that a vision such as that of Revelation 1 is an intellectual rather than a physical one, conveying an abstract meaning by symbols to the reader. There is then a further stage of intellectual interpretation, for which Johnston relies heavily on Mosheim's history: that of identifying these meanings with historical events. For instance, the horse and rider of Rev 6:2 represent 'the dispensation of divine providence', the whiteness showing the Church's purity and the bow the victory of the gospel, so the breaking of the first seal prophesies the spread of the gospel in the apostolic age; the darkness of sun, moon and stars in Rev 8:12 represents 'a state of great darkness and ignorance', so the fourth trumpet prophesies the growth of superstition and corruption from the end of the fourth century (I.169, 278). Though Johnston's anti-papal interpretations are scarcely novel (apart from fixing the fall of Babylon for the year 1999) he stresses that the full meaning of the dark sayings and detailed fulfilments of prophecy are evident 'to those persons only, who study it with competent knowledge, uprightness, and directness' (I.6f.).

Equal to Johnston's in hermeneutical confidence though surpassing it in rhetorical ambition is the commentary published in 1789 by William Cooke, Professor of Greek at Cambridge (Cooke's only other book of note was an edition of Aristotle's *Poetics*, which ended with a translation into Greek of Gray's Elegy). He begins his book – in sentences of Proustian length and considerably more complex syntax – with the claim that whereas Mede and other interpreters have been busy toiling and reaping in the field, now 'there are those [namely Cooke] whose it is to collect the sheaves, to set them in order, and tie them together, and put them up, and make them stand, and point towards heaven'. After this harvest the Apocalypse will be able to convert any infidel and can be seen to fill 'the measures of perfection, which are described by Aristotle for an Epic Poem or Tragedy'.[30] In fact, apart from some novel identifications of papal characteristics (for instance in Rev 18 the harpers are singing High Mass and the crowds on the vessels are 'the young fry of the clergy') there is little new in Cooke's exegesis. He is alone among English interpreters of the eighteenth century in slating Joseph Mede, though at the end of his Preface he does include some faint praise:

> And now I have returned favours to the learned Mede, and set him and his Synchronisms on their right legs. I shall always acknowledge and admire his deep penetration, uncommon genius, immense knowledge, probity, candour, and extreme diffidence of himself:- and I should be very glad to come as near to him in true modesty, as I find myself short of him in information and learning (p. lviii).

There is no indication that the professor ever gained this modesty. The *Dictionary of National Biography* records that (like an alarming number of interpreters of Revelation) Cooke ended his life 'deranged'.

But the new sensibility could not be ignored by preachers and exegetes, and it meant that as the century progressed the English suspicion of 'enthusiasm' gradually diminished. One can see the sensibility variously represented by Hurd's 'Gothicism', by Lowth's biblical scholarship, by the fervour of the Methodists and the extravagancies of the nascent Gothic novel. In each case there is a new kind of primitivism at work, a subtler notion of time and history that made it increasingly hard to believe (with Isaac Newton) that Noah or Daniel or Homer were separated from the modern world simply by the passage of chronological time. Rousseau's alternative Genesis was evocative for thousands of people in Europe and America for whom the Christian pattern of history and redemption had turned dry. It stimulated the researches already begun by Vico into the origins of language and culture, setting the biblical narrative in a far wider context. This widened still further with the oriental studies of Sir William Jones, while Lowth's empathetic approach to Hebrew poetry was followed by Herder, who deepened it into the sense of *Einfühlung* into the 'spirit' of past cultures. To sum up huge and disparate movements of thought and scholarship in a couple of sentences is foolhardy, but it would be fair to say that European thought in the decades before the French Revolution evinced a growing sense of Johnson's 'uncertain continuance of Reason', at any rate of the continuance of the straightforward rationalistic spirit of the previous generation. Instead there evolves the search for a cultural or poetic coherence through sympathetic engagement with the past or indeed the future, conducted now not through mathematical calculations but through imaginative leaps in evolutionary time and space. The new spirit in contrast with the old is seen at its most extreme in Blake's verbal and visual attacks on Newton, though it must be stressed that the Romantics generally did not disdain scientific thought – one thinks of the scientific interests of Goethe, of Coleridge and of Shelley. It was at this time too that Kant's new epistemology and his relativising of time and space became known; and at this time that biblical 'higher criticism' was born.

In *The Eclipse of Biblical Narrative* Hans Frei has outlined the failure in all the massive engine of eighteenth- and nineteenth-century biblical scholarship to retrieve the traditional sense of engagement with narrative as narrative: he depicts the almost constant hermeneutical pressure to relate the text to some 'ostensive reference' or meaning. Rationalism and historicism are equally inhibiting to a genuine poetics of the Bible, Frei suggests: whether the reference is to natural truths of reason, to dogma, moral principles or historical facts, the defining of extratextual meaning is an escape from its function as narrative. While apocalyptic writing is not 'narrative' in the ordinary sense of the word (certainly not Frei's 'history-likeness') we have seen this process at work with a vengeance in eighteenth-century English writing on Revelation. There is some sense now and again of poetic shaping of the Apocalypse and of its poem- or story-like effect on the reader – instances would be Whiston's diagram, Hurd's feeling for the 'sublime', Cooke's comparison of the book with classical tragedy – and poets and preachers who treat the text more allusively often use it to convey a personal religious appeal. But by professional exegetes the symbols, visions and events are nearly always pressed into reference to events or features of church and world history subsequent to the first century. Lowth's sense of the sublimity and spontaneity of Hebrew poetry, of entering the mind and environment of the original poet and of the place of emotion in conveying religious truth, seems to have had little impact on the interpretation of 'prophecy' or on English New Testament scholarship generally. Like 'Ossian', it seems, he came to life best when exported to Germany.

It was a pioneer of biblical higher criticism, Johann David Michaelis, who translated and annotated Lowth's Latin lectures. Some influence of them may be seen in another pioneer, Johann Gottfried Eichhorn, whose influential *Commentarius in Apocalypsin Johannis* was published in 1791. Eichhorn sees Revelation as a 'grand symbolic drama'. He lucidly portrays the literary structure of the book and is not unresponsive to its symbolic power. Yet the symbols of the book are for him merely artistic dressing or *Einkleidung*: its real matter is in what was to the writer recent history, namely the Jewish War and the fall of Jerusalem. From this historicist point of view, the Apocalypse's emotional and liturgical impact (and therefore, for Eichhorn, its canonicity) is an issue apart from its original and therefore real meaning.[31] To find a commentary written in the light of contemporary historical scholarship but evincing a genuine hermeneutical engagement with the text one must turn to Herder, whose *Maran Atha* was first published in 1779 and translated into English in 1821. The commentary had a curious

history. It originated in 1774 as a manuscript which Herder circu-
lated among friends (including Goethe and Lavater) and which has
fortunately been preserved and printed in Herder's collected
works. This included a vigorous German verse translation of the
Apocalypse with pithy and emotive comments between the
stanzas, unfolding both what Herder saw as the book's original
frame of reference – which was similar to that perceived by
Eichhorn – and more powerfully and convincingly its present function as a call to the immediacy of Christ's presence. Herder was
persuaded to abandon the translation and expand the commentary,
and moreover to ensure that John is still seen as a 'prophet' by
dating the Apocalypse in the 60s CE, referring to the events of the
Jewish War as future. It was in this rather unconvincing form –
though with the addition of a lengthy concluding evocation of the
poetic and existential power of the book – that *Maran Atha* was
published.[32] Interestingly, one of the finest nineteenth-century commentaries on Revelation, that by the erudite and sensitive
American Moses Stuart (1845), ends after a thousand pages of close
criticism with a further thirteen pages quoting part of Herder's conclusion *in extenso*, as though to say, 'Whatever you think of all the
scholarship above, read this if you really want to enjoy the last
book of the Bible'.[33] In expounding Herder's interpretation, I shall
refer indiscriminately to the 1774 and 1779 versions.[34]

Like Lowth, to whom he owed so much, Herder responds to the
prophetic text with emotion and enthusiasm. Unlike Lowth,
however, he is less concerned with literary forms than with access
to the 'spirit' of the writing and its historical context. The text of
the Apocalypse, he says in good eighteenth-century style, is not
'mystical'. Nor, however, does it require expert elucidation, since
John (like Eichhorn, Herder identifies the writer with the apostle
and author of the fourth gospel) speaks directly to the heart and
mind: he writes in 'images, not hieroglyphics, still less riddles, and
certainly not meaningless nonsense' (p. 6). 'Each whole image
speaks, each whole image is understandable. ... How natural are
these images! how clearly each one speaks and works on its own
account!' (pp. 10, 110). What they speak of is Jesus and his coming.
Again and again Herder stresses, with the urgency of a preacher,
the centrality of Christ and the closeness of his unveiled presence in
the text: 'Revelation is a book whose every word binds together
heaven and earth, blends into one both time and eternity; and the
central point, the germinating power of the whole, is *Jesus*, our

brother and our judge' (p. 98). So Herder is sensitive to the pace and language of the Apocalypse, filled as it is with 'speed, presence and coming' and repeating its refrain *Er kommt!* ('He is coming!') He is coming, Herder says, 'not to the fall of a royal city, but to those communities in Asia, he is coming to the whole earth' (p. 255). Interpreting the book symbolically means that it is not filled with *Schadenfreude und Rachsucht:* wrath and vengeance are swallowed up in the fraternal love of Christ and his prophet for the churches. The coming of Christ is 'tender and filled with love', entering 'with heart-breaking softness, rich in love' (p. 12). The approach to the modern reader is identical with that to the seven churches, and, quoting Luther, Herder maintains that the book's canonicity rests on its subjective impact; if that is lacking, or if Herder has failed to convince his readers, then let the Apocalypse 'remain what it is, deuterocanonical – for according to the Church's most ancient witnesses that is what it is and must remain' (p. 274).

Hans Frei, who judges Herder to have come closer to a genuine sense of biblical narrative than any other interpreter of the period, points out the reverse side of this subjectivity. Paradoxically, he says,

> this total surrender, which was the price of entry into the spirit of any specific past to which one was relating himself [*sic*], was necessarily accompanied by an equally pervasive detachment from it at every other level. The *Einfühlung* into another specific, historical spirit or age, though aesthetically uncritical, was confined solely to the aesthetic mode.[35]

While it is true that Herder's actual meaning is very hard to nail down – Coleridge put several scatological comments about the author on his copy of Herder's *Briefe, über das Studium der Theologie* to this effect – nevertheless Frei perhaps underestimates the extent to which Herder saw his writing as not academic but homiletic. It has the mellifluous tones of the court preacher that Herder was, and pointedly avoids any political application. Yet this tender Christ who comes to the seven churches comes also as judge to the moribund church of Germany, Herder implies – for if the spiritual voice that John heard is lost, if hope and rejoicing decay,

> then farewell, extinct Christendom! Your stem and your root are withered! You have nothing left but a story long ago worn out

and become a *Märchen*; no Christ beside you or addressing you, no Spirit of his eternal Word! (p. 125)

This is more than aesthetic, however pietistic a religion it springs from. There is the sense in *Maran Atha*, as in *The Spirit of Hebrew Poetry*, that access to the *Volksgeist* is to restore the decayed intuition of the eighteenth century, that for Herder this *is* redemption and the new Jerusalem.

Frei also points to the tension that Herder never resolves in his writing 'between the spatiotemporal reference of realistic accounts … and the unique, realistic, or historical spirit or consciousness of the Jewish people'.[36] The tension is bewilderingly evident in Herder's treatment of the Apocalypse, in that while he opens, as we have seen, by insisting that the text is self-explanatory and requires 'no key', he later says that a 'historical key' is necessary in order to unravel the origins of the events and visions in the history of the Jewish War, and the 1779 text is filled with references to Josephus and other historical detail. Rather unsuccessfully, Herder seems to be groping towards an interpretation which is, in the language of a later generation, both synchronic and diachronic, and towards the nineteenth-century writing of history as itself a symbolical narrative. In the end the very concern with history that informed the higher criticism may have been one of the sources of liberation from the obsessions with chronology and evidence that saturated earlier hermeneutical endeavours.

* * *

But there was another more immediate source, when in 1789 'history' became present as never before in the century. For many, providence was now no longer a matter of pious reflection but of news reports from Paris; prophecy not a matter of conjecture about past and future but of present experience; and in that experience poetry could find a new moral immediacy. Throughout Europe the events in France had an impact felt far beyond the world of politics in the narrow sense: poets, preachers and would-be prophets were all affected. That effect has often been seen in terms of a revival of apocalyptic. How far, if that is so, it is mediated through interpretation of the central apocalyptic text of Christian Europe is the subject of the following chapter.

4

Revelation and Revolution

From the world-historical calculations of Isaac Newton to the evidences of Bishop Hurd, eighteenth-century English readers of the Apocalypse turned to its baffling words for an assurance that was scientific as well as moral and religious. Given a correct understanding of their 'hieroglyphics', those words would provide a reasonable description of events past or future, in accord with the findings of natural religion. Certainly, as we have seen, among those who retained a belief in original sin there was a sense – sometimes unacknowledged – of darkness and mystery: the awareness of Swift and Butler and Law that meaning and reference in the biblical text were not as obvious as the Christian rationalists might wish. With the evangelical revival too there came a readiness to apply the symbols of Revelation in a looser and more emotional way to individual experience of conversion or expectation of heaven, while in Germany Herder began a systematic interpretation of the text in this vein. Yet such people still moved within a culture where light and clarity were the supreme intellectual values. For instance, despite Butler's and Wesley's reckoning with a mystery in the human personality and in the cosmos that reason could not completely fathom, the former's apologetics and the latter's biblical interpretation both assume and move within a 'rational' discourse where words are univocal signifiers that can eventually lead to the direct knowledge of the purposes of providence. Even Herder, with his sense of the Bible's emotive call to its readers' present spiritual situation, feels obliged to treat the text of Revelation as one of 'prophecy'. And 'prophecy' means prediction, an indication of the outworking of those providential purposes in measurable time.

The Greek word for 'time' in this sense is *chronos*. *Chronos* can be divided into years and months, into seconds and fractions of seconds. Measurable by the now highly reliable chronometer, but also on a larger scale by Newton's mathematics and astronomy and – he would add – by his research into 'prophecy', it extends unchangingly into the infinite past and the infinite future – or at any rate as far back as the first 'day' of creation and as far forward as the possible dissolution of time in the new Jerusalem where there is no night. The ceaseless, changeless ticking of *chronos* derives from and expresses the mind of God the supreme Watchmaker. Given the assumption that Scripture too is the Word of this almighty Calculator, and given its references to measured periods of time, especially in Daniel and Revelation, it was natural that such texts should be read as chronological information, affording meaning and shape to the apparently impersonal succession of time. But in the light of the historical criticism of the Bible that was born in the same century this appears to be a severe misreading of the biblical and prophetic sense of time. The biblical prophet is inspired not to 'tell the time' in an unusually accurate way but to announce a 'time' of judgement and salvation. In the New Testament such a moment is not *chronos* but *kairos*: the 'day' or 'hour' that is God's 'favourable time'.[1] Biblical time and *a fortiori* apocalyptic time are not the ticking away of *chronos* but a succession of revelatory *kairoi*. And the *kairos* is not for people to measure but for them to participate in and to respond to in repentance or in worship. From this perspective the events and visions of the Apocalypse – and of Zechariah and of passages like Mark 13 – are really approaching the swallowing up of *chronos* in *kairos*: the measurements, unlike perhaps those of Daniel, bear purely symbolic significance in the intertextual biblical structure, and while there clearly is reference to extratextual phenomena (the churches of Asia and the Roman Empire) all the stress is on the immediate or imminent apocalypse of the Lamb.

Herder's homiletic use of the Apocalypse, surveyed in the previous chapter, conveys something of this sense of *kairos*, as do some of Charles Wesley's hymns. Neither seems to be interested in chronology. But, writing before the French Revolution, they differ from the New Testament in avoiding any very confident association of this 'time' with public events whether historical or mythological. The *kairos* is that of the individual's conversion or illumination or death. 1789 was the year that was to enable readers of the Apocalypse to recover a dimension of the text that was both contemporary and political: 'A veil had been/Uplifted'.[2] The astonishing events of the subsequent decade in France created a visible *kairos*, what Schüssler Fiorenza calls a new 'rhetorical situation' in which the text can be reborn.[3] The coming of the French Revolution, writes Clarke Garrett, had the effect of giving awesome reality to what had before been only speculation. The surge of interest in prophecy of all kinds was one indication of the need to fit what was new and unprecedented into categories that were old and familiar ... Revolution and millennium both affirmed the possibility that heaven could be built on earth.[4]

Garrett is writing primarily of the more eccentric and proletarian millenarian movements that began or were rejuvenated in the 1790s; but, as he shows, the events of that decade led to the revival and republication of older scholarly interpretations of 'prophecy', often recasting them to put infidel France in the role of the Beast formerly held by the Pope.[5]

Such reactionary publications in Britain seem to have had the covert support of the government. They also drew on a strand of English 'world-historical' interpretation of the Apocalypse that encouraged a French as well as a papal demonology. As far back as 1734, for instance, Sayer Rudd had calculated the number of the Beast by Latin *gematria* to represent LUDOVICVS – that is, Louis, characteristic name of the Bourbon kings. Rudd was a Baptist minister in London who fled his recalcitrant congregation to study midwifery in Holland but later returned home to become an Anglican clergyman; his *Essay towards a New Explication of the Doctrines of the Resurrection, Millennium and Judgment* draws on Mede and assumes that Revelation is 'as generally confessed ... a perpetual history of the church', but also includes full chronological calculations to support the scheme of a 'spiritual reign' of Christ that will become the 'personal reign' of Rev 20 only after the overthrow of the eastern and western Antichrists (that is, the Pope and the Turk) and the Bourbon Beast.[6] Half a century later another English clergyman, Thomas Vivian of Devon, published a commentary on the Apocalypse 'In an historical View of the past and present State of the Christian World compared with the prophetic Visions', which also reads the number of the Beast as LUDOVICVS. But Vivian combines an anti-papal and anti-Bourbon historical reading with political liberalism. For him the Dragon is the Emperor, the first Beast is the Pope, and the second Beast, sustaining the power of the wounded papacy, is the King of France. He traces the corrupt history of French monarchy from the fifth to the eighteenth century, looking forward to its dissolution or possibly its repentance from support of the first Beast and so to the fulfilment of the prophecies of the bowls in Rev 16.[7] There are signs of this approaching fulfilment in the gradual decay of idolatry and intolerance, even in Austria the Dragon's lair, and Vivian welcomes any moves towards religious liberty, including that of Roman Catholics, desiring further progress such as the freeing of North American slaves and the independence of South American nations.[8]

Writing in 1785, Vivian could not detect in French events an actual apocalyptic *kairos*. Four years later, however, British liberals – and, not much later, their conservative opponents – discovered a new symbiosis of prophecy and event. For instance the prominent dissenters Richard Price and Joseph Priestley had long believed in progressive enlightenment leading to millennial liberty; but after the French Revolution 'they believed that God's everlasting kingdom of justice and peace was now imminent and that the spread of liberty throughout the world had truly cosmic dimensions'.[9] Beyond the world of preachers and would-be prophets, whether radical or reactionary, lay also what Marilyn Butler sees as 'the main English literary response to French events' which again takes apocalyptic form:

> [s]ymbolic narratives of the destruction and construction of worlds are told by the poets Blake, Byron and Shelley, and by the novelists Scott, Godwin, Radcliffe, Mary Shelley and Maturin ... a re-enactment of that devastating experience, a means of criticising, of containing, or of naturalising it.[10]

The mythical and the monstrous have now become a matter of contemporary public experience; they cannot so easily be bound in patterns of regular chronology or in a detached world of Gothic fantasy. And while preaching on and scholarly interpretation of the Apocalypse continue apace in this period, the sharp point of hermeneutical activity seems to move from the clerical study into the political arena and thence into the poetic imagination. In this chapter I wish to examine that trajectory, focusing on the years 1789–98.

* * *

When Britain joined the war against revolutionary France, Pitt's government and the English bishops ordered a Fast Day to be observed each February with special sermons, the object being to unite church and nation behind the war and seek God's blessing on the army and his overthrow of the infidel Jacobins. Unfortunately for Pitt and the ecclesiastical establishment, not all preachers saw it that way. For instance a Unitarian minister in London, successor to Richard Price whose welcome to the events of 1789 had spurred Burke into writing his counterrevolutionary *Reflections*, was happy to preach on the Fast Days of 1793 and 1794; but his sermons, far from supporting the government, hymned the fulfilment of biblical prophecy in the events across the Channel, with the national enemy being seen as in fact the instrument of God's liberation and of the approach of the Millennium. This minister was the renowned scientist Joseph Priestley, who a few weeks after the Fast Day of 1794 emigrated to Pennsylvania. From there, in the remaining decade of his life, he observed events in Europe with some disquiet; but the disquiet was not enough to quench his huge optimism nor his conviction that the events of the French Revolution were divinely ordained. His task continued of 'fitting its events into the scheme of biblical prophecy with the same single-minded tenacity that he brought to everything else he did'.[11] It was not that Priestley was not already a millennialist. His Hartleian doctrine of divine benevolence and necessary progress towards ultimate happiness required some such corollary, and Priestley was happy to express it in scriptural terms, including the restoration of the Jews to Palestine and the Pope as Antichrist. What the French Revolution did, for him as for many others, both radicals and Tories, was to make the possibility of fulfilment much less theoretical and more experiential.

In his millenarian poem 'Religious Musings', the young Coleridge pictures his revered Priestley driven from his native land (after the 'Church and King' riots of 1791 in Birmingham) by 'Statesmen blood-stain'd and Priests idolatrous/By dark lies mad'ning the blind multitude'; but the 'Patriot, and Saint, and Sage' was not deprived of hope; rather,

> ... calm, pitying he retir'd,
> And mus'd expectant on these promised years.[12]

The picture is an accurate one, as Priestley's letters from America bear out. He followed not only the events in France and England but also the attempts to interpret them in terms of providence and prophecy. While dismissing the homespun prophecies of Richard

Brothers, he expressed respect for the writings of James Bicheno, the Baptist minister at Newbury, whose *Signs of the Times* reached a wide readership and went through several editions. In his sermon for the Fast Day of 1795 (published as *A Word in Season)* Bicheno insists that the day is one not for sycophancy, complacency or chauvinism, nor for mere religious devotion, but for sounding an alarm. Religion and politics must not be separated, he says, in his exposition of Luke 21:36, which refers beyond the fall of Jerusalem to events in 'the latter days'. Those days, it appears, are now arriving, and the fulcrum is France. This had indeed been foreseen by Increase Mather, whose words of 1710 Bicheno quotes with the clear implication that the prayer is now being answered: 'May the kingdom of France be that *tenth part of a city* which shall fall! May we hear of a mighty revolution there!'[13] England too is being judged and called to repent for her national crimes – the slave trade, church patronage, alliance with Rome, bribery and above all the immoral and expensive lust for war. As with Priestley, pragmatic, apocalyptic and perfectibilist language are blended.

This, for Bicheno at any rate, was still the dawn when it was bliss to be alive. But though he later recognised that his interpretations of fulfilment had been 'precipitate', Bicheno's Christian millennialism and political liberalism were not to be destroyed. He produced a revised version of his scheme of fulfilment after Waterloo (*The Fulfilment of Prophecy farther illustrated by The Signs of the Times,* 1817), reminding his readers that even Napoleons, like Cyrus, can be 'the unconscious instruments of the Deity' and writing as eloquently as before against the folly and sin of war, with approval of the Quakers' pacifism. Providence has not abandoned the church or nation, despite temporary evil and the post-revolutionary revival of the 'two beasts' of civil and religious tyranny, for Rev 19:20 assures its readers that the beasts are to be cast down while still alive:

> Thus, though revived and again restored to power, yet we may hope it is but for a little while, and then they are to be utterly and for ever destroyed, as creatures cast into a lake of fire and brimstone – beyond rescue, even by British wealth, or British arms. [14]

The pattern may seem familiar from earlier overconfident interpretations of the Apocalypse. But with Bicheno and other preachers of the 1790s there is a new sense of urgency in the exhortations to a

nation at war and threatened by internal subversion, and there is a
new sense of the vividness and contemporaneity of the terrifying
events of John's vision. For

> the subject becomes vastly more interesting and affecting, if we
> ourselves, are acting a part in the great drama, witness the scenes
> of the fulfilment of the divine predictions, and are able to ascer-
> tain, with any tolerable degree of precision, their instant pro-
> gress. In prophecy we discern not the policy of men, but the
> councils of God. We behold the Supreme Being himself opening
> the volume of his divine decrees, and disclosing futurity to the
> world. In their fulfilment we see the proofs of the Being and
> Providence of Him who is wonderful in counsel, and excellent in
> working; whose wisdom is infinite, and who is greatly to be
> feared.[15]

'We see' is now a matter of literal 'witness', not of historical study
or eschatological speculation.

Bicheno is interesting not just because of his wide influence in
the world of liberal Dissent but because his preaching and writing
epitomise the different functions that the text of Revelation per-
forms in the revolutionary period. These are basically four, all of
which appear in *A Word in Season* and all of which draw on the
notion of a revolutionary *kairos:*

> the Apocalypse's continuing role as 'evidence' and proof-text;
> its provision of inspiration for belief in progress and for political
>   utopias;
> its supporting role in political rhetoric;
> its subversion of the logic of hermeneutical discourse.

I shall examine each of these functions in turn, taking Bicheno's
sermon as a way into more substantial writings of the 1790s.

PROOF BY APOCALYPSE

Despite the greater immediacy and urgency deriving from experience of the French Revolution's apocalyptic *kairos*, Bicheno does not
abandon the tradition of Mede and Whiston, the use of chronological calculations based on 'prophecy' or the treatment of Revelation

as *evidence* for the work of Providence. In *A Word in Season* he insists on the scholarly work of establishing the correct reference of each symbol and vision in Revelation and in the apocalyptic passages of the gospels. Certain sayings apply to the destruction of Jerusalem in the first century, others to the end of the world, and others to the intermediate period; and in working out which applies to which any double meanings are to be avoided (pp. 5–7). The predictions of the latter times are made in a 'figurative sense ... a manner of speaking derived from the ancient hieroglyphics', where the sun represents kings, clouds represent multitudes, and so on (pp. 12f.) In interpreting these hieroglyphics, Bicheno adopts the style and method of Mede and Newton, with one important difference that brings his actual application of the prophecies closer to those of the seventeenth-century radical millenarians: the 'latter times' are the present. So, he claims, the outpouring of the first bowl of Rev 16:2 upon the earth 'appears to have prevailed', and now (in 1795) comes fulfilment of the second bowl, the one poured into the sea, in God's present judgement on the maritime powers, especially Britain. It is a strange blend of biblical exegesis and journalistic speculation:

> Are the French the instruments which God is using for the chastisement of the nations...? ... Providence seems loosing them from their former restraints, and it is probable that, making peace with some of their continental enemies, they will be at liberty to bend their force more immediately against this country, and to exert all their power for the destruction of our navy (p. 44).

Hence the seas of blood seen by John; and hence the combination in Bicheno's sermon (and in writings throughout his life) of strong pacifist polemic with calm trust in God's providence.

James Bicheno and Joseph Priestley were not alone as radical dissenting millennialists. A fierier spirit than either was Joseph Towers, the Unitarian minister of humble origins who became Richard Price's 'co-adjutor' in Hackney in 1778. Towers was a member of the Revolution Society, addressing it with ardour on the centenary of the 1688 Revolution, a year before Price's famous speech. He also joined the radical Whig 'Society of the Friends of the People' and the more dangerous Society for Constitutional Information, writing an introduction to the latter's two-volume collection of tracts which led to his interrogation by the Privy Council. His *Dialogues concerning the*

Ladies, despite the condescending tone of their title, were an argument for the intellectual equality of women and men, and he published three volumes of other tracts on political and other subjects in 1796.[16] But in the same year he was in trouble again with the Privy Council for a book that Pitt appears to have succeeded in suppressing, as hardly any copies survive before an edition published in 1828 after Towers had become insane. Its full title was *Illustrations of Prophecy; in the course of which, many Predictions of Scripture are Elucidated; together with Numerous Extracts from the works of the preceding interpreters. Also, New Illustrations of Prophecy, in Five Dissertations, on an Infidel Power; the Abyss, or Bottomless Pit; the Symbolic Dragon; a Millennium; and the Coming of Christ.*

It hardly sounds like the world of liberal rational Dissent. Yet in his interpretation of Revelation Towers makes a traditional insistence on its usefulness in manifesting providence, in providing evidence for Christianity, in giving hope to the Church, and in upholding Protestantism; and to achieve this it requires 'decyphering' by a correct symbolical dictionary – he includes lengthy quotations from Mede, Whiston, Hurd and others. Numerological and chronological calculation lead to a more contemporary application than any of these provided, however – one in which he follows Bicheno quite closely. The two beasts are the civil and ecclesiastical tyrannies so closely united in prerevolutionary France. It is to France that the earthquake and the two witnesses of Rev 11 apply. The three and a half days when people gaze at the witnesses' bodies are interpreted as three and a half months, that is 105 prophetic days, that is 105 actual years, that is the interval between the Revocation of the Edict of Nantes in 1685 and the coming of liberty to France in 1790. Again, like Bicheno, he calculates the number of the beast by *gematria* to read LUDOVICVS, that is, Louis XVI. But all this ingenuity is placed in the service of a liberal political cause. Revelation's constant hostility to all monarchy, says Towers, is inescapable. Its martyrs crying out for justice are those whose conscience makes them defend 'the civil liberties of mankind'. Its millennium will follow the overthrow of the world's governments and be an era of 'knowledge', 'genuine Christianity', 'good government', 'virtue' and 'happiness'. And the 1828 edition closes with praise of Christianity as the religion of civil liberties and a quotation from Mrs Barbauld celebrating Christ as 'the Great Reformer, the innovator of his day; and the strain of his energetic eloquence was strongly pointed against abuses of all kinds'.[17]

In interpreters like Bicheno and Towers, then, there is a combination of the 'hieroglyphical' exegesis of the Mede tradition and the confident liberalism of the dissenting academies. There is also affinity with the political enthusiasm of the radical millenarians of the Civil War, but it is hard to show any very close contact between the eighteenth-century remnants of that tradition and the rationalism of the academies. What can be affirmed is, first, that seventeenth-century popular millenarianism never completely died out, and that, secondly, it underwent a revival in the heated political atmosphere of the 1790s. J. F. C. Harrison has elaborated not only the institutional survival of apocalyptic sects like the Ranters and the Muggletonians throughout the eighteenth century, but also the periodic rise of new 'prophets': the 'French prophets' early in the century, the Shakers in the middle part, and groups gathering in the 1780s around isolated prophetic female figures – Sarah Flaxmer and Mrs Eyre in London, Mary Evans in Meirionydd, Mrs Buchan in Ayrshire, the last of whom claimed to be the Woman of Rev 12 and also the Holy Spirit and assembled her followers for the Second Coming.[18] Harrison also shows from contemporary almanacs and chapbooks the continuing prevalence in folk culture of belief in magic, witchcraft, astrology and the prophetic interpretation of dreams, together with 'a simple, unintellectual type of neo-Platonism', concluding that 'millenarian prophets, no less than the early Methodist preachers, when they took their message to the people, found a basis for understanding and sympathy in some elements of folk culture and popular religion'.[19]

But before the 1790s such preaching barely engaged with political events. The French Revolution and the consequent wars gave it a new focus and a wider audience. Iain McCalman has shown the connections between radical politics, popular journalism, biblical interpretation and Methodism among anti-government activists in the 1790s; such people were perceived as a threat to established order out of all proportion to their numbers, and it was reaction to them that engendered the most repressive legislation in England since the Revolution of 1688.[20] Even the highly eccentric Richard Brothers gained serious attention among some Anglican clergy and had his apologist at Westminster in the oriental scholar Richard Halhed MP. Halhed's *Testimony on the Authenticity of the Prophecies of Richard Brothers* (1795) aimed to show 'by scientific proofs, and almost ocular demonstration' what Brothers showed by direct inspiration in his *Revealed Knowledge* of 1794 – that Daniel had predicted the destruction of the Royal Navy, that England was

Babylon, that the four kings of Daniel were in fact George III, Louis XVI, Catherine the Great and Friedrich Willhelm II, and that Brothers himself was 'the Prince of the Hebrews' raised up to lead the ten lost tribes back to Jerusalem for the Millennium. Brothers spent the next eleven years in an asylum and then lived until 1824, occupying himself mainly with elaborate architectural plans for the restoration of the Jews. His following largely dispersed after the military crises of the mid-1790s; but it is unlikely that it could have existed at all beyond a small circle of eccentrics if he had not both appealed to the authority of scripture and prophesied about the absorbing political events of the time. Much of Brothers's following later transferred to the less political but more organised Joanna Southcott, who died in 1814 in an imaginary childbirth believing she was the Woman of Rev 12 bearing 'Shiloh'.[21]

Unlike the Spenceans and the rational Dissenters, Brothers had no political philosophy, but his attacks on the king and the war led the government to see him as not only mad (which he undoubtedly was) but dangerous (which from their point of view was also true). For people to use religion to ally themselves with – or at any rate to fail to support the war against – the atheists and deists of the French Directory was to the mind of the civil and religious establishment blasphemous and absurd as well as subversive. So Tories and other government supporters were challenged to a 'prophetic' reading of contemporary politics; and many responded with enthusiasm, being if anything more ready than radicals to see in the revolutionary events an apocalyptic *kairos*. Thus Bishop Samuel Horsley, in a charge to his Rochester clergy in 1800, interpreted the French Republic as the Beast and saw the Methodists as the British fifth column of the Jacobins.[22] The bishop was drawing on such books as the widely read *History the Interpreter of Prophecy*, first published in 1799 by Henry Kett. Kett was a fellow of Trinity College, Oxford, and had been Bampton Lecturer in 1790, though later, according to the *DNB* – and not unlike others who had immersed themselves in the Apocalypse and written two lengthy volumes on it – 'his mind became unhinged, and he was found drowned at Stanmore, Middlesex, on 30 June 1825'. Examining the 'prophecies' of Paul as well as of John, Kett divides Antichrist into three 'branches', the papal, the Mahometan and the infidel; but he spends longer in expounding the third than the first two combined, observing that too many exegetes have misinterpreted prophecy by looking only at the first branch.[23] For Kett, the second Beast of

Revelation is Infidelity, allied with 'Democratic tyranny'. He relies heavily on Barruel, the exponent of the Jacobin conspiracy theory, to trace the origins of French godless republicanism in Voltaire and the Illuminati, but makes novel identifications of their prophetic types: the Beast's two horns, for instance, are German Illuminism and French Freemasonry. Now the prophesied 'last times' have arrived and the fourth vial has been poured on France; but England alone, thanks to the providential wisdom of her civil and ecclesiastical constitution, is escaping the general corruption of infidelity.[24] Kett's detailed historical exposition is combined with an apocalyptic tone that echoes Burke's but makes more direct inferences from scripture:

> may I not ask, whether we have not ourselves seen a Power gradually rise from its den, where it has long been strengthening itself, and from whence it has long sent forth the fumes of an intoxicating poison to prepare the world for its appearance, which exactly resembles this second beast? Have we not seen APOSTATE INFIDELITY, under the name of REASON, establish its dominion over the minds of men by its pretensions to a *refined* religion, a *pure* morality? Are not the doctrines of LIBERTY and EQUALITY, doctrines most perversely drawn from the *religion of the Lamb*, the HORNS of its *fascinating* power?... Has it not caused them that dwell on the earth to make an IMAGE to (or *like*) the beast which had the wound by a sword, and did live? (I.409)

A similar concentration on the evils of French atheism is found in Joseph Galloway's *Brief Commentaries upon such parts of The Revelation and other Prophecies as immediately refer to the Present Times*, those times now being 1802, when history has reached the verge of the seventh trumpet. Galloway believes himself to be living during the outpouring of the bowls of wrath (Rev 16). The first, with its painful sores, has destroyed the French *ancien regime*; the second has killed papal Rome; the third has been poured into the 'rivers' of Germany (the 'angel of the waters' probably being George III); the fourth on to the 'sun' of Louis XVI. The last three are soon to come, destroying the French atheistic republic ('the throne of the beast'), the Ottoman Empire ('the great river Euphrates'), and finally all the remaining enemies of God at Armageddon.[25] Different from Galloway's in detail as political events proceeded, but similar in its concentration on France and England, is the interpretation in Lewis Mayer's pamphlet of 1803, *A Hint to England; or, A Prophetic Mirror; containing An Explanation of Prophecy that relates to The French Nation, and the Threatened Invasion; proving Bonaparte to be The Beast that arose out of the Earth.* For Mayer, the first Beast is the French monarchy from Charlemagne and the second is Napoleon himself. The two horns are civil and ecclesiastical power; the falling star is Louis XVI and the bottomless pit the French nation; the fire from heaven is that of the French artillery and the locusts are Napoleon's armies. The number 666 belongs to Napoleon not by *gematria* but by adding together the number of all the Roman Emperors, all the Popes, the sovereigns of the 'ten nations' and Napoleon himself. The first woe is passed in the war of 1793, and the next two are soon to come. The prophecies' fulfilment so far ensures the English reader that his country will be 'exempt from the tyrannical power of France'; but Britain is not free from sin, which means that God will 'visit this country with a heavy scourge'. Then, after national repentance, comes the age of the British Empire prophesied in the most anti-imperial book of the Bible:

> ere long, the British nation will display her banners on the Gallic shores, extend her influence over the Continent of Europe and Asia, re-establish the Jews in their ancient possessions, and give universal peace to the world.[26]

Mayer was not alone in giving an Anglocentric slant to the apocalyptic history. It was present, as we have seen, in Brightman, and prevalent among readers caught up in the 'rhetorical situation' of the seventeenth-century revolution.[27] But its most ingenious practitioner was an Anglican clergyman, Frederic Thruston, who published in 1812 his *England Safe and Triumphant; Or, Researches into the Apocalyptic Little Book, and Prophecies, Connected and Synchronical.* Thruston wrote 'in that appointed time of the end' and as a member of 'that pure church and exalted nation' of England.[28] Indeed in his reading the national Church is represented three times in the Apocalypse by angels. In Rev 14 the first angel represents the Lutheran and the second the Calvinistic Church, but 'the third angel, pure and permanent' is the Church of England – neither too mild like the first nor too violent like the second but 'majestic and dignified' (I.458). It is this refined Anglican angel who, according to Thruston, gives the command to 'Come out' at

Rev 18:4f. (II.212) and the closing commands of the Apocalypse at Rev 22:8ff., demonstrating that 'in Protestant England alone, of all the powers of the Roman Earth, stands the Holy and Catholic Church' (II.426). The politics of Europe in 1812 fulfil the 'prophecies' of Rev 17: Napoleon's assumption of papal–imperial functions, combining 'infidelity' and 'Roman idolatry', is the fateful conjunction of Beast and Whore (II.173–8). But the prophecies dictate also Thruston's patriotic and optimistic conclusion: his 'great aim', he says, has been

> to prove that many of the mystic characters of the Revelation can only be referred to the pure Apostolic Church in England .... The discipline and doctrine of the Church of England will have received the divine sanction, and be made the foundation of the Church of the world .... Whenever,... throughout the Apocalypse we find any of these promises fulfilled upon any symbolic thing or person, therein we may confidently assert is there a regard, direct or indirect, to that Protestant England, who overcame by the blood of the Lamb (II.440–3).

The apotheosis of Napoleon also gave new life and ingenuity to calculations of the number of the Beast (a well-tested way of demonising one's contemporary enemies that continues apace in the USA at the end of the twentieth century). In his exhaustive survey of British interpretations between 1560 and 1830, David Brady counts no fewer than 147 different identifications, using dates, Greek and Latin *gematria* and Arabic and Roman numerals, with results ranging from religious foes like popes, Mohammed, Calvin, Luther, Laud and Wesley, to the political Pandemonium of LUDOVICVS, Cromwell, parliament and Tom Paine, and even including Cardinal Bellarmine transliterated into Hebrew. Not the least ingenious was Hester Thrale Piozzi, who calculated Napoleon's name to 666 by a study of Corsican dialect.[29] But Napoleon did not rule the field either as first or second Beast during the First Empire. In 1814 J. E.Clarke demonstrated that the number must be Greek *gematria* and went to the immense trouble of listing in Greek the names of all known nations throughout history, none of which adds up to 666 except *hē latinē basileia* ('the Latin kingdom'); this is the basis for a traditional anti-papal intepretation of Revelation.[30] More literal still in his approach was R. B. Cooper, the translator of Mede. In his 1833 commentary on Revelation, Cooper generally follows his master closely, but is not afraid to update him by seeing the fulfilment of the fourth bowl of wrath in the French Revolution and to support this from his own experience: on the day that Louis XVI was condemned to death Cooper saw spots on the face of the sun.[31] Clearly the age of evidences was not over.

Most systematic of all until the scholarship of E. B. Elliott was the Anglican evangelical clergyman George Stanley Faber. Faber began half a century's research into Revelation with his Oxford University sermons of 1799, in which he explained five of the seven bowls of Rev 16 by recent events. The sermons were refined in Faber's massive work *A Dissertation on the Prophecies...*, first published in 1805 and undergoing numerous revisions in the light of political developments until it reached 1400 pages in the 1828 edition, *The Sacred Calendar of Prophecy*. The final title betrays Faber's chrono-logical bent, but in the earlier editions from the Napoleonic period the calculations are centred clearly around recent history. Over 100 pages are dedicated to proving that the third woe-trumpet had sounded in 1789. The first bowl is the 'sore' of atheism, poured out on 26 October 1792; the second is the Terror of 1792–3; the third is the wars leading to the gathering in of the harvest with the peace of 1801; the fourth the French tyranny and military campaigns com-mencing in August 1802.[32] The objects of Faber's conservative wrath are made plain in his identification of the dragon's vomit of Rev 12:15 as

> a noisome *flood* of mock philosophers, German and French, illuminated and masonic ... philanthropic cutthroats, civic thieves, humane anarchists and candid atheists; enlightened prostitutes and revolutionary politicians; of popish priests and protestant ecclesiastics ... of Jews, Turks, infidels and heretics; of the *catharmata* of the prisons of Lyons and Paris ... in short, of *all* the filth and offscouring of *all* the kennels of *all* the streets of *the great mystical city Babylon*.[33]

While believing in the coming millennium, Faber was, as Oliver remarks, 'more interested in calamity than in happiness'.[34] Another Tory interpreter of Revelation, who like Faber was mocked by Coleridge, was the fashionable poet and preacher George Croly. Croly believed that interpretation of the book was generally a failure until the great clarification of prophecy at the 'end of the era' in 1793, that is 1260 years after the beginning of papal supremacy under Julian in 533. Now that things are clearer, he says, it can be seen that Napoleon was Abaddon, that the second woe was the four-fold alliance of 1813, and that the workings of providence culminated in the raising up of Burke, Nelson and Wellington.[35] Even more Anglocentric in its interpretation was Philip Allwood's thousand-page *Key to the Revelation of St John the Divine* of 1829.

Whether we are looking at radicals or conservatives, at Anglicans or Dissenters, at serious scholars or self-proclaimed prophets, we can find in much of the interpretation of the French revolutionary period the same concern with chronology and with 'evidence' in prophecy and its fulfilment of the working of providence and the truth of Christianity. There is the same lurching between literal and allegorical readings that was seen earlier in the century. But its calmness has largely gone. Apart from some rather tired anti-papal rhetoric and some conventional moralising, there was little polemical urgency among the interpreters surveyed in the previous chapter. Now the prophecies are not just demanding moral rectitude and a readiness to wait on God's intervention; they demand political decision in response to the apocalyptic events of the present that they are held to refer to. Whatever the calculations of past prophetic eras, the 'day' of judgement and salvation, God's *kairos*, has come near.

THE DAWNING MILLENNIUM

M. H. Abrams sees the Book of Revelation fostering in Christianity 'a strong historical prospectivism' that emerges in two main forms. One is the idea of revolution, traced by Abrams in the radical Reformation, the English, American and French Revolutions, and in Marx. The other is the idea of *progress*, which Abrams finds instances of in Joachimism, in Bacon and even in Robert Owen's use of biblical vocabulary.[36] But the idea was far from absent in the eighteenth century, sometimes existing in conjunction with that of revolution. Together with Bicheno's political radicalism and his traditional use of calculations and 'hieroglyphics' to apply the biblical text to present circumstances goes a firm belief in progress. 'O when will the time come that we shall all learn the lessons of Jesus Christ?' he asks in *A Word in Season*. Those lessons are of a day of universal happiness, assured by scriptural prophecy, and

It only needs that the great mass of mankind should be enlightened by the wisdom of the gospel ... that all governments should
be formed on the broad principles of justice and benevolence. ...
Were men thus enlightened, and governments thus constituted,
universal peace and happiness would follow of course.[37]

The coalescence of apocalyptic crisis-imagery and faith in human
perfectibility, seen also in Priestley, may seem an odd one. It
derives mainly from a thinker who was in the ordinary sense most
unapocalyptic and politically uninvolved, David Hartley. Hartley's
Observations on Man (1749) are an unusual combination – if not
exactly, as he intended, a synthesis – of mechanical psychology and
morality with fervent biblical religion. The lengthy first part exam-
ines the workings of the brain in terms of 'vibrations' registered in
its 'medullary substance'; these are the source of all sensation, of all
pleasure and pain whether physical or intellectual, and of all ideas
(which, as for Locke, are communicated by association). 'All
reasoning, as well as affection, is the mere result of association,' he
concludes; 'the moral sense is ... generated necessarily and
mechanically'.[38] But the necessity is a philosophical rather than a
'practical' one, he is at pains to point out; the mechanism derives
from and leads back to the benevolent God. So the reasoning, affection and moral sense of which he speaks need not be as dry as they
sound; the God-given vibrations actually create the 'tendency of
our natures to spirituality' (II.215), and in Hartley's own posthumously published meditations there is no doubt about his religious
fervour. If his necessitarianism is a secularised form of Calvinism,
then it is as capable of providing a sense of happy assurance as is
many a Calvinist's faith in predestination to salvation: Hartley's
own temperament bears this out, and Priestley's further radicaliz-
ing of it by his belief in the materiality of the soul actually
intensifies the optimism.

But how far the religious optimism actually follows logically
from the mechanistic psychology is unclear. Hartley endeavoured
to prove this in the almost as long second part of the *Observations*,
which covers natural religion, revealed religion, a 'rule of life' and
eschatology. He explains in his introduction to this part that

I do not presume to give a complete treatise on any of these subjects; but only to borrow from the many excellent writings, which
have been offered to the world on them, some of the principal

evidences and deductions, and to accommodate them to the fore-going theory of the mind; whereby it may appear, that though the doctrines of association and mechanism do make some alter-ations in the method of reasoning on religion, yet they are far from lessening either the evidences for it, the comfort and joy of religious persons, or the fears of irreligious ones (II.4).

One senses in these cautious words his uncertainty as to the co-herence of his project. As he implies, his theological apologetics are conventional for the first part of the eighteenth century, resting on arguments from design, from prophecy and miracles, and evincing a biblical latitudinarian faith rather than a thorough reasoning from the conclusions of his first part. Yet they contain a kind of prag-matic mysticism. The design of the scriptures, he says, 'is that of bringing all mankind to an exalted, pure, and spiritual happiness by teaching, enforcing, and begetting in them love and obedience to GOD' (II.131). The notion of 'purity' is a prevalent one, both in Hartley's 'practical rules' on things like diet, humour, sex and art, and in his philosophical tendency to monism. But this purity is fre-quently associated with happiness:

> The true and pure religion of CHRIST alone grows more evident and powerful from every attack that is made upon it, and con-verts the bitterness and poison of its adversaries into nourish-ment for itself, and an universal remedy for the pains and sorrows of a miserable, degenerate world (II.202).

The point is that since both the Christian gospel and the operation of association promote happiness, the world is becoming pro-gressively *less* miserable and degenerate. Developments in human thought, trade, medicine, philology and the interpretation of prophecy all favour this evangelistic progress and increase of happiness. Nevertheless, Hartley says rather surprisingly, 'it is not probable, that there will be any pure or complete happiness before the destruction of this world by fire' (II.388–93). In the final part of the *Observations* the imagery of Revelation predominates, and it becomes more apparent that the real grounds for Hartley's opti-mism and belief in 'benevolence' lie in his biblical teleology, based on fairly literal interpretations of the prophecies of the return of the Jews to Palestine and of the earthly millennium. The question 'of the terms of salvation' is 'whether at the resurrection we enter into

the new Jerusalem ... or whether we be cast into *the lake of fire'*
(II.417). Yet the lake is a purgatory rather than an eternal hell, and
Hartley ends his *magnum opus* by speaking of 'the final happiness of
all mankind in some distant future State'.

Hartley's psychology, ethics, theology of 'benevolence' and biblical interpretation were all influential in the second half of the eighteenth century, not least in the Unitarian tradition – where it could
be argued that the conscious rejection of the doctrines of original
sin and atonement was actually more significant than the rejection
of the doctrine of the Trinity.[39] But his teaching on progress and on
philosophical necessity were strongly politicised in that tradition,
first by the involvement in the radical Dissenters' campaign for religious liberty, but then more firmly by the reflections on civil liberty
arising from the American and more particularly from the French
Revolution. The rest of this section will survey the use of the
Apocalypse in the context of this belief in progress through the
writings of three prominent Unitarians: Richard Price, Joseph
Priestley and S. T. Coleridge.

Richard Price (1723–91) is best remembered as the preacher
whose sermon in November 1789 led to Burke's furiously eloquent
response in his *Reflections on the Revolution in France*. Burke portrays
him as a naive necromancer dabbling in politics, which is a travesty
of a man who was rational and judicious with great respect for
factual accuracy.[40] Forsaking his early Welsh Calvinism, Price
moved towards Unitarianism, though adopting an Arian position
(believing in Christ's pre-existence) rather than his friend Priestley's thoroughgoing Socinianism, and towards political liberalism,
playing a leading role in the 'Honest Whigs Club'. But Price's main
energies were spent in moral philosophy, where he adopted a rationalist and anti-voluntarist position, and in mathematics. The latter
was an essentially practical interest with (in Price's mind) important ethical consequences: Price became an expert in demography
and hence in insurance, serving for many years as technical adviser
to the Equitable Society, devising and advocating a universal
system of retirement pensions and undertaking a long-term study
of the National Debt. This hardly sounds like the wild orator of
Burke's caricature, who 'chaunts his prophetic song', countenanc-
ing 'delusive, gypsey predictions' and surrounded by 'the fumes of
his oracular tripod'.[41] In fact Price had no time for 'prophetic'
enthusiasm and was a stern opponent of what he saw as Methodist
irrationalism. It seems that he entered political controversy only

reluctantly, and principally as a result of the dispute with the American colonies, which in an old-fashioned puritan way he saw as leading a more virtuous and uncorrupted life than was possible in the mother country.[42]

Yet there is a strain of rather secularised prophecy running through his preaching and writing. In an early sermon for General Thanksgiving Day 1759, published as *Britain's Happiness, and the Proper Improvement of it,* Price indulges in fulsome celebration of his blessed island's progress in trade, military strength and religious liberty, rather in the style of James Thomson. It is 'a land which has the best constitution of government, the best laws, the best king and the best religion in the world'.[43] There is however still the need for moral improvement and for progress in 'virtue and religion', yet

> The world is now advanced far beyond its infancy. There are many indications of an approaching general amendment in human affairs. The season fixed by prophecy for the destruction of the *man of sin* cannot be far distant, and the glorious light of *the latter days* seems now to be dawning upon mankind from this happy Island (p. 12).

His language is usually less fervent than this, and his contentment with the state of the nation certainly diminished in the reign of George III. Yet the connection between a belief in progress and the action of Providence is a constant one in what Fruchtman calls his (and Priestley's) 'republican millennialism'. Thus Price's political argument in his *Observations on the Nature of Civil Liberty* (1776) and *Additional Observations* (1777) is almost entirely secular and far from apocalyptic: he reasons from moral principles, prudence and economic facts, with little reference to scripture. But when he asks of America and Britain at the climax of the first tract, 'Which side then is Providence likely to favour?' this appears as more than a rhetorical flourish. It is actually the undergirding of the whole rational argument, coming from a man who sees in the ineffective American Prohibitory Act of 1776 'something that cannot be accounted for merely by human ignorance. I am inclined to think that the hand of Providence is in them working to bring about some great ends' (p. 69).

Price is less cautious about the nature of those ends after the establishment of the United States, which he celebrates in 1784 as an empire which may be the seat of liberty, science and virtue, and from whence there is reason to hope these sacred blessings will spread till they become universal ... next to the introduction of Christianity among mankind, the American revolution may prove the most important step in the progressive course of improvement ... the independence of the English colonies in America is one of the steps ordained by Providence to introduce these times [of universal peace and the empire of reason, when the wolf shall dwell with the lamb] (pp. 117–19).

Here is a contemporary *kairos* that spurs its witnesses on to seek the promised millennium. But it is hailed in the language of the Enlightenment as much as in that of scripture. The same combination is seen in a more general vein when Price preaches at the founding of the new Hackney academy in 1787. The sermon, published as *The Evidence for a Future Period of Improvement in the State of Mankind*, takes for its text the petition 'Thy kingdom come', seeing it as referring 'primarily to the introduction of the christian religion among mankind'; yet 'the most glorious period' of this kingdom is still future, and signs of its growth are present now, fulfilling the prophecies of Isaiah, Daniel, Paul and of course Revelation. The signs are in the general, if not uninterrupted, progress of civilisation, reaching a peak in Isaac Newton, who was 'necessarily reserved for an advanced age of the world'. But there are still corruptions in Church and State, which must be purged before Antichrist can fall, and this purgation cannot simply be left to Providence: Christians, especially Dissenters and their academies, have an active role, bound 'to employ all the means in our power to cause the kingdom of God to come'. 'Reason and scripture' together lead to the expectation of a 'more prosperous state of things'. So Price concludes with the mildly apocalyptic imagery of 'a tide set in ... a favourable gale ... clouds scattering' in his appeal to 'seize the auspicious moment, obey the call of providence, and join our helping hands to those of the friends of science and virtue' (pp. 152–75). Clearly political events have led Price to a more vigorous expectation of the approach of the kingdom than Hartley could muster forty years before; nor does Price share Hartley's necessitarian philosophy and psychology. But his faith in progress is expressed in the same mixture of rational and scriptural language that Hartley used.

It was however in the events in Paris shortly before his death that Price saw the greatest *kairos* of God's liberating and progressive providence. The bulk of his famous sermon of 4 November 1789, delivered to the Society for Commemorating the Revolution in Great Britain and entitled *A Discourse on the Love of our Country*, is actually a sober assessment of the achievement of 1688 and the continuing need for reform, with Christians' natural love of their own country requiring 'regulation and direction' by reason and by Jesus' teaching of 'Universal Benevolence, which is an unspeakably nobler principle than any partial affections'. There is no new political theory in this sermon. What roused Burke's wrath was the final peroration, when Price moved from general principles to combine an ardent belief in progress with a scriptural salutation of recent events in France. As Laboucheix observes, those events inspire a new use of rhythm and metaphor in Price:

> What an eventful period is this! I am thankful that I have lived to see it, and I could almost say, 'Lord, now lettest thou thy servant depart in peace, for mine eyes have seen thy salvation'. I have lived to see a diffusion of knowledge which has undermined superstition and error. I have lived to see the rights of men better understood than ever, and nations panting for liberty, which seemed to have lost the idea of it. I have lived to see thirty millions of people, indignant and resolute, spurning at slavery, and demanding liberty with an irrespressible voice, their king led in triumph, and an arbitrary monarch surrendering himself to his subjects. After sharing in the benefits of one Revolution, I have been spared to be a witness to two other Revolutions, both glorious. And now, methinks, I see the ardor for liberty catching and spreading, a general amendment beginning in human affairs, the dominion of kings changed for the dominion of laws, and the dominion of priests giving way to the dominion of reason and conscience.[44]

Price ends by calling on all 'friends of freedom' to rejoice and all 'oppressors of the world' to tremble, using the language of 'starting from sleep' and of light being kindled. Nor was this an isolated instance of the new rhetoric inspired in him by the French Revolution. On the evening of the sermon Price moved a Congratulatory Address from the Revolution Society to the French National Assembly; the following month saw him proposing a toast to 'the Majesty of the People' at a meeting of the revived Society for Promoting Constitutional Information (he himself was toasted as 'the Friend of the Universe'), and a year later, chairing a meeting of the Revolution Society, he boldly proposed yet another toast, 'The Parliament of Britain, may it become a National Assembly'.[45] Yet it is interesting that, while Price continues to use scriptural language in his preaching at this period, he now rarely quotes from Revelation or speaks of the fulfilment of prophecy. He is rhetorical rather than exegetical, continuing no doubt to rest on Hartley's millennialist interpretation but shying away from direct application of text to event. And this is almost certainly not because he did not see the events as fulfilling prophecy but, on the contrary, because the fulfilment was so awe-inspiring that there was little need any longer to refer to its foreshadowing.

In this rhetorical use of the Bible Price contrasts with Joseph Priestley, who succeeded him as minister at Hackney after Price's death and after Priestley's own flight from Birmingham. Priestley is both closer to Hartley in his scientific interests and more concerned than Price with biblical exegesis.[46] He is also more interested in history and – in common with the English hermeneutical tradition outlined in the previous chapter – in fulfilment of biblical prophecy within the history of the church. But like Price he experiences the fulfilment of prophecy in a radical way through revolution, and even more firmly than Price he believes in the inevitable march of human progress under the hand of providence and with the assistance of liberal-minded Christians. The history of the church, however, is for Priestley largely that of 'the corruptions of Christianity', which began at a very early stage. Even the Reformation was only a very partial purge of those corruptions, in particular since it failed to banish religious establishments; and it required the further witness of Locke, Newton, Hartley and Priestley's own scientific work (investigating the nature of air and leading to his assertion of the identity of matter and spirit) to purge the world of superstition.

Like Newton's, Priestley's use of the Bible in this evangelical task of overcoming corruptions tends to operate with a 'canon within the canon' whose core is in Daniel and Revelation. Like Newton again, he attempts a univocal interpretation of their prophetic figures. So John Money writes of his 'proposal to purify religion by the millennial fusion of progressive experimental philosophy and Christian revelation'.[47] But the optimistic spirit of that fusion owes more to Hartley than to Newton's meticulous chronometry. Writing to his Unitarian colleague Theophilus Lindsey in 1771, Priestley says that 'everything looks like the approach of that

dismal catastrophe described, I may say predicted, by Dr Hartley
... and I shall be looking for the downfall of Church and State
together. I am really expecting some very calamitous, but finally
glorious events.'[48] In his influential *Institutes of Natural and Revealed
Religion*, published the following year, Priestley includes many
quotations from Revelation as proofs of the existence of a future
state and to show that the Pope is Antichrist and that the Jews will
literally return to Palestine.[49] There is a lengthy quotation from Rev
19 and 20, interpreting the millennium as earthly but not literally of
one thousand years: perhaps the prophet meant to signify 365 000
years, he wonders. But whereas Wesley had thought that the millennium might last such a time because it would take God so long
to judge many millions of souls, Priestley's extension of it is
because he reckons that, although progress in science is now more
rapid, a thousand years would be scarcely sufficient to bring the
world to its 'mature state'.

Yet the Millennium's actual beginnings are near, he concludes
from the present political situation:

> The present kingdoms of Europe are unquestionably represented
> by the feet and toes of the great image which Nebuchadnezzar
> saw in his prophetical dream.... From Daniel's interpretation of
> this vision it may be clearly inferred, that the forms of govern-
> ment, ecclesiastical and civil, which now subsist in Europe, must
> be dissolved; but that something very different from them,
> and greatly superior to them, more favourable to the virtue and
> happiness of mankind, will take place in their stead (II.370).·

As noted above, the American and French Revolutions, which
occurred after these words were written, sharpened Priestley's
perception of this new political state prophesied in the Bible.[50]
Reflecting on recent events in his Fast Sermon for 1793 and again
quoting both Hartley and Revelation, he asserts that

> I am led by the present aspect of things, to look forward to events
> of the greatest magnitude and importance, leading to the final
> happy state of the world.... It is a great and momentous aera to
> which we are brought. A great improvement will, no doubt, be
> finally made in the condition of man, and happy will be the
> willing instruments of it.... To those who are usefully and prop-
> erly employed, nothing can come amiss (XV.513–16).

The following year's Fast Sermon has a much firmer conviction that the apocalyptic troubles are 'now commencing' and also contains a much more detailed application of biblical texts to contemporary events: the French Revolution was the earthquake of Rev 11:13, the present wars mean that the seventh trumpet is near, whereas the prevalence of infidelity may be the fulfilment of Luke 17:8. But

> Happily, this infidelity is, in its turn, destroying those *antichrist-ian* establishments which gave birth to it; and when this great revolution shall be accomplished, genuine, unadulterated Christianity, meeting with less obstruction, will not fail to recommend and establish itself, by its own evidence, and become the religion of the whole world.... This was the idea of the great Sir Isaac Newton, as appears from the evidence of the excellent Mr Whiston (XV.547).

With this extraordinary blend of fundamentalism, rationalism, evangelism and optimism, Priestley set sail for America where for the remaining 16 years of his life he 'mus'd expectant on these coming years'. His letters and those of John Adams make it plain that, though political events altered his detailed interpretations, his 'millennial fusion of progressive experimental philosophy and Christian revelation' continued unchanged.[51]

For a time, however, one of the most ardent Unitarian millennialists in England was Samuel Taylor Coleridge. In 1796 he published his first collection of poetry, culminating in the political and millenarian 'Religious Musings', and some time in the same year he wrote in very Preistleian vein in a notebook:

> Millenium [*sic*], an History of, as brought about by a progression in natural philosophy – particularly, meteorology or science of air & winds – Quaere – might not a Commentary on the Revelations be written from late philosophical discoveries? (*CN* I.133)

Like many of Coleridge's projects this was never achieved. But the fascination with the notion of the millennium and with the Book of Revelation recurred throughout his life. They did not abandon him when he soon turned his back on his radical and millenarian views, any more than did his fascination with 'natural philosophy' (that is,

1. William Blake, 'The Angel of Revelation'

3. Blake, *America*, plate 10

2. Blake, *America*, plate 8

4. Blake, *Europe*, plate 1

5. Blake, *Europe*, plate 15

6. Blake, *Jerusalem*, plate 22

7. Blake, *The Book of Urizen*, plate 1

8. Dürer, *The Woman and the Dragon*

9. Dürer, *The Battle with the Dragon*

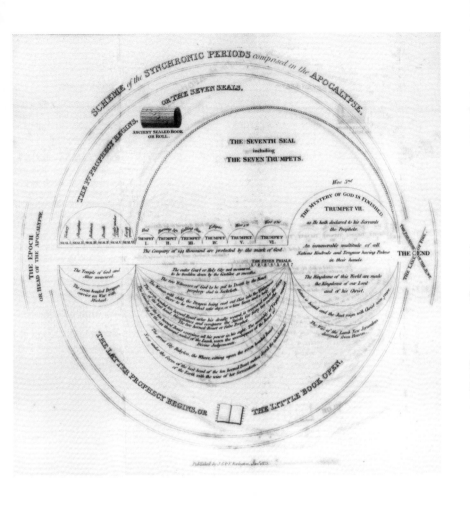

10. Joseph Mede's synchronisms (from *Clavis Apocalyptica*, 1833 edition)

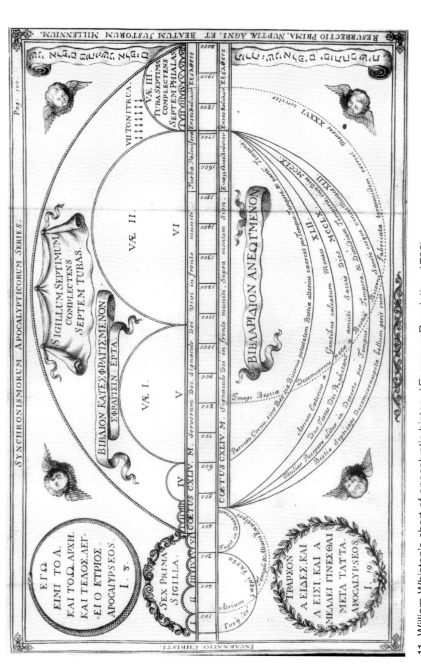

11. William Whiston's chart of apocalyptic history (*Essay on Revelation*, 1706)

natural science) or his attempt to apply a scientific and philosophical mind to the doctrines and symbols of traditional religion. In
1794–96, however, Coleridge was a convinced disciple of Hartley
(after whom he named his son in 1796) and the belief in progress
and its support from biblical revelation were at the forefront of his
mind. With Southey he planned the 'Pantisocratic' venture, in
which they, the Fricker sisters and others would form a utopian
commune in America. And with great mental and rhetorical energy
he undertook a series of lectures in Bristol on religious and political
subjects.

One thing that emerges from these lectures of 1795, says his bio-
grapher Richard Holmes, is

> the profoundly religious impulse behind all Coleridge's Panti-
> socratic radicalism. Unlike Paine or Godwin, he never appeals to
> 'the Rights of Man', but always to a fundamentalist view of
> 'Christ's teaching' about wealth, property, temporal power, and
> the brotherhood of man.[52]

His *Conciones ad Populum* of February 1795 open with a satirical
'Letter from Liberty to her dear Friend Famine', in which Liberty
approaches first Gratitude, then the Court, and then Religion:

> but alas! instead of my kind Mistress, horror-struck I beheld 'a
> painted patched-up old Harlot.' She was arrayed in purple and
> scarlet colour, and decked with gold and precious stones and
> pearls, and upon her Forehead was written 'MYSTERY'. I
> shriek'd, for I knew her to be the Dry-nurse of that detested Imp,
> Despotism (*LPR*, p. 30).

Similar language from the Apocalypse is used of State religion in
'Religious Musings', as it is by William Blake. But despite the corruption of ecclesiastical Christianity, Coleridge, like Priestley,
insists on the necessity of a pure (that is, Hartleian and Unitarian)
religion. His anti-government stance and political ends may be
similar to Paine's or Godwin's, but whereas the latter's appeal to
disinterestedness may move the few, 'the over-worked Labourer,
skulking into an Ale-house' can be moved only by Religion; so

> 'Go, preach the GOSPEL to the Poor.' By its Simplicity it will meet
> their comprehension, by its Benevolence soften their affections, by

its Precepts it will direct their conduct, by the vastness of its
motives ensure their obedience (*LPR*, p. 43f.)

This evangelical concern distinguishes Coleridge from Southey and
Wordsworth as well as from Paine and Godwin, while his belief in
common property distinguishes him also from Priestley. But the
theological content of his Bristol *Lectures on Revealed Religion* comes
from Hartley *via* Priestley. The evidence of design in the universe
points unfailingly, says Coleridge, to a Deity of 'total *Benevolence*'.
Yet Paine's deism is an inadequate faith: the Mosaic dispensation,
miracles and all, is necessary to preserve a people from idolatry,
and prophecies too are 'necessary to Revealed Religion as perpetual
Testimonies' (*LPR*, p. 152). Coleridge draws also on Paley and
Michaelis to find 'a mass of direct Evidence in favor of the Truth of
Revelation' so strong that, imagining himself a stranger to Christendom, he concludes that on a dispassionate examination of that
evidence 'I must become a Christian on the same principles that I
believe the doctrine of Gravitation' (*LPR*, pp. 186, 176). He appeals
to the Gospels and Acts rather than to Paul or Revelation, but the
belief in religious and political liberty is a firmly progressive and
millennial one, where the true patriot 'looks forward with glad-
dened heart to that glorious period when Justice shall have established the universal fraternity of Love' (*LPR*, p. 13).

The millennialist and religious impulse is evident not only in the
1795 lectures but also in Coleridge's correspondence, notebooks,
journalism and poetry of 1794–96. In an extraordinary evangelistic
letter of 17 December 1796 to the radical John Thelwall (whom
Coleridge had not at the time met) he asserts in opposition to
Thelwall's atheism that

> the Religion, which Christ taught, is simply 1 that there is an
> Omnipresent Father of infinite power, wisdom, & Goodness, in
> whom we all of us move, & have our being & 2. That when we
> appear to men to die, we do not utterly perish; but after this Life
> shall continue to enjoy or suffer the consequences & [natur]al
> effects of the Habits, we have formed here, whether good or
> evil. – This is the Christian *Religion* & all of the Christian
> *Religion* (*CL* I.280).

Even Isaac Newton might have found this a bit jejune; but
Coleridge, while denying that this religion appeals to the 'fancy',

goes on to celebrate the visions of the 'innumerable multitude of angels & archangels' given by this religion, with lengthy quotations from the Apocalypse. The necessitarian, materialist, optimistic religion of Hartley and Priestley is anything but cool and dry in this young disciple, who writes to his fellow-Pantisocrat Southey on 29 December 1794:

> I would ardently that you were a Necessitarian – and (believing in an all-loving Omnipotence) an Optimist. That puny Imp of Darkness yclept Scepticism – how could it dare to approach the hallowed Fires, that burn so brightly on the Altar of your Heart?

But the following year Southey's fires were smouldering and the future of Pantisocracy bleak, expiring in the bitter letter to Southey of 13 November 1795. Before that, in early August, Coleridge had written, '– Southey! Pantisocracy is not the Question – it's realization is distant – perhaps a miraculous Millenium'.[53] And clearly the Millennium – whether distant or close, whether Pantisocratic or democratic – was much on his mind in this year when he was expending so much labour on the writing of 'Religious Musings' and on his unsuccessful foray into political journalism in *The Watchman*.

Writing under the masthead 'That all may know the truth; and that the truth may make us free!', Coleridge is determined in *The Watchman* to preserve a bias 'in favor of principles, not men'; and those principles are to him Christian ones. So the essay on fasts in the second issue has the air of a sermon rather than an article; that on 'modern patriotism' in the third issue satirises non-religious bourgeois radicals like Godwin and Thelwall, insisting that 'you must give up your sensuality and your philosophy, the pimp of your sensuality; you must condescend to believe in a God, and in the existence of a Future State!' (CC II, pp. 98–100). His powerful essay 'On the Slave Trade' in the fourth issue uses practical and moral arguments, but intriguingly its starting-point is an issue of theodicy (the evident evil of such a trade discouraging belief in a benevolent God) and its climax is again a religious argument (the hypocrisy of 'Christians' profiting from the trade) (CC II, pp. 130–40).

The Watchman also contained verse, including the lines on 'The Present State of Society' that were to form the central section of 'Religious Musings'. The musings, like the journalism, are both religious and political; but the two elements are more clearly held together by a rather frantic attempt at a Miltonic version of the Apocalypse. It was a very important achievement for Coleridge: 'I rest for all my poetical credit on the *Religious Musings*', he wrote in April 1796.[54] Though he was soon to repent of much of its bombastic language and later of its religious doctrine, the poem is clearly an important and carefully constructed statement of a not quite coherent political and religious position.

The musing focuses on the omnipotence of 'The Great Invisible' God, which evokes a depiction of cosmic worship. At first this is connected to the Christmas angels; but they are soon left behind, as is the Christ they hymn, in a more vigorous depiction of the militant Elect who 'marching onwards view high o'er their heads/His waving banners of Omnipotence'. Despite the section praising the crucified and 'despised GALIAEAN', the prominent imagery of the poem comes from the Apocalypse and (as throughout Coleridge's poetic career) from light and the sun. The revelation of the 'Omnipresent Sire' is like sun dispersing mist.[55] Here is the progressive 'enlightenment' of providence as seen by Hartley, assuring the believer of ultimate happiness and of the passage from evil to good, which includes the emergence of freedom out of science and science out of war, avarice and trade (ll. 227–50). It derives from

> The SUPREME FAIR sole Operant: in whose sight
> All things are pure, his strong controlling love
> Alike from all educing perfect good.
>
> (ll. 62–4)

But this same benevolent Deity is also the agent of apocalyptic vengeance, and Coleridge's notes to the poem make explicit the frequent allusions to and actual quotations from the Apocalypse and their reference to contemporary politics. As in the letter to Thelwall quoted above, the vision of the one seated on the 'jasper throne' evokes both reverence and reforming energy. So from the 'dreadless awe,/A solemn hush of soul' comes the vision of the 'Seven Spirits' who 'fill their seven Vials with salutary wrath' (ll. 82–96), while after the lurid depiction of human poverty and oppression the seer proclaims:

> Yet is the day of Retribution nigh:
> The Lamb of God hath open'd the fifth seal...
>
> (ll.316 f.)

In the lines following, images of the destruction of the mighty are piled up from Revelation. 'Ev'n now the storm begins' – and the poet makes it clear in a note to this line (328) that the storm is the French Revolution and that 'the Babylon of the Apocalypse does not apply to Rome exclusively; but to the union of Religion with Power and Wealth, wherever it is found'. Foul spirits shriek at the fall of the scarlet-clad 'old Hag', the gates of Paradise open, the Millennium begins and the Elect dead rise, prominent among them the 'Coadjutors of God' – Milton, Newton and Hartley – followed by the still living Priestley.

The poem's incoherence may seem to derive from the combination of apocalyptic and necessitarian language; though that, as seen above, is present in Priestley the 'Patriot, and Saint, and Sage', and also in Hartley ('of mortal kind Wisest'). Perhaps Coleridge's translation of the doctrine from calm prose to fiery verse does the service of uncovering the logical inconsistency of the necessitarian philosophy *per se*, and in particular of the rhetorical difficulty of combining images of crisis with those of progress. To hold them calmly together requires a mind like Priestley's that interprets symbols in a literal way and sees words corresponding directly to historical realities. Coleridge's mind was too imaginative to rest for long in such a correspondence. At the very time he was writing the progressivist effusions of *The Watchman* and 'Religious Musings', the symbolic edifice was beginning to crumble in his mind. As I hope to show in the final section of this chapter, this was a result of his exposure both to political developments and to the symbolism of the Bible itself.

THE RHETORIC OF PATMOS

As well as using Revelation and other biblical texts to provide evidence for the workings of providence and to put flesh on a belief in progress, James Bicheno's preaching often alludes to prophetic and apocalyptic writings in a *rhetorical* rather than a hermeneutical way to urge political and moral decision. 'What are a great part of the writings of the prophets but moral politics?' he asks at the beginning of *A Word in Season* (p. 4). The main topics of his preaching in this sermon are not biblical texts but the national 'crimes' of the slave trade, bribery, religious establishment and war, and it would be quite possible to draw a coherent moral argument from it if all the exegesis of apocalyptic texts were omitted. But without the weight of rhetorical allusion to those texts the argument would be a very plain one and the appeal to repentance greatly weakened. 'The clouds have already begun to darken our hemisphere – they roll towards us – they groan with the weight of vengeance which they bear', he says when speaking of the need for the renewal of the Church (p. 47): the very lack of the precise reference that he otherwise often provides makes the words more rather than less effective, since they can be associated with a whole range of situations in his hearers' experience and imagination and imbue them and possible moral responses to them with a biblical authority. The same is true of his final appeal in the sermon, which is addressed in prophetic style to more than individual listeners:

> O ye nations! ye nations! prepare to meet your God. He cometh in his power, to rejudge the cause of the dead. He will break his enemies with a rod of iron, and dash them to pieces like a potter's vessel. Then ye servants of God, ye afflicted followers of Christ, look up, and lift up your heads, for your redemption draweth nigh. HE THAT TESTIFIETH THESE THINGS SAITH, SURELY I COME QUICKLY, AMEN. EVEN SO, COME LORD JESUS (p. 53).

The words are a catena of allusions from Amos, Isaiah, Jeremiah, Psalm 24 and Luke 21, but the climax consists of the closing words of the Apocalypse, used both to lend authority to the preceding sermon and to direct the political opinions, prayers and actions of the listeners. Again, the lack of precise reference heightens the rhetorical effect.

Such techniques of biblical allusion are familiar from sermons throughout Christian history. But in the battle of books, pamphlets and speeches that the French Revolution engendered in England during the 1790s they are used widely in apparently secular contexts, addressed to a culture whose symbolic world was still largely formed by biblical typology. The Apocalypse plays a particular part in this battle since both its narrative and its visual elements provide rhetorical support for arguments against or in favour of the Revolution. Its narrative is used to underscore the sense of a *kairos*, a time of judgement and decision; its depiction of chaos and monsters to visualise the extraordinary nature of revolutionary upheaval.

The battle really began with Edmund Burke's *Reflections on the Revolution in France*, published in November 1790 as a response to Price's sermon of twelve months previously. It is a book that ranges far beyond that particular controversy to adumbrate and advocate an organic vision of a settled, hierarchical society, to which the French restructuring forms the antithesis: it brought forth over 80 written responses, and British political debate for the next quarter of a century was embroiled with interpretation of events in France, many of which seemed to be justifying fears of Burke that had seemed rather wild in 1790.[56] In Burke's thought and rhetoric there is tension between order and disorder, which is partly the result of the ambiguity of 'nature' for him. The gradual organic historical growth of a society or nation is like that of a tree, so that Burke sees things like the British constitution as 'natural': though apparently highly complex and disordered, it is in fact the living fruit of the supreme divine ordering of nature. Burke positively delights in the dependence of such order on 'natural' prejudice. It contrasts with the apparently ordered but really highly unnatural and artificial philosophical spirit represented by Price – and represented more ominously by the French rulers, measuring their country out into its precise administrative squares and so destroying the venerable growth of centuries centred on hearth and altar:

> In England we have not yet been completely embowelled of our natural entrails.... We have not been drawn and trussed, in order that we may be filled, like stuffed birds in a museum, with chaff and rags, and paltry, blurred shreds of paper about the rights of man. We preserve the whole of our feelings still native and entire, unsophisticated by pedantry and infidelity. We have real hearts of flesh and blood beating in our bosoms. We fear God; we look up with awe to kings; with affection to parliaments; with duty to magistrates; with reverence to priests; and with respect to nobility. Why? Because when such ideas are brought before our minds, it is *natural* to be affected (p. 182; cf. pp. 119f.)

The power of such a passage – at any rate over those readers who formed what Burke called 'the British public', which was actually as he recognised a small educated minority of the total population – rests on rhythm and alliteration, but also on the use of metaphor from nature; yet, as so often with Burke, the 'natural' image is a grotesque or ugly one. The 'stuffed birds' are like 'the little shrivelled, meagre, hopping, though loud and troublesome insects' to which Burke likens the English radical cabals, failing seriously to disturb the settled constitution of 'thousands of great cattle, reposed beneath the shadow of the British oak' (p. 181). Again, as seen above, Burke depicts Price as a magician, perverting nature for his sinister purposes. In accord with his earlier aesthetic theory in *A Philosophical Inquiry* (1757), the sense of the sublime depends on feelings of fear and on the instinct for self-preservation.[57] So the contemplative delight in the hierarchical order that he advocates can be both heightened and undercut by Burke's evident horrified delight in the *dis*order of the grotesque. In this he is very close to the rhetorical effect of Revelation: both Burke and John of Patmos (like Milton in *Paradise Lost)* take great risks in their use of monstrous imagery, for the strategy may rebound upon its author to make the derided monsters more alluring than the sublime political or heavenly order. Satan becomes more powerful than God, the chirping grasshoppers more attractive than the ruminating cattle, the great Whore more impressive than the heavenly court.

Despite his adherence to the protestant constitutional settlement, Burke rarely quotes the Bible, and his allusions to it, through frequent, are usually oblique. He does not actually say that the revolutionary French are the Whore or that British radicals are followers of the Beast; but he allows the monstrous apocalyptic images to take root by referring to people pledging 'the societies of Paris in the cup of their abominations' (p. 204), or, when speaking of Price and his colleagues, to 'the confused jargon of their Babylonian pulpits' (p. 115). As he says of the French situation near the beginning of his book, in one of several allusions to *Macbeth,*

> Every thing seems out of nature in this strange chaos of levity and ferocity, and of all sorts of crimes jumbled together with all sorts of follies. In viewing this monstrous tragi-comic scene, the most opposite passions necessarily succeed, and sometimes mix with each other in the mind; alternate contempt and indignation; alternate laughter and tears; alternate scorn and horror (p. 92f.)

The passage is revealing: the dramatic chaos is both in the actual events across the Channel and in the spectator's or commentator's mind. Burke's first readers were very aware of this. Tom Paine, for instance, mocks Burke's 'mob of ideas' and 'pathless wilderness of rhapsodies', and alludes ironically to the words just quoted when he refers the chaos and crimes not to the people of Paris but to the usurpation of William the Conqueror and its continuing effects.[58] And in the rhetorical high point of Burke's meandering argument, the much praised and much mocked eulogy of Marie Antoinette, there is veering between veneration for the beautiful symbol of monarchical order and an almost pornographic fascination with 'all the decent drapery of life ... rudely torn off', when 'a queen is but a woman; a woman is but an animal'.[59]

It is in this passage, where the language of the sublime, the beautiful and the monstrous are constantly mingled, that Burke's sense of the French Revolution as an apocalyptic *kairos* is most in evidence. Not only is the revolution a time for decision in British politics, it begins a new era in world politics. '[T]he age of chivalry is gone. – That of sophisters, oeconomists, and calculators, has succeeded; and the glory of Europe is extinguished for ever' (p. 170). The hyperbole is increased in Burke's use of the apocalyptic language of cosmic upheaval to express the seriousness of the *kairos*. Thus the godless philosophers of France threaten 'to sweep the earth with their hurricane, and to break up the fountains of the great deep to overwhelm us' (p. 149); if they succeeded 'the commonwealth itself would, in a few generations, crumble away, be disconnected into the dust and powder of individuality, and at length dispersed to all the winds of heaven' (p. 194). In a calmer passage, Burke asks himself why he feels 'so differently from the Reverend Dr Price', and characteristically answers, 'because it is *natural* I should'. He draws again on his earlier reflections on the sublime and the beautiful to speak of the effect of events on feelings and the moral value of feeling:

> because in events like these our passions instruct our reason; because when kings are hurl'd from their thrones by the Supreme Director of this great drama, and become the objects of insult to the base, and of pity to the good, we behold such disasters in the moral, as we should behold a miracle in the physical order of things. We are alarmed into reflection; our minds ... are purified by terror and pity; our weak unthinking pride is humbled, under the dispensations of a mysterious wisdom (p. 175).

The irony here is that the words could almost have been written by Price himself, who for all his un-Burkean rationalism was just as concerned with the moral effect of political events. In both men the concern leads to a contemporising of apocalyptic events – and also to a certain caution in directly identifying the action of God in the 'great drama'.

As events in France developed in the final years of Burke's life and often seemed to fulfil his predictions, his use of the language of apocalypse and monstrosity and his insistence that Europe has reached a time of judgement both increased. So in his self-justificatory *Letter to a Noble Lord* (1796) he writes of 'the revolution harpies of France, sprung from night and hell, or from that chaotick anarchy, which generates equivocally "all monstrous, all prodigious things"', again using ornithological metaphors to depict them as adulterous cuckoos and as birds of prey defecating over tables, to 'leave nothing unrent, unrifled, unravaged, or unpolluted with the slime of their filthy offal'.[60] The *Letters on a Regicide Peace* of the same year mix reasoned pragmatic and statistical arguments with violent, obscene and supernatural language, for, to Burke's mind, all else must pale before the priority of war against the 'vast, tremendous, unformed spectre,... that hideous phantom' that has arisen 'out of the tomb of the murdered Monarchy in France' (IX.190f.) The war is not a territorial one – Burke mocks the British government's peripheral engagements in the Caribbean – but an intellectual and religious one against 'the evil spirit that possesses the body of France', against 'the Synagogue of Anti-Christ ... that forge and manufactory of all evil, the sect which predominated in the Constituent Assembly', of a character 'the most restless, the most enterprizing, the most impious, the most fierce and bloody, the most hypocritical and perfidious, the most bold and daring that ever has been seen, or indeed that can be conceived to exist' (IX.243, 292). But if this is a religious war, what part (if any) does God play? Burke uses the language of providence and of apocalypse to bolster the importance of his cause. But the possibilities of divine intervention or direction or of the unambiguous fulfilment of prophecy are effectively sidelined when one comes to the actual conduct of policy: it would be 'mad and impious presumption for any one to trust in an unknown order of dispensations, in defiance of the rules of prudence, which are formed upon the known march of the ordinary providence of God' (IX.269). And this 'known march' centres on the known order of Church and King. All that is needed to be known of God is available in nature and reason and tradition; and the main function of scripture for Burke – as to some extent for the more scholarly Lowth – is to rouse the passions into moral commitment to preserve the known order. He is ready to do this quite shamelessly, unlike the generally judicious Price, whose precise and measured rhetoric Laboucheix contrasts with Burke's use of *'une ironie aggressive, une poésie créatrice de mythes, et une déformation systématique du vocabulaire de la philosophie pour en faire l'instrument d'un pouvoir affectif occulte'.*[61]

There is a contrast here not only with Price but also with Burke's most successful antagonist Tom Paine, whose *Rights of Man*, according to its author, sold up to half a million copies in ten years (Part I appeared in 1792, part II the following year).[62] Paine's style is vigorous, aphoristic, but deliberately plain, appealing to readers far beyond the cultivated landed circle of Burke's 'British public'. James Boulton, stressing as ever the inseparability of 'matter' and 'manner' in political writing, says:

> Paine is indeed a conscious artist ... his style and literary methods embody his political and moral values as effectively as Burke's quite different style and methods are an embodiment of his.... Paine's distinction ... is that he perfected an idiom appropriate to his deceptively simple philosophy as well as to his culturally unsophisticated readers; his manner of defiant abruptness suited the urgency of the times and the seriousness of the issues from the standpoint of the oppressed members of society.[63]

Of the urgency of the times there is no doubt for Paine, and ironically (for Paine was a deist, later to undertake a thorough attack on the Bible in *The Age of Reason)* his proclamation of an apocalyptic *kairos* is grounded more explicitly than Burke's on theology and even on scripture. This is already true of his response to the incipient American Revolution in *Common Sense* (1776). 'The time hath found us', he exults; 'a situation, similar to the present, hath not happened since the days of Noah until now. The birth-day of a new world is at hand'.[64] The argument against monarchy in this pamphlet is not only from nature and reason but also from scripture (the story of Samuel resisting its institution). With the arrival of the French Revolution, *Rights of Man* similarly speaks of 'a new era to the human race' and of the present generation appearing to the future 'as the Adam of a new world' (pp. 162, 268). This transformation is of course a political but also a mental and religious one, since for Paine human rights and equality are based at least partly on 'the Mosaic account of the creation' and their revolutionary enactment 'rises into a Regeneration of man' and constitutes 'a renovation of the natural order of things' (pp. 66f., 114, 144). Paine abjures Burke's use of classical allusion and quotation, having 'no occasion to roam for information into the obscure field of antiquity.... We are brought at once to the point of seeing government begin, as if we had lived in the beginning of time' (p. 185). In fact, practically his only references to other writings (apart from the Declaration of the Rights of Man) are to the Bible. These are generally oblique and ironic. 'Lay then the axe to the root, and teach governments humanity', he appeals in an echo of John the Baptist (p. 58). Like the young Coleridge, he rejoices in the 'death-wound' dealt to 'the affectation of mystery' by courts (pp. 208f.; cf. Rev 13:3; 17:5). And humorously he asserts that 'Mr Burke, by proving against the Rights of *Man*, proves in behalf of the *beast*; and consequently, proves that government is a beast' (p. 195). While denying it theologically, he still rests gently on a sense of scriptural authority to heighten his readers' awareness of the monstrosity of traditional government and of the God-given radical newness of the French and American achievements.

While Paine cannot really be called a millennialist and, unlike Hartley or Price or Priestley, does not recognise the Bible as revelation, he nevertheless uses millennial language in a secularised form. *Rights of Man* celebrates 'a morning of reason rising upon man on the subject of government' and its second part closes with a parable of buds appearing on twigs in winter (Paine remarks that it is February as he writes). Even if only one bud is visible, experience and reason lead the observer to conclude that such generation is not isolated,

> and though the vegetable sleep will continue longer on some trees and plants than on others, and though some of them may not *blossom* for two or three years, all will be in leaf in the summer, except those which are *rotten*. What pace the political summer may keep with the natural, no human foresight can determine. It is, however, not difficult to perceive that the spring is begun (p. 273).

In that political spring of the 1790s many of the more proletarian English radicals who seized on Paine's *Rights of Man* were less at home in his rational deism and seized also on the seventeenth-century millenarian tradition and on Methodist spirituality. Iain

McCalman has analysed the interpretative 'matrix of popular Puritanism and biblicism' of an activist like Thomas Spence, whom he sees as a millenarian 'bricoleur'.[65] Spence saw God as a leveller and himself as a Moses forming a people to instruct by popular means in 'Canaan'; many of his followers were or had been Methodists, and McCalman shows how their writings have frequent recourse to the Bible for rhetorical support in the levelling cause.

In his secularisation of the millennial language Paine is however joined by other deist or atheist opponents of Burke. The first response, appearing only three weeks after the *Reflections,* was from Mary Wollstonecraft. Her *Vindication of the Rights of Men* bears the marks of hasty composition and also of the contagious effect of Burke's rhetoric. There is no doubting her humanitarian passion, but she undermines her own rationalism by the prodigal use of adjectives and of grotesque or apocalyptic imagery. So, for instance, she rounds on the landed Burke:

> Man preys on man; and you mourn for the idle tapestry that decorated a gothic pile, and the dronish bell that summoned the fat priest to prayer. You mourn for the empty pageant of a name, when slavery flaps her wing, and the sick heart retires to die in lonely wilds ... Hell stalks abroad; – the lash resounds on the slave's naked sides; and the sick wretch, who can no longer earn the sour bread of unremitting labour, steals to a ditch to bid the world a long good-night.[66]

Paine was to say more in nine plain words: 'He pities the plumage, but forgets the dying bird'. Wollstonecraft herself was able to give a more measured assessment of the revolution four years later in *An Historical and Moral View of the Origin and Progress of the French Revolution and the Effect it has Produced in Europe*, which describes the events of 1789 with a personal commentary. She opens the first book of this work in progressive tones, claiming that 'the image of God implanted in our nature is now rapidly expanding', and attempts a sketch of world history as a gradual enlightenment culminating in the French Revolution.[67] As Harriet Devine Jump observes, 'the "first principles" to which she continually returns in the *Historical and Moral View* are clearly more moderate and secular expressions of the millennialist belief, common at this period, that both men and political systems were naturally moving towards a more perfect state'.[68] But – as in parts of the *Vindication of the Rights of Men* and as with the Pantisocratic Coleridge – one senses that her heart is more in a pastoral paradise where the intractable structures of civil society can be left behind.

A more single-minded secular rationalist was the man who was to become Wollstonecraft's husband, William Godwin. His *Enquiry Concerning Political Justice, and its Influence on Morals and Happiness* (1793) was by far the most substantial testament of English radical political theory. In the thorough utilitarianism of his ethics and the studied rationalism of his rhetoric, Godwin also anticipates Marx by hailing a secular millennium when, after the necessary present political reforms, 'one of the most memorable stages of human improvement' arrives with 'that auspicious period, the dissolution of political government' (V.24). Before that stage of moral perfection it is likely, though regrettable for Godwin, that revolutions must occur, but in his chapter 'Of Revolutions' he envisages this happening as a natural process of decay and regeneration rather than of violent upheaval:

> There is a period, at which [imperfect institutions] may be expected to decline and expire, almost without an effort.... Men feel their situation; and the restraints that shackled them before, vanish like a deception. When such a crisis has arrived, not a sword will need to be drawn.... The adversaries will be too few and too feeble, to be able to entertain a serious thought of resistance against the universal sense of mankind (IV.2).

In this austere liberal vision of the process of earthly salvation there is neither theological substructure nor biblical dressing; yet the actual political expectation and ethos differ little from the religious Priestley's. It is as though the Bible and the Apocalypse, having conveyed their teleological impetus, can now be laid aside. The intellectual project of Hartley has been taken to its logical conclusion, and apocalypse is mechanised.

THE COLLAPSE OF INTERPRETATION

None of the writers surveyed in the section above was setting out actually to interpret scripture in the systematic way of preachers like Priestley or Bicheno. But the frequently unselfconscious way in which either images from Revelation or quasi-millennial expectations surface in their writings witnesses to the deep effect wrought by the Apocalypse in both scholarly and popular English hermeneutical traditions and to the power of revolutionary experience to resurrect elements of them. As W. H. Oliver shows, 'prophecy, both explicit and implicit, was a normal intellectual activity in early nineteenth-century England', and, especially among evangelicals, 'prophetic' exposition a normal way of engaging in polemic and of undergirding missionary activity.[69] Ironically, however, it was at the same period of the French Revolution that those traditions themselves were most clearly threatened with dissolution – their internal incoherence exposed not only by the failure of the revolutionaries' aims but also by the impact of German philosophy and biblical criticism and of the English poetic imagination.

James Bicheno's attempt to use the Book of Revelation as rhetorical undergirding for his liberal political views eventually foundered. There was a mismatch between political events in the Napoleonic period and his millennial hopes; a mismatch too between the crisis language of the Apocalypse and his belief in earthly progress directed by providence; and a mismatch between the aim to discover direct historical reference in John's vision and the evidently mythopoeic energy of that vision. So when his *Fulfilment of Prophecy farther illustrated by The Signs of the Times* appeared after Waterloo it lacked the conviction and passion of his sermons and exegesis of the 1790s. Not that it lacks persistence or ingenuity, as for over 250 pages it tries to relate the 'prophecies' to the conflicts and chronology of recent history and to ascertain whether the seventh angel is about to empty his bowl. But the hermeneutical and homiletic conclusions he reaches are limp ones. 'The impression on my mind is, that that shaking is begun, and that although there is at present a pause, yet that this pause is only that short one intimated in Rev. xvi.13–16'; and in order to escape the probable consequences, his readers are urged as before to come out of Babylon by repenting of immorality, superstition, intolerance and so on.[70]

For other radicals a hermeneutical Waterloo had arrived before 1815. Godwin and Wollstonecraft had never attempted a theological interpretation of events. In America, Paine became disillusioned with French politics and sensed that the political summer was longer in coming than he had hoped, although the optimistic Priestley was still able to 'muse expectant'. Not so his former devotee Coleridge, who was already growing restless with Hartleian progressive millennialism when 'Religious Musings' appeared. This poem was published only two years before the *Lyrical Ballads*, and it was not long before Coleridge had abandoned not only the high-flown style but also the beliefs in necessitarianism, millenarianism and radical politics – Morton Paley convincingly shows that it was for these latter rather than for stylistic reasons that Coleridge prevented its reprinting between 1803 and 1828 (when it appeared among his 'Juvenile Poems').[71] In the eighth issue of *The Watchman* (April 1796) Coleridge wrote a 'Remonstrance to the French Legislators', and two years later he expressed his continuing but altered faith in Liberty in the 'poem of recantation', 'France: An Ode'. Here he looks back on his ardent radicalism of the mid-1790s, when genuine loyalty to French ideology had tested his patriotism:

> For ne'er, O Liberty! with partial aim
> I dimm'd thy light or damped thy holy flame;
> But blessed the paeans of delivered France,
> And hung my head and wept at Britain's name.
>
> (*CP* p. 214: ll. 39–42)

But French imperialism and militarism drove the poet to ask Freedom's forgiveness for this misplaced zeal, and the poem ends with his rededication to Liberty in another form:

> … there I felt thee! – on that sea-cliff's verge,
> Whose pines, scarce travelled by the breeze above,
> Had made one murmur with the distant surge!
> Yes, while I stood and gazed, my temples bare,
> And shot my being through earth, sea and air,
> Possessing all things with intensest love,
> O Liberty! my spirit felt thee there.
>
> (ll. 99–105)

It is simple therefore to read Coleridge's development between 1795 and 1798 as a retreat from the public to the private realm, from concern with politics to concern with nature and domestic life. And certainly most of his best early poetry (from 'The Eolian Harp' of 1795 to 'Frost at Midnight' of 1798) does centre on the latter concerns. But there is no straightforward progression, and in fact the concerns overlap and struggle with one another, as Coleridge tries to create a language that will relate nature, the mind, apocalypse, politics and salvation in one poetic achievement – a language he comes closest to in the fragmentary 'vision in a dream' of 'Kubla Khan'.

At the very time he was working on the confidently millennial 'Religious Musings', Coleridge also wrote his fine poem 'Reflections on Having Left a Place of Retirement'. Here the newly-married poet has resolved to leave his 'pretty Cot' to return to the active life in Bristol, expressing it in the language of *The Watchman:*

> I therefore go, and join head, heart, and hand,
> Active and firm, to fight the bloodless fight
> Of Science, Freedom, and the Truth in Christ.
>   (*CP* p. 81:ll. 60–2)

But at least part of his heart stays behind at the 'Cot'; the poet tries to transform this nostalgia into altruistic eschatology, but significantly it does not really work, and the poem ends by pining for the domestic tranquillity, adding,

> And that all had such!
> It might be so – but the time is not yet.
> Speed it, O Father! Let thy Kingdom come!
>   (ll.69–71)

Here the 'kingdom' seems to be not a new political order but the sharing of a pastoral haven; and the energy to achieve it, whether in Paris, Pennsylvania or Somerset, seems to have been resigned into the hands of Providence.

Yet still Coleridge worked on the 'Religious Musings', and even later (at Christmas 1796) returned to the apocalyptic theme in his 'Ode to the Departing Year', a poem whose rhythmic vitality and evocations of the spirit world anticipate Shelley (*CP*, pp. 93–7). Here again there is reference to the heavenly court of Revelation ('wheeling round the throne the Lampads seven') and, in violent language, to contemporary events – the Empress of Russia is the 'insatiate Hag' of the Apocalypse. Yet now Christ is completely absent, and the most violent upheaval is the one taking place in the visionary's own mind and senses (in section VI). And this poem too ends not in redemptive action for threatened 'Albion' but in renunciation:

> Away, my soul, away!...
> Now I recentre my immortal mind

In the deep Sabbath of meek self-content;
Cleans'd from the vaporous passions that bedim
God's Image, sister of the Seraphim.

(ll. 149–61)

The 'vaporous passions' seem to include the very involvement with
radical politics and reflection on international events that inform
the writing of the poem. But the mental quiet of the Sabbath was
not so easily obtained by Coleridge, even in the stimulation of the
developing friendship with Wordsworth the following year. He
was unable to rest in the confident tranquillity with which his
friend looked back over early years in *The Prelude* and to which he
himself was to respond with envious awe after hearing that poem
read by the 'Friend of the Wise! and Teacher of the Good'. And this
is at least partly due to the fact that his attention continued to be
held not only by nature and the self but also by scripture, apocalypse and myth. Like Blake, he was conscious of the power of the
text of Revelation and wished to relate it to epiphany or event
while being unwilling to take a secular or purely subjectivist path;
like him, he attempted a new myth using elements of the old biblical one. But whereas Blake was able to sit loose to biblical authority
and scholarship, Coleridge's mythopoeia is both constrained and
stimulated by his respect for the canon and his interest in biblical
criticism. Hence it emerges only in fragments.

*   *   *

Clearly the events in France stimulated on the other side of the
Channel great hermeneutical as well as political energy. The text of
Revelation was given renewed exegetical attention, it played a
significant part in the political debate, and the millennialist and
perfectibilist traditions variously authorized by it were enlivened
by the sense that 1789 was a *kairos* revealing the approach of the
millennium or political summer. The older interpretation based on
a gentler providence working out its purposes through *chronos* was
increasingly though never completely sidelined. It is more than a
'drastic simplification' and actually misleading to maintain with
M. H. Abrams that 'faith in an apocalypse by revelation had been
replaced by faith in an apocalypse by revolution, and this now gave
way to faith in an apocalypse by imagination or cognition'.[72]

Yet still one sees the text itself resisting attempts – whether by Bicheno or by Brothers, by Priestley or by Coleridge – at moral or historical interpretation of it. John had created a coherent and powerful mythological world that invited association with both personal and political experience in later history. But even at a time when those associations seemed most obvious, with revolutionary upheavals and with a new sense of the authority of poetic vision, his world provided most of its interpreters with only fragments of poems or commentaries, or with elaborate constructions left stranded by events or by experience. As the biblical text looms more immediately, as it even lures its readers in to become fellow-seers, its solidity is dissolved, and with it is dissolved the hermeneutical task.

This fragility of hermeneutics as applied to the Book of Revelation will be examined further in the next two chapters. The first will deal with the later Coleridge's attention to scripture and the Apocalypse in dialogue with his other literary work and with his friend the millenarian preacher Edward Irving. The next will deal with the unique achievement of Blake in moving beyond a hermeneutics into a poetics of Apocalypse.

5

Coleridge and the Limits of Interpretation

Could Coleridge ever achieve his resolve to be 'Cleans'd from the vaporous passions that bedim/God's Image'? In this chapter, moving from the time of his disillusionment with revolutionary France to his death in 1834, I plan to show that he persistently sought a *redemption* both personal and cosmic and that this necessarily involved for him also the search for *meaning*. In this dual search the role of *the Bible* was crucial.

Coleridge wrote towards the end of his life that in the Bible 'there is more that *finds* me than I have experienced in all other books put together'; they are words that 'find me at greater depths of my being; and … whatever finds me brings with it an irresistible evidence of its having proceeded from the Holy Spirit.' (*CIS*, p. 43) These statements from his 'letters on the inspiration of the scriptures' avoid asserting a difference in kind between scriptural and other inspired writing, an assertion Coleridge saw as leading to the superstition of 'bibliolatry': while purporting to represent true Christian faith, such a superstition was for him actually destructive of faith as well as of human reason, destructive too of the human redemptive pattern of 'scripture history' itself. But here a strange tension arises. Believing that God *was* Reason, Coleridge was with part of his mind determined to apply to the biblical text the modern critical practices he had learnt from German scholars. But believing also in original sin he was with another part determined to seek a personal and cosmic saviour. So the primary imagination is, in his famous definition, 'a repetition in the finite mind of the eternal act of creation in the infinite I AM' (*BL* XIII). Again, the human trinity of his mature thought mirrors and participates in the divine trinity, with Holy Spirit as the 'mesothesis' mediating the two; but the whole geometric–metaphysical structure collapses without the 'prothesis', the 'Identity' which in *Aids to Reflection* he defines as the Pythagorean point that is 'transcendent to all production, which it caused but did not partake in ... the Supreme Being ... the INEFFABLE NAME, to which no Image dare be attached'.[1] In the 1820s Coleridge's respect for traditional Anglican theology and his acute sense of the reality of evil combined to underwrite the necessity for adherence to the independent original will. Without that origin there is for him no hope for reason or therefore for humanity, only eternal fall into the 'positive Negation', the substance behind death pictured (in his manuscript poem of 1811, *'Ne Plus Ultra'*) as 'the Dragon foul and fell' (*CP*, p. 326).

So the genuine and effective arguments against 'bibliolatry' in *Confessions of an Enquiring Spirit* are hedged about with protestations of the writer's belief in the transcendence of divine speech and therefore in the uniqueness of the biblical canon; and even with these caveats Coleridge felt unable to publish the letters in his lifetime. As he admitted, 'I take up [the Bible] with the purpose to read it for the first time as I should read any other work, – as far at least as I can or dare. For I neither can, nor dare, throw off a strong and awful prepossession in its favour' (*CIS*, p. 41). Like almost all Romantic poets, Coleridge is an *apocalyptic* writer, believing in the possibility of new vision. As a student of Kant he is also a *subjective* writer, insisting on the necessity of inner apprehension if knowledge is to be real. But as a sinner seeking redemption he is also inescapably a *hermeneutical* writer, looking to interpret and to preach from an authoritative Will and an authoritative text. His sense of tradition as well as his sense of sin, above all his sense of the continuing possibility of apocalypse, make this interpretation a particularly acute and agonistic one.

Parts of the Bible that appear to him historically dubious, literarily inadequate or ethically dangerous he is prepared to treat simply as evidence of the prevalence of superstition and therefore deutero-canonical – legends like those of Balaam's ass, the first six chapters of Daniel and the nativity stories fall in these categories – and at times, citing Luther, he threatens the Apocalypse with a similar relegation. But he is nervous and furtive about such heretical tendencies. He is also haunted by the seer figure of Patmos and takes claims to vision with great seriousness. John's is a book that will not let him go.

In tracing its place in his thinking, I shall first examine Coleridge's intellectual and artistic responses to the works of three other men. For each of these – William Wordsworth, the biblical critic Johann Gottfried Eichhorn and the Scottish preacher Edward Irving – he professed friendship, and from each he claimed to have learned; but with each he became aware of fundamental differences over the nature of inspiration. Admiring *Wordsworth's* apocalypse of the human mind, Coleridge nevertheless felt unable to achieve that experiential synthesis of subject and object, of vision and redemption, and constrained to continue with the more prosaic and laborious task of interpretation. On the other hand, while admiring *Eichhorn's* historical and exegetical scholarship, Coleridge dismissed his poetic sensibility: Eichhorn had missed the 'spirituality' of the Apocalypse and indeed of the Christian faith, which Coleridge attempted to express in his own apocalyptic theory of 'symbol'. *Irving* read the Bible, and particularly Revelation, with astounding immediacy, his passionate rhetoric and single-minded faith again drawing Coleridge's admiration; but they were seen by him as woefully misdirected by 'the dead letter of the senses'. Instead, *Coleridge himself* tries haltingly in the last decade of his life to interpret Revelation as a symbolic microcosm of the structure of cosmic redemption. The attempt demonstrates the limits and the limitations of interpretation.

WORDSWORTH AND THE DISPLACEMENT OF APOCALYPSE

The reality and the decay of vision are both treated at length in Wordsworth's *Immortality Ode,* to which Coleridge's less confident *Dejection* is probably some kind of response. Again, at many points in *The Prelude* there is bold proclamation of the apocalyptic powers of the human, or at least of the poetic mind, while the friend for whom it was written was aware on hearing it that he could no longer share such a degree of visionary confidence. Yet Coleridge himself had produced the most haunting visionary text of all English Romanticism in *Kubla Khan.*

The possible 'sources' of this poem and the possible meanings of its prefaces have been exhaustively studied; but in relation to Coleridge's reading of the Apocalypse the most important aspect may be that of German 'higher criticism', the scholarly investigation of the biblical books in their original historical context that began to flourish in the late eighteenth century in the wake of Spinoza's and Lessing's researches. Acquaintance with such criticism was part of Coleridge's Unitarian culture, and there are signs of its influence in *The Watchman* (for instance in the 'Essay on Fasts' in the second issue). The critics' destabilisation of the Bible's value as an historical record and realisation of the part played by 'myth' in its construction led some to seek religious power in a new kind of 'mythologised history', and among their number were two scholars closely involved in interpretation of Revelation, Herder and Eichhorn.[2] When combined with the contemporary 'Romantic' fascination with 'bard' figures and with dreams and grotesquerie – both of which Coleridge evidently shared – it is not surprising that this scholarly work led some writers to see John of Patmos as the archetypal bard and the model for a new visionary poetry. E. S. Shaffer presents the process as one of the subjectivisation of history, including biblical history:

> Evangelists became antique Oriental bards, and John the philo-sophic and poetic genius among them ... The Apostle John ... who saw Jesus with his own eyes, and the Evangelist John who philosophized His teaching, merge in the apocalyptic style. Epic objectivity is transformed in the epic subjectivity of vision: intens-ity of perception and profundity of doctrine are one and the same. The extraordinary but typically romantic conjunction begins to emerge: primal historical fact can be known only through visionary eyes. The apocalyptic bard gives us the histor-ical milieu and the milieu of Christian belief as the landscape of mythology.[3]

Eichhorn saw the historical origin of the Apocalypse as a mytholo-gical interpretation of the recent fall of Jerusalem, a subject whose poetic potential clearly fascinated Coleridge and on which he intended to write an epic. Investigating his notes on this, Shaffer claims that they

> suggest that 'Kubla Khan' is based on his epic plan, and that his 'dreamwork' condensed the three Acts of the Apocalypse into the climactic moment of the First Act, when the sixth seal is opened. It is no wonder he never set pen to paper to write the 'last poss-ible' epic; he himself had already gone beyond it and made it impossible.[4]

Thus, she says, through a radical alteration of the concept of 'event' was invented a new genre, the 'epic fragment'.

When Coleridge eventually published *Kubla Khan*, however, it was not as a new genre but 'rather as a psychological curiosity'.

Moreover Shaffer's assertion that Coleridge made Revelation 'the locus of [the] synthesis' of Judaism with gnosticism, Platonism and the Mysteries is not demonstrated.[5] His attitude to the Bible was in many ways less radical than she claims. It is unclear, for instance, how far his concern for authoritative redemption as well as subjective vision allowed him actually to emancipate himself from the historical questioning of the Enlightenment, whether in the 1790s or in the 1820s – though clearly he desired such an emancipation and wearied of the labour of historical evidence. He was never able to treat the Gospels as 'philosophemes' as he did the Mysteries.

Nevertheless, reading *Kubla Khan*, one can with Shaffer recognise John in the persona of its visionary poet. It is not simply that Coleridge combines with other mythical material in the poem elements from the Apocalypse – the sacred river, the measuring, the prophecy of war and the milk of Paradise. In the bard himself, with 'his flashing eyes, his floating hair', is also a glimpse of that visionary certainty that enabled John to say 'Then I saw...' But, transmitted through the centuries, the prophetic vision becomes elusive and fragmentary, and the whole of the final section of the poem is conditional upon 'Could I revive within me...' So Coleridge is both claiming and disclaiming visionary insight. The claim and disclaimer are both heightened by the 'preface' to the poem, purporting to give an account of its origin: like the glosses to 'The Ancient Mariner' and unlike those to 'Religious Musings' (or Blake's claims to vision), this is highly ironic. It is fairly clear that Coleridge was at least reluctant to make the claims to bardic insight that Shaffer makes in his name. And this raises the question whether any prophetic *kairos*, any revelation is still available. For the mythological landscape of *Kubla Khan* hints at the possibility and the authority of apocalyptic dream only to withdraw the hint, so that an unambiguous reference of the poetic text is no more accessible in the poet's subjective experience than it is in the objective events of the French Revolution.

This casts some doubt on the application to Coleridge of the thesis that Romanticism retained the biblical visionary tradition by moving its reference from external to internal 'event'. M. H. Abrams, for instance, writes of

the tendency, grounded in texts of the New Testament itself, to internalize apocalypse by transferring the theatre of events from the outer earth and heaven to the spirit of the single believer, in which there enacts itself, metaphorically, the entire eschatological drama of the destruction of the old creation, the union with Christ, and the emergence of a new creation.[6]

Abrams is right to point to St John and St Paul as initiators of this process of internalisation, continued in Origen, in St Augustine's *Confessions* and in the Christian mystical tradition; right to see Wordsworth as one of its most tenacious practitioners. But is it right to place Wordsworth in such a paradigmatic role as his book does? For St Paul at least, apocalypse remained external and future and corporate, however important was 'the spirit of the single believer'. And for a reader of the Bible as reverent as Coleridge the process of internalisation could not be limitless. Whereas one senses that Wordsworth's response to nature was pantheistic and that he spent much of his later life trying to cover his heretical tracks as an orthodox Christian, with Coleridge the situation is different: though 'a compulsive monist', he is engaged nearly all his life in a conscious struggle with his pantheistic tendencies.[7] He is a poet not primarily of *anamnēsis* but of *agōn*, engaged in a struggle for *redemptive* vision, not the more tranquil apprehension of 'spots of time'.

This can be seen even in the poem where he comes closest to a direct endorsement of 'internalized apocalypse', *Dejection* (*CP*, pp. 280–3). There are indeed echoes of the probably contemporaneous *Immortality Ode* of Wordsworth:

> I may not hope from outward forms to win
> The passion and the life, whose fountains are within...
> Ah! from the soul itself must issue forth
> A light, a glory, a fair luminous cloud
> Enveloping the Earth...
> (ll. 45f., 53–5)

This light or glory or 'strong music in the soul' is hymned in the tones of the apocalyptic marriage of Rev 21:

> Joy, Lady! is the spirit and the power,
> Which wedding Nature to us gives in dower
> A new Earth and new Heaven,
> Undreamt of by the sensual and the proud
> (ll. 67–71)

Yet two features of the poem prevent it from fully endorsing the affirmations of Wordsworth's ode. First is the representation of the natural world itself. Whereas Wordsworth gives a generalised picture of mountains, birds and meadows, with the childlike joy of communion an integral part of the whole, Coleridge's observation of nature is much more precise and much more sombre – 'the dull sobbing draft ... the slant night-shower ... its peculiar tint of yellow green'. For all its beauty, nature alone is 'that inanimate cold world'; nor does the human soul enter the world, as for Wordsworth, 'trailing clouds of glory'. Rather, the bridal apocalypse of man and nature is a hard-won moral victory, constantly threatened by relapse into dejection. Secondly, Coleridge does not sustain the affirmations of his two central stanzas and unlike Wordsworth does not end his poem with a hymn of praise centred on himself as experiencing subject. Instead his own thoughts of joy and of dejection are interrupted by the sinister wind, hinting at the constant rupture of the possibility of 'wedding Nature'; and – as at the end of 'Frost at Midnight' the poet had transposed on to the baby Hartley his trust for communion through nature with God – so *Dejection* concludes with a prayer for Sara Hutchinson. Coleridge transposes on to another human being the hope that

> To her may all things live, from pole to pole,
> Their life the eddying of her living soul!
>
> (ll. 135f.)

For himself, as in *Kubla Khan,* the possibility of any such clear apocalypse or redemption in the body is highly fragmentary.

The same sense of contrast was felt by Coleridge on hearing *The Prelude* read for the first time, as recorded in his poem 'To William Wordsworth' of January 1807. His friend's 'long sustained Song' had celebrated not only 'the growth of a poet's mind' but also his vocation as a 'dedicated spirit'. At Cambridge the poet

>   ... was a chosen son.
> For hither had I come with holy powers
> And faculties, whether to work or feel....
> I was a freeman, in the purest sense
> Was free, and to majestic ends was strong –
> I do not speak of learning, moral truth,
> Or understanding – 'twas enough for me
> To know that I was otherwise endowed.[8]

Later, in the time of his residence in France, he likens himself to the Hebrew prophets ('So did some portion of that spirit fall/On me').[9] Such conviction is founded in the poem on visionary experiences, whether as a boy on the lake sensing the 'Wisdom and Spirit of the universe' vivifying lifeless forms and images, or as a young man responding to the unveiling of nature in the Alps, where

>   ...the sick sight
> And giddy prospect of the raving stream,
> The unfettered clouds and region of the heavens,
> Tumult and peace, the darkness and the light,
> Were all like workings of one mind, the features
> Of the same face, blossoms upon one tree,
> Characters of the great apocalypse,
> The types and symbols of eternity,
> Of first, and last, and midst, and without end.[10]

The use of prophetic and apocalyptic language is particularly marked in the pivotal tenth book of the 1805 *Prelude*, where the events of the French Revolution in which 'A veil had been/Uplifted' are traced in the poet's mind.[11]

Coleridge's response to the poetic achievement and the visionary claim is warm, admiring the 'great Bard's' rehearsal

>   ...of moments awful,
> Now in thy inner life, and now abroad,
> When power streamed from thee, and thy soul received
> The light reflected, as a light bestowed

from which the poet emerges filled with Hope that is

>   ...thenceforth calm and sure
> From the dread watch-tower of man's absolute self,
> With light unwaning on her eyes, to look
> Far on...
>
>   (*CP*, 300, ll. 16–19, 39–42)

Coleridge celebrates this internalised apocalypse, recalling his own sharing with Wordsworth in some of the experiences that nurtured it. But he is equally clear that his own poetic and religious path must be elsewhere:

> That way no more! and ill beseems it me,
> Who came a welcomer in herald's guise,
> Singing of Glory, and Futurity,
> To wander back on such unhealthful road,
> Plucking the poisons of self-harm!
>
> (ll. 76–80)

This is not so much a rejection of prophecy or even of some kind of prophetic role for himself as an admission that, for him, the synthesis of object and subject in the individual mind cannot be as instinctive as it was for Wordsworth. Revelation is more oblique, the veil never fully uplifted. Wordsworth's visionary confidence could not be shared, any more than could the confidence of political revolutionaries or of biblical prognosticators or even of his own 'conversation poems'.

'Wedding Nature to us' is still an aim of Coleridge's thinking and writing after 1807; but the marriage will be a tortured one as he embarks on a more restless search through literature, science and metaphysics, seeking assurance from outside of the redemption that he knows he must experience within. The possibility of vision is not denied, but the interpretation of vision is almost an impossibility. And the poet-seer, the ancient mariner with his 'glittering eye', undergoes a curse that derives not from failure of vision but from the paradigmatic sin of the killing of the albatross. Redemption begins for the mariner with the transformation of vision in his blessing of the water-snakes; but even after the shriving it is not complete, the curse is not removed and still forces him to rehearse his uninterpretable story.

For Coleridge, therefore, apocalypse, whether external or internal, does not constitute redemption or displace the need for redemption. It is a rather inadequate intimation of it, experienced in fragments and subject to suspicion even if it is incorporated in the biblical canon, since apocalypse does not *per se* inhabit the moral order. And when he himself becomes the poet of apocalypse, his work is either uncompleted – as in the case of *Kubla Khan*, *Christabel* and to some extent *Dejection* – or is ironically unravelled by a prose gloss like that to *The Rime of the Ancient Mariner*. As David Jasper comments on the reading of all these poems,

> there is a sense of a wholeness, vast beyond human comprehension, which the poet momentarily inhabits in his imagination.

The revisions tend to create new narrative levels which force poet and reader to become spectators of themselves as the poetry is experienced, and which open the way for a pattern of reflections pointing to an infinity, and to the glimpsed completeness and unity.[12]

This suggests a self-consciousness in both the poet's and the implied reader's method that is at odds with the internalising of apocalypse by Wordsworth – or by Blake or Shelley. Coleridge refuses to locate the 'completeness and unity' within his own mind, as he refuses to locate it without remainder in any poetic or biblical text; nor, unlike the other three poets, does he attempt any writing of a new apocalypse beyond the fragment of *Kubla Khan*. The reason for all these hesitations is his insistence, again unlike the other three, on believing in a transcendent Will, in original sin and in moral Law. For him, vision and redemption cannot be equated. And it is not until the 1820s, when he embarks on more sustained study of theology and the Bible, that he approaches any kind of resolution of the tension between them.

EICHHORN AND PROPHETIC HISTORY

The German higher critics' investigation of the New Testament encountered difficulties when it tackled the Apocalypse, a book shunning almost all historical or factual reportage yet almost certainly referring to and arising from historical events in the life of the early Church. An example is J. D. Michaelis, the editor and translator of Lowth, a man well respected among the few 'advanced' biblical scholars in England. Michaelis's own erudite scholarship confesses itself baffled when it reaches the end of his *Introduction to the New Testament*. Revelation, says Michaelis, is 'the most difficult and the most doubtful book in the whole New Testament'. He quotes Luther, whose 'opinion of the Apocalypse is delivered in terms of the utmost diffidence, which are well worthy of imitation', and reviews the mixed patristic reception of the book, suspecting that 'it is a spurious production, introduced probably into the world after the death of St John'.[13] He dismisses arguments for its authenticity based on the fulfilment of its 'prophecies', pointing to the vast range of meanings attached to these. Commentators 'have been frequently guilty of almost inconceivable absurdities', which is not surprising since they have lacked most of the requirements for judicious interpretation: these Michaelis lists as knowledge of the original languages, understanding of history, especially Asian history, and 'a taste for poetry and painting' (IV.507–11). But though he himself possesses all these, he still ends by confessing that 'during this enquiry, my belief in the divine authority of the Apocalypse, has received no more confirmation, than it had before' (IV.544). He suspects that the book relates in some way to the destruction of Jerusalem, but is on firmer ground when he comes to examine its language. Because of the solecisms and Hebraisms, he doubts whether its author can also be that of the fourth Gospel, but responds in the manner of the Enlightenment to 'beauties of a very different kind' from the Gospel's, which is written like a 'rivulet' in comparison to the 'torrent' of Revelation: 'the language of the Apocalypse is both beautiful and sublime, is affecting and animating ... [it] has something in it, which enchants, and insensibly inspires the reader with the sublime spirit of the author' (IV.528–34).

Michaelis's historical investigation of the Apocalypse, as well as his conventional aesthetics, were carried forward by the younger scholar Johann Gottfried Eichhorn of Goettingen. Unlike Michaelis, Eichhorn considered the book to come from the same pen as the Gospel, and more confidently than him he (like Herder) treated it as a symbolic poem on the destruction of Jerusalem. It was Eichhorn whom Coleridge came to know during his stay in Göttingen in 1799 (eight years after the publication of the *Commentarius in Apocalypsin Johannis*), recording at the time that the German scholar paid him 'the most *flattering* attention' and recalling many years later that 'Eichhorns's lectures on the New Testament were repeated to me from notes by a student from Ratzeburg'.[14] And it was Eichhorn to whose commentary he turned many times when studying Revelation in greater detail – particularly, it appears, in 1810, 1818, 1827 and 1833.

Eichhorn's commentary sees the book as a 'grand symbolic drama' in three acts, with prologue (Rev 1:4–3:22), prelude (4:1–8:5) and epilogue (22:6–11), written by the apostle as a 'poetic' interpretation of the fall of Jerusalem a generation after the event. But the actual subject reaches far beyond the happenings in Palestine to a cosmic representation of the triumph of Christianity. In the first act (8:6–12:17) 'Jerusalem falls, or Judaism is conquered by the Christian religion'; in the second (12:18–20:10) 'Rome falls, or the Gentiles are conquered by the Christian religion'; and in the third

(20:11–22:5) 'The heavenly Jerusalem comes down from the sky, or
the bliss of future life which will last eternally is described'. Far from
being obscure, says Eichhorn, John aims throughout at clarity, using
his considerable poetic powers to present a clear historical and doctrinal thesis; and noting the common reticence among scholars concerning the book and its effects, Eichhorn trusts that both its readers'
literary sensitivity and their appreciation of its historical accuracy
will redeem its canonical place and status.[15] The *carminis nostri ratio* is
the same as Paul's and the fourth Gospel's, namely to expound the
glory and divinity of Christ (I.li). Eichhorn stresses the unity of
the whole *carmen* or *drama*, admiring 'the poet's artifices' such as the
numerological patterns, and his 'wisdom' and use of Graeco-Roman
and cabbalistic imagery in the service of Christ. Thus the *prolusio* to
the drama (chapters 4–7) is summed up as 'the stage is prepared',
and the author's use of the Hebrew prophets is described as

> much that they had announced before he did not simply repro-
> duce; he inverted it, elaborated, adorned, amplified or changed
> it, and dignified it with much worship, so that, elaborated with
> greater skill, the language should come forth with greater orna-
> ment, elegance and beauty (I.xxxi).

In his use of Eichhorn's commentary over a period of thirty years,
Coleridge generally accepts the German's description of the book's
genre and the main thrust of his historical arguments. What he disputes – in different ways at different times – are the commentary's
aesthetic response to Revelation and its valuing of its canonicity
and authority.

Eichhorn's influence may lie behind Coleridge's plans of 1803 for a
poem on the destruction of Jerusalem (*CN* I.1646). It is certainly clear
in the plan for a verse translation of the Apocalypse with a prose
commentary, which he refers to as 'an intention long and fondly
cherished' in a footnote to his second *Lay Sermon* of 1817. Here he
regrets the abuse perpetrated by millenarian Christians from 'the
primitive Church to the religious Politicians of our own times'
(among whom he presumably includes the young Coleridge) on
what he calls 'this sublime and magnificent drama'. Paraphrasing
Eichhorn, Coleridge says that

> My own conception of the Book is, that it narrates in the broad
> and inclusive form of the ancient Prophets (i.e. in the prophetic

power of faith and moral insight irradiated by inspiration) the successive struggles and final triumph of Christianity over the Paganism and Judaism of the then Roman Empire, typified in the Fall of Rome, the destruction of the Old and the (symbolical) descent of the New Jerusalem. Nor do I think its interpretation even in detail attended with any insuperable difficulties (*LS*, p. 146).

In 1829 Coleridge was again to describe the book in Eichhornian terms as 'this sublime poem ... the most perfect specimen of symbolic poetry ... this sacred oratorio' (*C&S*, p. 139f.) Yet his comments in the margin of Eichhorn's *Einleitung in das Neue Testament*, which may date from 1816, dispute not only the identification of the author with the apostle but also its status as 'Poem' rather than 'Vision':

If ever there was a Vision (of which the 6th or ecstatic state of zoomagnetism supplies recent proofs) the Apocalypse was a Vision, not a Poem. – Whether divine and bona fide prophetic, I do not here determine (*CM* ii, p. 458f.)

In fact Coleridge differed strongly from Eichhorn both in his experiential and scientific understanding of 'Vision' and in his definition of 'Poem'. Eichhorn saw the biblical symbols and visions as mere embellishment of an historical subject: 'mere drapery, mere poetical fictions' (*blosse Einkleidung, blosse poetische Dichtungen*) are how he defines the visions of Ezekiel in his *Einleitung in das Alte Testament*, which Coleridge probably read in 1818/19 and in whose margin at this point he exclaimed:

It perplexes me to understand, how a Man of Eichhorn's Sense, Learning, and Acquaintance with Psychology could form, or attach belief to, so cold-blooded an hypothesis. That in Ezechiel's Visions Ideas or Spiritual Entities are presented in visual Symbols, I never doubted; but as little can I doubt, that such Symbols did present themselves to Ezechiel in Visions – and by a Law closely connected with, if not contained in, that by which sensations are organized into Images and mental sounds in our ordinary sleep.[16]

There is no doubt that Coleridge responded to the language of John of Patmos as a fellow-poet, and at least in the sense suggested above as a fellow-visionary too. Yet doubts about Revelation's canonicity and morality as well as irritation at its abuse by millenarians meant that his attitude could be ambiguous. In a lengthy notebook entry of 1823 he sympathised with Luther's reservations, contrasting the Apocalypse with his beloved and 'spiritual' fourth Gospel and regretting that 'it does not seem to have been blessed to a source of edification':

> O for a Luther on earth! To him I could appeal without fear of being accursed as a Blasphemer – whether from beginning to end [of the Apocalypse] the evangelical Idea & true Character of Christ are not so overborne by the red and glowing Marks of the Jewish Spirit, that would have called fire from heaven, as to appear only now & then (*CN* IV.5069).

It was probably in the same year that he wrote in his copy of Henry More (the Cambridge Platonist and disciple of Joseph Mede):

> At one time Prof. Eichhorn had persuaded me that the Apocalypse was authentic.... But the repeated Perusal of the Vision has sadly unsettled my Conclusions – The entire absence of all *spirituality* perplexes me ... and then the too great appearance of an allusion to the fable of Nero's return to Life & Empire ... & the insurmountable Difficulties of Joseph Mede's [hypothesis] – &c. on to Bicheno and Faber ... in short, I feel just as both Luther & Calvin felt – i.e. not know what to make of it, so leave it alone (*CM* iii, p. 922)

The lack of 'spirituality' is sometimes laid at the door of John himself, sometimes at his interpreters'. For Coleridge this term, though definitely a religious one, is akin to poetic imagination more than to piety. Spirituality, epitomised in the fourth Gospel, is the antithesis to the 'mechanical philosophy'; and despite his attention to poetry Eichhorn proves himself an adherent of such unspiritual religion. A test case is Eichhorn's interpretation of Rev 11:1–3, where he interprets the 1260 days or 42 months as simply representative of a long period of calamity. In the margin of his commentary Coleridge writes that Eichhorn

> stands here on the very same [Line of] Error, only at the other end of the line, as the prognosticating Commentators... The

symbolic *hebdomas hēmerōn* [seven days] is measured by the Horologe of divine Predestination, by Epochs & [the] Procession of the Plan of Providence – not subject to any *external* measure, but like the Sun & Planets self-measured by their own movements.[17]

This suggests that the opposite of 'spiritual' is neither 'historical' nor 'literal' – in his heart Eichhorn is just as much a literalist as Bicheno or Faber – but 'allegorical'. What Coleridge calls 'the essential spirituality of the Christian Faith' is not an allegorical extrapolation of biblical narrative or doctrine. Nor is it a denial of historical grounding. But it entails an insistence that the real grounding is neither in historical event nor in any other kind of 'external' measuring but in a kind of internal coherence, without which Christianity decays into mechanical 'evidences' rather than redemptive faith. It is this coherence of story and spirit that Coleridge finds in, say, Genesis, in the prophets, the fourth Gospel and St Paul – and at times in the Apocalypse. As a hermeneutical principle it operates in a similar way to the early Christian Fathers' *regula fidei* or to Luther's Christ-centredness, but the more sophisticated reading of history in Coleridge's day meant that he had to struggle with himself and even more with his contemporaries for such a spiritual reading. In May 1826 he writes:

> I begin to question much, whether the Age can bear the whole truth respecting the essential Spirituality of the Christian Faith, and the necessity of keeping it constantly before our minds in the interpretation of the *historical* Form. Now interpretation *kata pneuma* requires that every historical Fact should be *symbolically* integrated.[18]

Underlying this was a theological conviction concerning the true nature of 'prophecy' that Coleridge clung to but had difficulty substantiating. For, in the spirit of many of the Fathers but without their recourse to allegory, he endeavoured to see the

> whole Jewish history, in all its details,... so admirably adapted to, and suggestive of, symbolical use, as to justify the belief that the spiritual application, the interior and permanent sense, was in the original intention of the inspiring Spirit, though it might not have been present, as an object of distinct consciousness, to the inspired writer (*NED* I, p. 337).

Such inner symbolical coherence is what he had expounded to the nation in *The Statesman's Manual* and the second *Lay Sermon* of 1817. Another public presentation of the spirituality of Christianity was made more in terms of philosophical or moral coherence in the much more widely read *Aids to Reflection* of 1825. In both these homiletic works there is an attempt to interpret history that betrays impatience with the intractability of 'every historical Fact' and even more with the unspiritual interpreters of such facts.

For instance the two 'lay sermons' of 1817 are designed to combat the national threat of a 'moral *necrosis*', which will commence 'if its causes are not counteracted by the philosophy of history, that is, by history read in the spirit of prophecy'.[19] Without this philosophical–prophetic reading of both history and the Bible, education degenerates into mere instruction, and Reason is replaced by 'mechanical understanding'. So Coleridge sees himself engaged on a programme of moral and political redemption, one that is both practical and spiritual, requiring a 'more manly discipline of the intellect', not just a revised approach to literature or history or religion. The role of the Bible in incarnating and propagating this programme is a crucial one, since in the biblical writers words flow directly from 'principles and ideas that are not so properly said to be confirmed by reason as to be reason itself' and from 'the emotions that inevitably accompany the actual intuition of their truth':

> The imperative and oracular form of the inspired Scripture is the form of reason itself in all things purely rational and moral. ... Hence it follows that what is *expressed* in the inspired writings is *implied* in all absolute science.... The great PRINCIPLES of our religion, the sublime IDEAS spoken out everywhere in the Old and New Testament, resemble the fixed stars (*LS*, pp. 18–24).

The idealistic and dogmatic tone of such assertions is mitigated somewhat when Coleridge pays attention to the actual text of the Bible in *The Statesman's Manual* – though interestingly it is only fleetingly and it is by means of a visionary rather than an historical passage, one that gave rise to the esoteric Jewish *merkabah* ('chariot') mysticism. This is used to contrast biblical concreteness with the abstractions of 'the histories and political economy of the present and preceding century', which are, he says, the *product* of an unenlivened generalizing Understanding. In the Scriptures they are the living *educts* of the Imagination; of that reconciling and mediatory power, which incorporating the Reason in Images of the Sense, and organizing (as it were) the flux of the Senses by the permanence and self-circling energies of the Reason, gives birth to a system of symbols, harmonious in themselves, and consubstantial with the truths, of which they are the *conductors*. These are the Wheels which Ezekiel beheld.... The truths and the symbols that represent them move in conjunction and form the living chariot that bears up (for *us*) the throne of the Divine Humanity. Hence ... the Sacred Book is worthily intitled *the* WORD OF GOD (*LS*, p. 28f.)

It is from this sacramental and purportedly biblical theology that the famous contrast between allegory and symbol (or 'tautegory') is developed on the next page. The two constituents (wheels and cherubim) are distinct but indivisible, hence the 'translucence' and poetic power of the symbols.[20]

The problems with this arise from several angles, and they are particularly acute with a text as 'symbolical' as that of Revelation. First, Coleridge is unable to show except in very subjective terms how the *difference in kind* that he had earlier implied between the Bible (the 'fixed stars') and other inspired writing is apprehended or defined: indeed his various reflections on the canonicity of books like Daniel and his more rounded later position on biblical inspiration in the *Confessions of an Enquiring Spirit* both seem to undermine such a difference. Secondly, the notion of Coleridge and of other Romantic and post-Romantic critics that a symbol is *self-authenticating* needs questioning – and Coleridge himself was aware of the difficulty, compounded by his resolute rejection of 'associative' thinking. The failure of a 'symbol' to be 'translucent' for an educated reader may not be evidence of that reader's moral *necrosis* but simply an indication that the reader's own symbolic universe or language is a different one. Thirdly, much of the biblical text seems to invite an '*allegorical*' reading or – as in the case of Paul and the Letter to the Hebrews – to contain allegorical interpretation of other scripture. Crucially this is true of the Apocalypse. What Eichhorn describes and Coleridge accepts as a 'symbolic drama' is actually, in Eichhorn's interpretation and in Coleridge's terminology, an allegorical one: it refers outside itself, whether to other texts, to historical events or to spiritual beings. In his

continuing dialogue about this book with various kinds of histor-
icising or prognosticating literalists and with himself, Coleridge
will attempt to discover whether a genuinely 'symbolic' reading of
Revelation as of Genesis is possible – and if so, it will be necessary
for him to cast off all traces of Eichhorn's historical criticism
together with the aesthetics of 'embellishment' that he instinctively
rejected. As I hope to show in the final section of this chapter, his
vestigial concern with historical fact (arising partly from his stance
as Christian apologist) and his theological impulse towards an
authoritative text deriving from an authoritative creating and
redeeming God both made this move a difficult one. And finally,
Coleridge's concern for a *redemptive* pattern of prophetic history
makes it impossible for him to follow through the logic of his presentation of symbolic apocalypse in *The Statesman's Manual,* just as
it forced him to part company with Wordsworth's notion of
prophetic inspiration. What is 'the throne of the Divine Humanity'
borne up on the chariot of truths and symbols? For Blake, the
Divine Humanity symbolised in Jesus is a matter of direct experience, and the dissolution and redemption of Albion transcend
history. But for Coleridge, with his sense of original sin, such
radical incarnationalism or realised eschatology was not possible.
The Divine Humanity is only a glimpsed *parousia,* however con-
crete are the symbols through which it is mediated, and the poet is
left like Ezekiel gazing up at the chariot and falling on his face, or
like the blind visionary of 'Limbo' who 'seems to gaze at that which
seems to gaze on Him' (*CP,* p. 325). Salvation is not just revealed, it
must be worked out. This may still be a visionary stance, but it is
also an uncomfortable one, and a deeply moral one.

'The Bible is *all* Prophecy and *no* Prognostication', Coleridge
wrote in 1828 (*NB* 37, fol. 25). Here is a cry not just against the historical calculations of Faber or Croly but also against the historical
investigations of Eichhorn and his colleagues. They have only a
lowly place in the service of a truly spiritual religion and of
prophetic or symbolic reading. As he wrote in the margin of
Eichhorn's *Einleitung in das Neue Testament,*

> let me leave on record that as far as sound and extensive book-
> learning, unfettered research, and acute judgement, in determin-
> ing the Age of Writings and the grounds of their attribution to
> this or that traditionary Name are concerned, I gladly & thank-
> fully take Eichhorn, as my Guide. But as to the philosophy, the

religion by the performed comprehension of which alone the Contents of these Writings can be interpreted, I would soon [*sic*] trust a blind man in a question of Colors (*CM* ii, p. 491).

Coleridge could not bring himself to ignore the historical arguments by means of which the Bible was criticised and Christianity defended or rejected. But he wearied of them, seeing history unvivified by prophecy – like Nature unvivified by Reason – as an 'inanimate cold world'. 'Higher' criticism had served its lowly purpose, but there remained the task of prophetic and redemptive reading: to discover and so to empower 'the passion and the life, whose fountains are within'.

IRVING AND THE RELIGION OF IDEAS

Coleridge was eventually driven to a closer and more critical reading of Revelation by a friend who was one of the most ardent of 'prognosticators', the Scottish minister Edward Irving (1792–1834). He heard Irving preach soon after the latter's arrival in London in 1822, describing him as 'the present Idol of the World of Fashion ... the super-Ciceronian, ultra-Demosthenic Pulpiteer of the Scotch Chapel', and more kindly a fortnight later as 'certainly the greatest *Orator* I have ever heard ... however, a man of great simplicity, of overflowing affections and enthusiastically in earnest' (*CL* V, p. 280, 286f.) Coleridge's response to Irving's preaching was not untypical, nor was his depiction of him as idol of fashion exaggerated. In a rhapsodic description of scenes at the little church in Hatton Gardens, George Gilfillan pictured the carriages with coronets waiting outside while within were assembled Canning, Peel, Wilberforce, Brougham, Bentham, Godwin, Hazlitt, Macaulay, 'and in a corner, Coleridge – the mighty wizard'.[21] In the wizard's notebook of July 1823, however, was a critical comment that was to be amplified in the years ahead and to encapsulate much of Coleridge's sadness over what he saw as his friend's growing madness: 'Mr Irving's Error. Declamation (high & passionate Rhetoric not introduced & pioneered by calm & clear Logic)' (*CN* IV.4963).

Irving's passionate rhetoric was in marked contrast both to the moralising pulpits of the Church of England and to the orthodox Calvinism of his own national Church, which was eventually to

turn on him for heresy, expel him from his ministry and excommuni-
cate him. Margaret Oliphant's sensitive biography of Irving, which
reproduces much of his original correspondence, portrays him as an
apostolic enthusiast, 'a man who trusted God to extremity, and
believed in all Divine communications with faith as absolute as any
patriarch or prophet'.[22] His immersion in Scripture is evident both in
the extraordinary declamatory style of his letters (including those to
his wife) and in his refusal to compromise with modern concerns –
he was as whole-hearted an opponent as Coleridge of 'mechanical
understanding', although for different reasons and with very different results. And it was his literal interpretation of the Bible that led to
his three 'heresies': his Christology grounded on the clear evidence
of Jesus' full humanity in the gospels, his pentecostalism and
unusual church polity grounded on the *charismata* and ministries in
Paul's letters, and his millenarianism grounded on literal reading of
the Apocalypse. From his exceptional sense of contemporaneity with
the primitive Church he developed his high theology of baptism and
of orders (including what Mrs Oliphant called his own 'priestliness')
as well as his judgements on the 'gifts of the Spirit' that were manifested in his congregation from 1830.[23] A systematic and expository
preacher, he also spoke at extreme length and with extreme fre-
quency – even while they were on holiday in Ireland, for instance his
wife recorded that 'Edward preached thirteen times in eight days'.[24]
The unusual blend of ritualism and Pentecostalism in the Catholic
Apostolic or 'Irvingite' Church founded in 1833 preserved much of
its 'angel's' convictions and idiosyncrasies; but it never recovered the
'high and passionate rhetoric'.

It was not long before Coleridge was introduced to Irving by
Basil Montagu, and from 1824 the preacher became a regular visitor
to Highgate for meals and discussions, where Coleridge declared
himself 'not the only person who thinks Mr Irving more delightful
still at these times than even in the pulpit' (*CL* V, p. 368). In 1825 he
was to write of Irving's 'vigorous & ... *growing* mind' and 'manly'
character – words very similar to those often used of his revered
Luther, to whom he compared Irving more than once ('my Luther-
hearted friend' with 'high heart and vehement intellect').[25]
Regretting that Irving was not an Anglican, Coleridge described
him in the same year as 'more earnest in his love of Truth & more
fervent in his assurance that what is *truth must* be Christianity ...
than almost any man, I have met with – and with fewer prejudices,
national or sectarian' (*CL* V, p. 476).

The friendship was not broken but the respect was sorely tested by Irving's growing interest in and study of 'prophecy' from 1825. In that year he was approached by the keen student of apocalyptic interpretation, Hatley Frere, who found in Irving's evangelical spirit and biblical literalism a ready disciple for his chronological and ecclesiastical speculations. Mrs Oliphant saw this encounter as fateful:

> Henceforward the gorgeous and cloudy vistas of the Apocalypse became a legible chart of the future to his fervent eyes ... he had found in prophetical interpretation a study which charmed him deeply, and had felt himself drawn, as was natural, into a closer, exclusive fellowship with those who pursued the same study and adopted the same views.[26]

From this fellowship grew in the following year the 'Albury House Group' of mainly Anglican students of 'prophecy', in which Irving played a leading part.[27] Members met for house parties at which lengthy and learned expositions of prophecy and its fulfilment were made, many of these finding their way into the group's journal *The Morning Watch*, founded by John Tudor in 1829 and lasting until the birth of the Catholic Apostolic Church in 1833. It ceased publication then since the editor believed that all was now in place for the final conflict between Christ and Satan (that is, between 'the true Church' and 'Liberalism'). The editor himself signed off by resolving to devote himself wholly to the 'higher calling' of 'feeding and overseeing a sixth part of the flock of Christ in London', but the previous lower calling of exposition of prophecy is itself described in apocalyptic terms:

> We have torn the veil which has been cast by man over the Prophetic Volume; we have battered down the walls of the modern Babylon; the children of God are able to read the title-deeds of their inheritance, and are free to go in and take possession.[28]

The words express well the world that Coleridge's friend inhabited during those eight years – its intellectual earnestness, its religious exclusivism, its political conservatism, and its immediacy of expectation, which was greatly heightened after the beginnings of charismatic manifestations in the west of Scotland in 1829. When in 1825 Irving dedicated his volume of sermons *For Missionaries*

after the Apostolical School to his 'dear and honoured Friend'
Coleridge, the latter read them with respect but at times with alarm
and embarrassment at the way that snatches of conversation at
Highgate or passages from *Aids to Reflection* had been half understood by the preacher and pressed into the service of a less spiritual
religion. While affirming his agreement with Irving 'respecting the
Second Coming of our Lord', he remarked on the book's end-paper,
'I cannot help, believing, that his imagination that the XXth Chapter
of the Revelations favors the doctrine of a future Millennium prevents him from seeing, that it is a mere imagination' (*CM* iii, p. 9).

Irving's two volumes of exposition of Daniel and Revelation that
appeared the following year under the title *Babylon and Infidelity
Foredoomed of God* considerably expanded such expectations (and
Coleridge's alarm). They follow Mede in style though not in
detailed identification of fulfilments, since Irving sees the 1260
years of Babylon's – that is, the papacy's – ascendancy as ending in
1792, after which the bowls are being poured out on it by Infidelity
(the combined forces of the Jacobins, Napoleon and modern
Liberalism). Now, in 1826, with deceptive signs of a revived
papacy,

> the hoary Man of Sin, the dotard of the triple crown, is talking,
> like a drunken lustful braggart, against the word of God.... And
> Infidelity, under the name of liberalism in politics, of expediency
> in philosophy, and under the name of education in knowledge ...
> is dissolving the faith of the people.... The seventh vial hangs
> trembling in the air, in the angel's hand, the sixth thunder
> already hurtles in the heavens, and its hollow roar reverberates
> among the upper clouds of the sky ... we are now standing upon
> the narrow isthmus between the two seas of woe.[29]

Infidelity, on whose approaching doom Irving dwells in his second
volume, is the great and final rebellion, the protestant apostasy that
outdoes the sins of the papal and Muslim apostasies. Now that
Armageddon is near, the true Church has been formed, and its missionary task is simply to call people to 'come out': 'The time for
conversion, the time for building Churches, is gone ... occupy your
position ... by prophesying unto the Babylonish nations', expecting
biblical persecutions, not success (II.443). The whole scheme is
erected on close exposition of Daniel and of apocalyptic passages in
the New Testament, but particularly on Revelation, whose author

Irving depicts as a 'hoary man exiled far away from the habitation of the church', seized by the Spirit that 'possessed him with a prophecy' of all future ages and then 'in words of awful and terrible solemnity, closed the canon of revelation' (I.22).

With Irving engaged on these labours of study, preaching and writing, in addition to the pastoral care of his rapidly growing congregation, Coleridge grew worried by his friend's overwork and even more by its fruits. Writing to their mutual friend Basil Montagu on 1 February 1826, he confesses,

> I do not at all understand our Friend's late excursions into the prophecies of a sealed Book, of which no satisfactory proof has yet been given whether they have already been or still remain to be fulfilled ... for myself, I am not ashamed to say, that a single Chapter of St Paul's Epistles or St John's Gospel is of more value to me, in light & in life, in love & in Comfort, than the Books of the Apocalypse, Daniel & Zachariah, all together (*CL* VI, p. 550).

But he notes elsewhere that the rumours of his friend's 'Aberrations' impelled him to a closer study of the Apocalypse, which he undertook with the help of Cocceius's and Eichhorn's commentaries (*CN* IV.5323). And only a week after the letter to Montagu, when he has 'studied it verse by verse in the original', he is writing to Edward Coleridge that

> the whole scope of [the Apocalypse], and all the main stages of it's magnificent March are perfectly clear to me – and I have no doubt of establishing for all competent Inquirers the Conclusion, which I have drawn for myself – that the Apocalypse is truly the Supplement to the three preceding main divisions of the New Testament, and the requisite Complement of the Christian Faith – of high interest, use and edification for *all* Believers, and without which the New Testament would not be what it *is*, the compleat Quadrature and Antitype of the Old (*CL* VI, p. 558).

Similar language appears in the notebook entry of the same month referred to above, where Coleridge sees the book as 'the Supplement to the New Testament and the Complement of the Christian Faith' (*CN* IV.5323).

After this close reading of the text Coleridge made an appointment with Irving 'to go through the Apocalypse with him, chapter by chapter – if so I might withdraw him from what I cannot regard other than a Delusion' (*CL* VI, p. 570). Unfortunately another guest appeared at Highgate at the same time, and it is not clear whether this thorough mutual examination ever took place. If it did, Coleridge cannot have dissuaded Irving, since his millenarian and charismatic preaching continued. But not long after this time, the confidence that Coleridge had expressed in the letter to his nephew – that 'there are not a[bove] 4 or 5 *words* in the 22 Chapters, the meaning and intention of which are dark or doubtful to me' – seems to have been dispelled, and doubts about the spirituality and canonicity of Revelation recur. Fuelled by the vaticinations of another London preacher, George Croly, he wrote in May 1827 to H. F. Carey (assistant keeper of printed books at the British Museum) asking him for as many commentaries as possible on Revelation. His aim was to expose the wild variety of 'fulfilments' as '*one* way of opening men's eyes' to the folly of a prognosticating interpretation of the book. His real difficulty, it is clear, is not in reading or enjoying the book but in treating it as scripture. Just as, he says, he would happily read Daniel if it were placed in the Apocrypha, so

I should read the Apocalypse with unqualified delight and admiration, if it took the Lead of the 'Shepherd' [of Hermas], St Barnabas, and St Clement, and (for I will confess to the whole extent of my Offending) the 3 Pastoral Epistles ... in a Volume by itself under the modest name of *Antilegomena*.[30]

A year later Irving presented his friend with a copy of his *Sermons, Lectures and Occasional Discourses,* and during the winter of 1828/9 Coleridge made extensive notes on it: like his annotations to the Spanish Jesuit Lacunza's *On the Coming of the Messiah* (translated by Irving) these often echo the strictures on biblical interpretation given fuller form in the *Confessions of an Enquiring Spirit.* Messianic interpretation of Old Testament prophecy, on which so much Christian apologetic rests, he sweeps away as founded on 'ruinous and fleshly fancies ... a carnal Superstition' (*CM* iii, p. 34). The same is true of New Testament 'prophecy', which Irving and Lacunza would have done better to keep 'in the back ground', treating Revelation as deuterocanonical (*CM* iii, p. 418) – though, he adds, 'as a Symbolic Drama' the Apocalypse must ever soar as much above [the NT apocrypha] as the Eagle above the Bat and the Owl. I know indeed no Poem ancient or modern, unless it be the Paradise Lost, that can be compared with it either in the felicity of its Structure, or the sublimity of the parts (*CM* iii, p. 453).

Coleridge's comments here and elsewhere in his copy of Lacunza betray the continuing influence of Eichhorn, and in a notebook of 1829 he draws up a sketch based on Eichhorn's structure in case he 'should ever attempt to realize my long ago thought of translating the Apocalypse into a Symbolico-dramatic Poem sui generis' (*NB* 39, fol. 32). Yet in the same notebook he again contests Eichhorn's attribution of the Apocalypse to John the evangelist and belief in 'the identity of Doctrine' of the two books, regretting the 'spirit of stern Judaism' accompanying Revelation's 'incomparably sustained Symbolism' (*NB* 39, fols 11–14).

Irving's own mind, however, was moving further and further in the direction of literal fulfilment of prophecy and of seeing the Apocalypse as the primary text of the New Testament. It is, he claims in his Edinburgh lectures of 1829, the 'KEY-book' of scripture, armour against 'liberalism' and 'the chart, and the pole-star, and the light of the Christian Church'; he rounds on the 'scoffers' who treat Revelation 'as a sealed book, as a dark riddle, as an unintelligible hieroglyphic'.[31] The lectures were published in 1831 as a commentary on the Apocalypse, although in nearly 1500 pages they covered only the first six chapters. At times, in order to present 'the emotions of my soul', Irving turns to verse, though (as he rightly says) 'I am no poet'; his tone is both pastoral and polemical, expressing his ardent incarnationalism and trinitarianism (which Coleridge saw as tritheism) and – in his treatment of the 'angels' of the seven churches – the nascent polity of the Catholic Apostolic Church and 'the dignity of the ministerial calling'.[32]

As in *The Morning Watch*, Irving is proud to quote in his lectures 'Coleridge, that precious relict of the school of sages, in his "Aids to Reflection"', and – in an un-Coleridgean way – to stress the absolute clarity of Revelation.[33] Such misguided homage, like the earlier dedication of Irving's sermons to him, caused the 'relict' some embarrassment, and he was prepared to go into print to explain his relationship with this disciple. To his *On the Constitution of the Church and State* (1829) Coleridge appended a lengthy footnote on 'the simplicity and grandeur of the plan, and the admirable *ordonnance* of the parts' of the 'sacred oratorio' of the Apocalypse, and the note had appended to it in turn a longer still 'P.S.' on 'my valued and affectionately respected friend, the Rev. Edward Irving' (*C&S*, pp. 139–44). In it he professes 'no faith in his prophesyings' and 'small sympathy with his fulminations' but still compares Irving with both Luther and St Paul, not least for an intellect 'too instinct with life, too *potential* to remain stationary'. The note continues:

> I look forward with confident hope to a time when his soul shall have perfected her victory over the dead letter of the senses and its apparitions in the sensuous understanding; when the Halcyon IDEAS shall have alit on the surging sea of his conceptions.

The words were significant, though they were to prove too sanguine. Significant, in that they express the nub of Coleridge's dissatisfaction with Irving's thought in the context of a work that contrasts 'ideas' and 'conceptions' as well as 'Reason' and 'Understanding'; over-sanguine, since the 'dead letter' ruled Irving's thinking more and more completely in the last five years of his life. While he was hailed in *The Morning Watch* as a new Samson, with his ejection from his church in 1832 marking 'an era of far greater importance than the ejection of Luther from the Papacy' and his new church as 'THE sign of the times', his ever more literalist interpretation of scripture and church polity demonstrated that for all his regard for Coleridge he had entirely missed the point of the 'spiritual religion' of *Aids to Reflection* and of the 'religious history' of *Church and State*.[34] So in late 1830 Coleridge writes of his 'highly gifted but undisciplined and *idealess* mind' (*NB* 48, fol. 20^v). A meeting between the two men is recorded in 1831, and to the end of his life Coleridge expressed friendship for Irving and distress at his fall – both his trial for a Christological 'heresy' that Coleridge regarded as perfectly orthodox and the fall of his mind into what he saw as near-madness.[35]

Whatever a clinical judgement might make of Irving, in Coleridge's terms he did become nearly mad. For his was a religion with power, emotion and understanding but no 'ideas'. Belief, Coleridge wrote, 'must be grounded on Ideas and severally and collectively united with Ideas' (*CN* IV.5421); or again, 'my *System* ... aims to prove, that Christianity is true Reason/namely, that the fundamental *Doctrines* of Christianity are *Ideas*, Truths having in themselves their own evidences' (*NB* 51, fol. 23^v). The literal understanding that dallies with the symbols of such Ideas risks being crazed by the light that it can 'see, not feel'. To move from the potentially trans- lucent images of the biblical text to historical event – whether of the first century, as with Eichhorn, or of the nineteenth, as with Irving – was to break Coleridge's unwritten commandment 'Thou shalt not commit allegory'. It was not just a hermeneutical digression but a theological transgression, a fleeing from a genuinely subjective apprehension of Ideas and Reason and God (the three are insepara- ble), and therefore from the possibility of redemption.

Yet what Coleridge has difficulty in demonstrating is that all the biblical text really is capable of such 'spiritual' interpretation. With passages where 'myth' and 'history' can be read as one and where there is no offence to morality – such as the early chapters of Genesis, Ezekiel's vision or St John's Gospel – he has no problem. But much of the Bible is more intractable, involving events that appear trivial, or miracles that seem incredible, or – as in the case of Daniel and the Apocalypse – narrative that is histor- ically dubious and ethically dangerous. In the last eight years of his life, at the same time that he was working on his letters on the inspiration of the scriptures, Coleridge amassed hundreds of pages of notes towards his projected commentary on the whole Bible, often tackling such issues in considerable detail. Frequently one can sense his weariness with historical argument and his relief when he can immerse himself again in Isaiah or the fourth Gospel. But ironically it was the literal-minded Irving who, by Coleridge's own admission, impelled him to move from the generalities of *The Statesman's Manual* to close study of the biblical text, and in particular of the Book of Revelation. And it was in the copy of Irving's second volume of sermons presented to him by the author that he tentatively began to work out a way of relat- ing the symbolic narrative of the Apocalypse to his own science, polar logic, trinitarian theology and understanding of prophetic history.

THE SPIRITUALITY OF HADES

Writing in his copy of Irving's second volume of sermons, probably in 1828, Coleridge confessed to beginning 'to fear that I ought to regret my intercourse with Mr I. on his own account'. The reason given is more precise than the one suggested above:

in my conversations with Mr Irving I have repeatedly endea-
vored to fix his attention on that main *hinge* on which my whole
System turns, & without which it is worse than senseless, a rank
fomes [*sic*] of mischievous errors – viz. that what he calls
Creation was the first Act of Redemption: which, of course, supposes an antecedent *fall*.... But this was not stuff for the Pulpit: &
on this account, tho' I fully believe not with his own consciousness, my friend always turned short off from my discourse on the
Chaos.... Hence his ignorance respecting the Absolute, the
abysmal Ground of the Trinity (*CM* iii, p. 66).

Yet if it was not stuff for Irving's pulpit Coleridge barely treated it as
stuff for his own. If it had been consistent 'with the wants and
preparatory studies of those for whose use [*Aids to Reflection*] was
especially intended', the writer 'could have entered into the momen-
tous subject of a Spiritual Fall or Apostacy *antecedent* to the formation
of man – a belief, the scriptural grounds of which are few and of
diverse interpretation, but which has been almost universal in the
Christian Church' (*AR*, p. 290f.) But he refrained, instead operating
the 'reserve' that the Tractarians were to advocate. For not only was
the 'discourse on Chaos' very difficult to communicate, he sensed
that it could not avoid unscriptural speculation; and while this might
have its place in the freedom of a poem like *Paradise Lost*, it hardly
suited the pronouncements of the preacher and Christian apologist
that Coleridge increasingly saw himself called to be. So although
there are mentions in *Aids to Reflection* of the 'mystery of death' which
is 'not the mere negation of life, but its positive opposite', and
although his summary of the creed at the beginning of *Confessions of
an Enquiring Spirit* lists, between the *stasis* of the eternal Trinity and
the *anastasis* of earthly redemption, the *apostasis* ('The Eternal Possibilities; the actuality of which hath not its origin in God: *Chaos spiri-
tuale*'), no more is said about these mysteries in either book.[36] Nor
were Coleridge's powerful poems on Hell, 'Limbo' and '*Ne Plus
Ultra*', ever published in his lifetime. The public preacher and the
private philosopher were at odds, yet sensing that somehow, in the
tautegories both of scripture and of polar logic, all must cohere, there
must be a hard-won apocalypse of hell as of redemption.

In his spiritualising of the doctrine of hell, Coleridge is keen to distinguish it as a timeless state of 'Eternal Death' from notions of
'Everlasting Torment; everlasting Consciousness; &c' which are 'all
arbitrary and illegitimate Consequences drawn by Divines' – not

least, doubtless, from the images of the Apocalypse (*CM* ii, p. 559). His own tentative consequences are drawn from the scriptural hints that Milton had also heeded (especially Gen 1:2 and 6:1–3), from his reading of Boehme and the kabbalists, but more assiduously from his personal experience of despair and from his doctrine of 'contraries', which meant that belief in an absolute Good required the positing of absolute Evil, belief in eternal life required the positing of eternal death. So in a long notebook entry of September 1823 Coleridge uses the opposition of chemical 'Substances' to contest the popular notion of Evil as simply *privatio boni;* what he presents instead is

> the abysmal Mystery of the Devil, the Evil One – the Contrary of God, absolute emptiness as God is the absolute Fullness, mere Potence as God is a pure Act, wherein all is that actually is – a hidden Fire, for ever seeking a base in which it may actualize & finding it only to convert it into its own essences, which is necessarily baseless (*CN* IV.4998).

He likens this to the picture in 1 Peter of the devil 'roaming about, like an hungry Lion', its 'eternal Hunger' generating 'Eternal Death', and concludes that 'the Disbelief of the Devil is but a hollow Bravado' and that without such belief the mysteries of divine Will and of human redemption are severely diminished. All must follow logically from belief in the reality of God, but the tracing of this logic beyond the world of time is almost impossible:

> What remains to be shewn, I see indeed, or believe myself to see, in its main Outline – tho' the line be dim and dissolving, my Eye traces it. But I find it most difficult to express myself in words: and for the majority of my readers I almost despair of conveying my thoughts intelligibly.

As seen in this note, Coleridge uses the traditional image of fire to represent evil and hell. Notebook entries from later in the same year take this further, with haunting speculation that begins to tie the imagery more closely to biblical language and which could be influenced by Irving's preaching. For instance,

> God is a consuming Fire – but there riseth up out of the Fire & cloatheth it as with an outspread garment the lightsome triumphing & dancing Flames. The torment and the tormented one? The

evil spirits = the Fire.... Evil is antipathy to the One.... It is the *dark* Fire: and the Wrath of God is the Fire in the Holy Will against the evil Will of the Fire.... As long as the *Mass* (the Antagonist of *the Spirit*) continues, so long will Evil find a *Being* – and the Logos (Forma Formarum) the subject of redemption. When that is utterly overcome & the Form is the Substance, the Evil becomes *eternal*, preventing all evil from *being* – the pledge that no evil thing shall be (*CN* IV.5076).

There are clear echoes here not only of the new heaven and new earth of Isaiah and Revelation but also of the Apocalypse's lake of fire where evil is to exist eternally but powerlessly. But the task of synthesising biblical imagery and polar logic is an elusive one, for Coleridge is trying to use the teleological biblical narrative to express ideas of timelessness. He needs, as it were, to go back before Genesis and on after Apocalypse; and not surprisingly it is these two books that he alludes to in his doctrine of Chaos. Not only is there delight in paradox and delight in redemption, there is explicit reference to Genesis, 1 Corinthians and Revelation in the note that continues the one quoted above:

Hell or the eternal Fire of Darkness is the ultimate Object and final Cause of the Creation, or the calling forth of the World from Chaos, as set forth by Moses ... the Fire of Hell eternal is the last, deepest, and blessedest Mystery of Love! It is the Echo from the Depths to the Wisdom in the Highest. The Heaven of Heavens saith, It shall be: and Hell answereth, It shall be. Eternity calleth to Eternity: Alleluia! the Lord God omnipotent reigneth. And again they said – Alleluia. Amen! And the Abyss resounded, Amen! And the smoke of the Burning rose up for ever and ever! (*CN* IV.5077).

It was perhaps with such images before him that Coleridge spoke later of the Apocalypse as being 'the requisite Complement of the Christian Faith'.

In his mature thought (though not in works published in his life-time) what Coleridge calls 'the spirituality of the Hades' is there-fore a necessary part of his doctrine of the divine trinity and of creation and redemption, building on the theologies of Paul and John. The Word breathing on the Chaos forms Nature; the same Word spoken in Christ redeems into the new creation; and these, though placed at different points in the biblical narrative, are in truth a single operation of both creation and redemption. He writes in a note of 1833 of 'the Mystery of Darkness, the contradiction, (the Chaos, Genesis I.2), which by the redemptive Word was made to become Nature' (*NB* 51, fol. 2ᵛ). Similarly the fall symbolised in the story of Genesis 2 is of a piece with the cosmic or angelic Fall. The language Coleridge uses of the human and moral and the cosmic dimensions of sin is remarkably similar, both reaching back behind Genesis. So in his manuscript 'Thoughts of Consolation for a frail but salvation-seeking Mortal' of 1830 he writes of the high calling of true human selfhood 'as a distinct subsistence, in the Fullness of the Logos' but continues:

> In the mystery of the evil Will I sought or willed to have, a Self in Myself – to be absolute in the Non-absolute. I fell – into the Indistinction. I became absolutely *nothing* – and nothing remained but the indestructible potential derived from the transcendence of the Eternal Will. I existed only for God – as an *evil* ground of a future Being. He awakened me into actual Being ... that I might be spiritually transubstantiated to, and born again into, the Living Word as the Divine Humanity, the God Man! (*NB* 44, fol. 31).

The same pattern appears, but this time in a universal context, in another notebook of the same year:

> The ground of the intelligibility of the whole is the *spirituality* of the Hades. The Spirit *was* Light of Light as long as it abode *in* the Light – and *fell* into Darkness, self-precipitated into blank potentiality, which but for the absolute Will would have been equal to mere non-essence, and which antecedent of the condescension of the Spirit, and the lucific Word was equivalent to non-existence – but which by the Word successively *actualized* is restored (*NB* 43, fols 35ᵛ, 36ʳ).

Similarly, the same language is applied in the same way to the individual self – 'that Phantom, that ens non vere ens ... which I *was*' – and to Nature 'as the Ens non vere ens, the Opposite of God, as the Spirit of Chaos'.[37] And both dimensions are often expressed in a spirit of orthodox Christianity and personal penitence before the absolute Will of the redeeming God:

> O absolute Good, Eternal I AM, the Holy *One*, the Father who with thy only-begotten Son, and thy Spirit, Life & Love essentially

art the one only living God – Glory and thanksgiving to thee, and for thy dear Son's sake, the Mediator, God of Mercy, Mercy for me, poor Sinner! Mercy! Mercy! Mercy! (*NB* 54, fol. 16).

In Coleridge's sketches towards a biblical commentary at this period the themes of Chaos and the Fall of the angels ('a most fruitful Contemplation') appear in many different canonical contexts – in 1829, for instance, not just in the notes on Genesis but also in those on Matthew and Paul.[38] There is naturally considerable difficulty in narrativising – in making readable – a pattern that appears to burst the canonical scheme of redemption, pushing behind Genesis and beyond Apocalypse. Coleridge wishes to see the Bible as paradigm of all redemptive history, an expression in time of the austere 'pentad of operative Christianity'. Yet in the Apocalypse and in the early chapters of Genesis there is hardly any 'natural' narrative, rather myth on a universal scale. This makes them more amenable to transposition into a symbolic theology or philosophy; and so it seems at times that he wishes to see Genesis and Apocalypse as a paradigm of the biblical canon itself.

An important element in this transposition is the term 'the Ground', which he distinguishes carefully from 'Cause' – God is not 'First Cause' (which would mean his ceasing to be absolute Will and becoming part of creation) but 'the Ground of Life', and Christ is 'the Base, Ground, or antecedent Unity of our proper Humanity'.[39] But in an intriguing addition to this last note (written in 1830/31) Coleridge speaks also of Hades becoming another kind of Ground, or rather a 'Floor', in the pattern of both Fall and redemption:

The fall out of Christ as before out of the Pleroma, into Hades the *fruitless* Branch is taken away – it is no longer known by the I AM as in his *mind* – therefore not according to his Will – therefore no longer having *actual* Being –. Hades – Hell the elastic Floor of Heaven, the counterstriving Will (as potential Being) the sure & constant suppression of which constitutes the *Life*, the Victory, and the triumph of the Angelic Love & Bliss.... Objectively, Hades is the material Nature of Heaven – and subjectively the Hell of Nature (*NB* 49, fol. 21ᵛ).

But the fullest, if still tentative, attempt at a presentation of chaos, creation and redemption in a symbiosis of scientific, philosophical and biblical language is one that draws heavily on the symbolism of the Apocalypse as well as of Genesis and the fourth Gospel. It comes in a long note of 1828/9 on the copy of Irving's second volume of sermons referred to above. This begins by speaking of the tension between 'Ground' and its manifesting 'Form' (as in Light/Life; Father/Son), then continues:

> In whatever Subject ... the *Ground* of Life is not, or no longer is, for that Subject Light ceases to be constructive, and becomes Destruction. The Light, which is the beatitude (visio beatifica) of Spirits – whose Will is the Will of the Father, is a consuming Fire to all Iniquity. The distinctive becomes *separative*, and works in both forms of Indistinction, the liquefying ... and the pulverizing. It is the great Agent in the processes of Sloughing, ejecting, excommunicating: and for each of these we find express declarations in Scripture, and facts equally express and declarative in Nature. But further: every great Epoch of Reproduction, (Recreation, Re-generation, New Birth) is preceded by a Destruction. The world (aevum, aeon) is brought to an end – a day of Judgement takes place – a new Ledger or Book of Life is opened, and only the Balance, the Net Profits are carried over. It is rendered highly probably by the recent investigations of Geologists that so it has been in each of the five great Epochs enumerated by Moses, as preceding the creation of Man. But most observable, and of most profitable Observation, is the Fact, that the two great Revolutions, the dread destructive moments of the existing Epoch, the one recorded, the other predictively denounced, in Holy Writings [the Flood and the lake of fire], present the two forms of Death, above-mentioned, the two modes of destructive disorganization; the first, namely, the liquifactive or fluidific, a form of Death which is however the matrix of future Life, & the second, the pulverizing or incinerative Power which is, however, at the same time the purifying, which reduces the substance to a harmony with Light ... The Lamb, Agnus, the spotless, *agnos*, the consuming Fire, and the purifying Water are one and the same with the Light of Life, the Living Light, whose indwelling Life is the alone true Light of Man. But in the likeness and the difference of Water and Fire a yet deeper Mystery is involved = the suspension, the witholding of Mercy: to the bursting forth of Wrath. In the diluvial Devastation, the Figure of the Son, the Articulation of the Word, is withdrawn; in the *final* conflagration the Will of the Ground is stirred up – the Distinctive Power no longer neutralizes its negative (-Elect'y = Oxygen) and positive force (+El'y =

Hydrogen) but receiving into itself the bitter will of the Ground shall oppose them in the fury of Conflict, the dilative shall be the fuel of the Contractive, and all shall be bound up in the utter darkness, sealed up in Death, & shall have no *place* more [cf. Rev 20:11]. Yet I doubt not that God will be glorified therein. The flameless Fire burns inward: the Contraction is absolute: and for this very cause there can be no contagion, no pollution. The evil is incommunicable, hath no *objective* Being & by its absolute heterogeneity separated from the Good and immiscible, may be nevertheless the Hades, the hidden and dark Ground of the Glorified New Earth – the enemy placed for ever under the feet of the Blessed, the elastic Spring of their mystic Dance, the Rebound of their ever fresh Triumph – the Ref[l]ection of the Light of the Lamb, which maketh the City of God resplendent, and filleth it with the reflexes of his Glory. – So it may be – & such are the forms which I seem to see dimly in the Mirror of Symbols, the laws and processes of corporeal World organic and inorganic, as interpreted by the Revealed Word. – And I speak only as I see-: seeing dimly I speak uncertainly (*CM* iii, pp. 60–2).

In these uncertain yet fascinating visions Coleridge responds to the 'great symbolic drama' of the Apocalypse in a way that obliterates neither the eternal reality of evil nor the joy of human and cosmic redemption. In the style of the eighteenth century, but with much philosophical and scientific water under the bridge, he again perceives a harmony between the Bible and the 'Book of Nature'. But the confident progress of 'Religious Musings' has given way to a sophisticated doctrine of hell; 'One Life' as a democratic reflection of the unity of God has given way to the dialectical dance of good and evil below the Light of the Lamb; apocalyptic symbolism as a politico-religious code has given way to the use of biblical and mythological narrative in a far more energetic teleology; and 'the mirror of symbols' is reflecting eschatologically as well as translucently. Here is an engagement with the Apocalypse that is both religious and poetic, attending to a structure that is ultimately not historical nor predictive nor political, but incorporating all three dimensions in a redemptive liturgy, the mystic dance of the blessed upon the elastic spring of conquered evil.

Such interpretations, however, raise in acute form the suspicion long attached to Coleridge that in the formation of his 'System' he is really an intellectual magpie, using scraps of the Bible, Christian theology and German philosophy as respectable but precarious underpinning of a structure that was actually esoteric if not solipsistic. He desperately needs the underpinning; without it he is left as the stranded seer yearning to revive within himself the symphony and song once heard in vision. He needs a canon to bring some kind of grammar to his own imagination and to form an agreed platform from which to undertake his homiletic task. But can the biblical canon really provide what he asks of it? Does this 'Mirror of Faith' work with the symbolic cohesion of the wheels and the cherubim, or can he actually use it only by committing allegory?

PROMETHEUS BOUND

In the meticulous study of the Bible that occupied much of the last ten years of his life Coleridge had two conflicting objectives. The first is a public, apologetic one: to be able to give more substance to the claims made for the Bible in the *Lay Sermons* and to expound for an intelligent, sceptical world the '*Bible*, the Code and Organ of the Instruction of all Men, learned and unlearned' (*NB* 55, fol. 16ᵛ). This involves attention not just to the text itself but to theories of inspiration and to historical criticism, bearing in mind the traditional foundation of Christian apologetics on miracles, prophecy and inspiration. With regard to this part of his intention, *Confessions of an Enquiring Spirit* can be seen as a kind of preface to the proposed commentary – an inauspicious one, since even when it was posthumously published in 1840 it was poorly received.

But there was a second, more private intention, one whose fulfilment or success is much harder to measure: namely to find corroboration in the traditional authority of the protestant world, the Old and New Testaments, for what he inwardly perceived as the truths of Reason. The assumption he works on is a belief that he recognises in a note of 1831 to be rejected by 'Infidel' and 'Bibliolater' alike, whereas for himself,

> in regard to the sacred Scriptures, the purest and most venerable product of the living and productive Reason, the Reason may be used as *a solar microscope* of powers increasing, as our knowledge increases, and enable us to descry and find a form and symbol for every truth, which in the course of our intellectual development

and research we have successively brought into the light of our consciousness (*NB* 50, fol. 25).

It is possible that for Coleridge this assumption raised no *practical* difficulties – that his immersion from an early age in Bible and Church was such that he intuitively sensed that scripture is, as he puts it in the same note, the outgrowth of reason as the oak is of the acorn. But it could hardly fail to raise *theoretical* difficulties – both about the formation and boundaries of the biblical canon, and more importantly about the degree to which a Coleridgean reader of the Bible is actually bringing 'truths' to consciousness from uncanonical sources (the 'fancy', or unbiblical writers like Kant or Schelling, or esoteric biblical writers like Boehme or the kabbalists) and then attaching them allegorically to biblical 'symbols'.

The connection between this process and Coleridge's first object-ive, the public and apologetic one, is that he aimed to prove by col-lecting his notes on the Bible into a coherent sequential commentary the value of the biblical canon

> as Books of no time because *for all times* – not so much what David consciously meant or understood himself to mean, but what *we* may and ought to understand by the Words. This is indeed the noblest & indeed the only philosophical sense of the *Inspiration* of the S[acred] S[criptures] (*NB* 46, fol. 34ᵛ).

This clearly foregrounds the present reader far more than did either the higher critics, with their concern for the original historical context, or the literalists, with their concern for the authoritative transmission of objective truth. 'What are words', Coleridge asks in 1830, 'even the *words* of God, unless the Spirit of Dictation in the Writer or Utterer be likewise present as the Spirit of Understanding in the Hearer or Reader?' (*NB* 47, fol. 4) In fact, as the *Confessions of an Enquiring Spirit* show, the Spirit is really for Coleridge one neither of dictation nor of understanding but – as for Lowth and Herder before him – of human communion across the ages. But the ghosts of Eichhorn and Michaelis haunt his notes as well. For insofar as a commentary requires 'understanding' of the text, and insofar as apologetics require arguments about prophecy and mira-cles as well as answers to the secularists' scepticism about Christian origins, Coleridge has also to attend to the particular historical issues raised by 'the sacred penmen'.

It is an unwelcome task for him, as one would expect for someone who approached history and politics in the broad-brush style of the *Lay Sermons, The Friend* and *Church and State*. Coleridge admits that 'But for Christ, Christianity, Christendom, as centres of convergence, I should utterly want the *historic* sense. Even as it is, I feel it very languid in all particular History' (*NB* 51, fol. 19^v). He sees this as a 'defect', contrasting his response to history with those of Scott and Wordsworth; one that must however be rectified if, for instance, he is to vindicate the authority of the synoptic gospels.[40] So he investigates thoroughly Eichhorn's thesis of an *Urevangelium* lying behind the canonical gospels; but he then asks himself, 'When the Ideas rise up within me, as independent Growths of my Spirit ... why should I trouble myself with questions about the precise character, purpose and source' of the gospels? (*NB* 35, fols 26^v, 27^r). The question is rhetorical, but a reasoned answer could only be, 'To address those who are still practising a religion of Understanding rather than Reason'.

Coleridge's weariness with historical arguing is much in evidence in his consideration of miracles.[41] But it is a weariness particularly oppressive when it comes to the question of 'evidence' from prophecy and its fulfilment, an issue that can hardly be evaded when studying the New Testament. 'I feel that the investigation of this subject has an unfavourable ungenial effect on my best feelings', he bewails; 'and yet I cannot continue my study thro' the Bible without having the subject forced on my notice'.[42] It is forced on him because most English Christians of his time took it for granted that the Old Testament contained numerous clear prophecies of a coming Messiah, which were perfectly fulfilled by Jesus – indeed, as Coleridge reluctantly admits, Jesus himself appears to have validated such interpretation in passages such as Luke 24. Forced on him also because the New Testament too – mainly in the Book of Revelation – contained prophecies of the coming end and judgement, if not the entire course of history. The first kind of fulfilment, that of supposedly Messianic prophecies, Coleridge sees as distressingly literal-minded. It restricts the prophetic text to a single meaning and means that once that meaning is discovered the text itself is no longer prophecy but merely 'evidence'; on the contrary, he senses when reading Isaiah that he is 'about to be visited by new Powers of Insight', for 'Is there not a *double Sense*, the one exterior and shifting, and now contracting, now enlarging, and the other stedfast, and unmoving, the *Idea* of the former!... May we dare to hope for a *sane* Swedenborg?' (*NB* 52, fol. 19^v) Strictly speaking, this is a multiple rather than a double sense; for while, like Origen, Coleridge is suggesting the primacy of a 'spiritual' meaning, unlike him he sees the other ways that the text speaks as not simply divisible into 'literal' and 'moral' but as endlessly fluid. One sense need not negate another, nor can they necessarily be ordered hierarchically.

In these notebooks from the last year of his life (numbers 52–5) Coleridge is still ploughing through the Bible, though the possible completion of his commentary seems to be receding. And he turns again to Daniel and Revelation, still considering the first six chapters of the former book as spurious and regretting the constant mangling of the latter book:

> It would be difficult, nay, rather impossible to determine, whether the Commentators on the Apocalypse hitherto have failed, more from the want of poetic Sight or of philosophic Insight. For both are alike indispensable conditions of a right understanding and making understood this sublime Poem: and of both alike the Commentators from Irenaeus to Parson Croley have been gifted with a superabundant Lack (*NB* 54, fol. 3ᵛ).

Coleridge presumably considered himself not to share this lack and therefore to be equipped to communicate such 'right understanding'. That is to say that hermeneutical authority is still possible, whether the text be considered as poem or as scripture. But is this really so for him, or does the inclusion of the Apocalypse in the biblical canon, with its uncompromising closing words, mean that its interpretation is going to be inevitably constrained or distorted when undertaken by Christians who are committed to perceiving harmony in the scriptures – even those with 'poetic Sight' and 'philosophic Insight' as keen as Coleridge's? And is the reason he remains hesitant about the canonicity of the 'sublime Poem' not primarily one of authorship or reception or morality, but that he cannot reconcile the symbolic and poetic and philosophical authority that it wields over him (the 'idea' of the book) with the teaching of the Church, even when the latter is interpreted in his own idiosyncratic way? In the general terms of *Confessions of an Enquiring Spirit*, the inspired authority of the whole canon can be affirmed; when it comes to the unravelling of specific texts the affirmation is harder to achieve.

Yet in a way the Apocalypse, with the first two verses of Genesis and the first two of St John's Gospel, was saying something he could find nowhere else in the Bible. For these passages stand outside the historical narrative of redemption while still speaking of the absolute Will, the eternal Logos and (in the case of Revelation) the conquest of evil. The Apocalypse actually narrativises this primal dialectic of creation and redemption. But precisely because it stands in the canon and is sucked into that historical framework, precisely because it does refer to Christ rather than to Apollo, Coleridge is nervous of interpreting it in public. In it lie the nightmare visions of Chaos and Evil, 'the Dragon foul and fell'; and – as with the ancient mariner's visions and his final pious advice – these can be incorporated into the Christian scheme of moral redemption only at the cost of a severe disjunction. Coleridge was drawn over many years to the esoteric scriptural interpretations of the kabbalists, which he saw as preserving patriarchal oral tradition.[43] In them he tried to see 'a sane Swedenborg', discovering spiritual sense in the canonical text without dissolving it in allegory. But the kabbalists hardly provided a convincing support for Christian apologetics in age that still sought 'evidences'.

The irony is that when Coleridge does try to interpret to the public a symbolic narrative of this dialectical 'mystic dance' of the blessed upon the 'floor' of vanquished darkness, it is not to the Bible that he turns but to Aeschylus. In a note of 1821/2, building on an unsuccessful attempt by his son Hartley at a poetic interpretation of the Prometheus myth, he sees this story as a supreme metaphysical attempt at the solution of 'the riddle which Man as Man is for himself', for which more traditional attempts are made through 'the chaos, the Fall or Degeneracy of Man, and the Deluge' (*CN* 4839). These thoughts were developed in terms of polar logic and redemptive *agōn* in his lecture of May 1825 to the Royal Society of Literature 'On the Prometheus of Aeschylus'. The myth is seen as a 'philosopheme', equivalent to that of Genesis; but whereas the latter's presentation of the fall is 'an allegory', 'The Prometheus is a *philosopheme* and *tautegorikon'*, and 'the ground-work of the Aeschylean mythus is laid in the definition of Idea and Law, as correlatives that mutually interpret each the other'.[44] Jove is the symbol of law (*nomos*), Prometheus of idea (*nous*). The kinship of the two gods shows that idea and law are inseparable. Their schism shows that idea and law are thesis and antithesis: Promethean resistance is necessary to maintaining the transcendence of *nous*, while Jovian control is necessary to maintaining order and actuality. As in *Prometheus Bound*, the reconciliation, involving the divulging of

Prometheus's secret and his liberation, lies in the future: for the present the polarity is preserved. Coleridge is careful to distinguish this from the account by 'Moses', to which he bows as revealed authority (pp. 392–4, 398). But Aeschylus and the Greek mysteries have the great advantage for him of not identifying the absolute will with the Creator; whereas Yahweh is an actor in the biblical story of creation and fall, Prometheus and Jove are antagonists distinct from the 'Identity' or prothesis (*to theion*). So Coleridge is liberated to interpret a myth of fall and redemption with philosophical precision and conviction and in a public (if somewhat élitist) sphere. This he was never able to do when the object of interpretation was the Bible, with its huge weight of canonical authority, with its historical particularity, with the absolute Will inescapable in its pages. And yet it was just such a representation of redemption through the struggle of idea and law that he was attempting to articulate in his tortured notes on Genesis and Revelation and other areas of 'the Mirror of Faith'.

What Coleridge was straining towards was a rewriting of scripture, a *kabbalah* of transcendental philosophy, a new apocalypse – perhaps the completion of *Kubla Khan*. Had he achieved this it might have been the release of his 'genial spirits' after the years of dejection. He might have shown, moreover, that the Bible was genuinely a 'system of symbols' and, by articulating those symbols, have dispensed with the need for interpretation. But he failed, or refrained, because of his hard-won adherence to the dogmatic framework that drew its authority precisely from the Christian canon, and indeed his personal adherence to the transcendent God who presides over it. In the trailing confusion of the canon (and of Coleridge's own life and writings) vision was dispersed, and the demon of allegory was inescapable. The fact that Coleridge was not, so to speak, redeemed from the Christian scheme of redemption meant that he continued to the end of his life as a hermeneutical explorer, testing and reaching the limits of interpretation.

6
Rewriting Apocalypse: Shelley and Blake

Prometheus underwent something of a reincarnation in early nineteenth-century England, and Coleridge and his son were far from being the only people studying Aeschylus or using the Titan as a symbol of freedom, enlightenment, resistance or intellectual energy.[1] Most enduring – and raising many of the most acute moral questions about the 'Promethean' spirit – was Mary Shelley's *Frankenstein, or the Modern Prometheus* of 1818. Her Prometheus, Victor Frankenstein, steals the spark of life by his scientific brilliance, but his 'new creation' consumes both its creator and his world. He is one 'imbued with a fervent longing to penetrate the secrets of nature' (I.ii), a man 'alone ... reserved to discover so astonishing a secret' as that of animation (I.iv) – and the words 'discover' and 'discovery', frequent in *Frankenstein*, still retained in Shelley's time their more active and literal (and apocalyptic) sense of 'uncovering'. Indeed, in her preface of 1831 the author unveils the origin of the story as an 'acute mental vision' in which '[m]y imagination, unbidden, possessed and guided me', the writing being simply 'a transcript of the grim terrors of my waking dream'.[2] But what is unveiled in this Swiss Patmos is not life but death. Prometheus is a destroyer, and this is an apocalypse without redemption.

It was not long after the writing of *Frankenstein* that Shelley's husband turned to a more positive but highly complex treatment of the Prometheus myth in his 'lyrical drama' *Prometheus Unbound* (1819). This is, in its syncretistic way, a fusion of Hellenic with Enlightenment but more significantly with biblical yearning. It is well known that for all his hostility to Christianity Percy Shelley was a fervent reader of the Bible; and in this poem, according to M. H. Abrams, Shelley

> renders the universal history of man in the dramatic form of visualizable agents and their actions, and ... represents man's

accession to an earthly paradise not (in the usual eighteenth-century pattern) as the terminus of a long and gradual progress but (by a reversion to the Biblical design of history) as a sudden, right-angled breakthrough from misery to felicity.[3]

Abrams also rightly sees the sounding of the shell by the spirit of the Hour in Act III as Shelley's equivalent of the seventh trumpet, while Michael Ferber describes the play's 'timeless last act' as 'his own version of the Book of Revelation'.[4] But in fact the whole of *Prometheus Unbound* can be seen as a rewriting of John's Apocalypse. In what he says is not an 'exhaustive list', Bryan Shelley has recently counted no fewer than 33 allusions to or echoes of Revelation in this poem (among numerous ones to other biblical passages).[5] More than that, I wish to suggest that the actual structure of the poem is modelled on that of Revelation and that Shelley, like Blake, is consciously writing a post-Christian apocalypse while still being haunted by the old one, with whose spirit he engages polemically. Unlike Aeschylus, and unlike Coleridge, Shelley was, as he confesses in the Preface to his poem, 'averse from a catastrophe so feeble as that of reconciling the Champion with the Oppressor of mankind': Jupiter/Yahweh/*Nomos* is destined for 'the bottomless void' (*SPP*, pp. 133, 182). By their prophetic proclamation of the death of God both Shelley and Blake make the move beyond interpretation that Coleridge could not make.

PROMETHEUS AND THE DEATH OF GOD

The dialogue of the first act of *Prometheus Unbound*, during the whole of which Prometheus is 'bound to the Precipice', begins when four Voices each speak twice. The pattern is reminiscent of the beginning of the action in John's vision with the release of the four horsemen (*PU*, I.74–106; Rev 6:1–8). The Voices come from the mountains, the springs, the air and the whirlwinds, rather as the judgements delivered by the first four trumpets of Revelation are directed at the earth, the sea, the springs, and the sun, moon and stars (Rev 8:7–12). Then at the end of the first act, four Spirits speak in turn, arriving 'On a battle-trumpet's blast. ... From the dust of creeds outworn' to address Prometheus (I.694–751). As after the first four trumpets of Revelation, there is a pause before the next two spirits come; and as after the sixth trumpet, a much longer interval before the 'mighty music. ... As thunder mingled with clear echoes' of the Spirit of the Hour (I.752–9; III.iii.80–2). The sevenfold pattern is consummated in Demorgogon's final seven invocations before his proclamation of the new Earth formed by 'the seals of that most firm assurance/Which bars the pit over Destruction's strength' and of the 'spells' by which the 'serpent' can be quelled (IV.519–78).

What is proclaimed by these spirits, however, is a reversal of Revelation's trumpets of judgement. Whereas the pause after the fourth trumpet is occupied by the eagle's cry of Woe to the earth, the pause after the fourth Spirit's words has Ione perceiving the approach of the next two with their 'soft smiles' and 'sweet, sad voices'. These announce not locusts, cavalry and plagues but 'Wisdom, Justice, Love and Peace' (Rev 8:13–9:19; *PU*, I.752–800). In contrast to the exclusive resurrection and vindictive judgements of Rev 20, the powers by which the pit is sealed and 'Conquest is dragged Captive through the Deep' are Love, Gentleness, Virtue, Wisdom and Endurance; and final glory rests not in repentance but in continued defiance and the refusal to repent (IV.554–78). Above all, in this drama without a single human character, salvation is won through the 'Heaven-defying minds' of earthly human spirits (II.iii.39). Prometheus himself, though immortal, arises 'a spirit of keen joy' from his mother Earth, whilst the six spirits of Act I are summoned by Earth as 'those subtle and fair spirits/Whose homes are the dim caves of human thought'; what they announce to Prometheus is 'the prophecy/Which begins and ends in thee', not in the transcendent throne of the Apocalypse.[6] So revelation comes from the human mind to the immortals, not the other way round, and the unveiling achieved by the fall of Jupiter and announced by the Spirit of the Hour in Shelley's original conclusion is the reverse of the unveiling of God's throne:

> The loathsome mask has fallen, the man remains
> Sceptreless, free, uncircumscribed – but man:
> Equal, unclassed, tribeless and nationless,
> Exempt from awe, worship, degree, – the King
> Over himself; just, gentle, wise – but man...
>   (III.iv.193–7)

Although in his Preface Shelley compares Prometheus to Satan, the actual imagery used of the crucified Titan in Act I aligns him with

Jesus; as often in Shelley's thought, Jesus is portrayed positively, with Christianity and the Church as satanic betrayals of his moral and poetic vision.[7] But like Blake, Shelley sees Jesus/Prometheus triumphing through resistance and forgiveness, not through the military conquest of the Apocalypse. The downfall of Jupiter in Act III is possible because in Act I Prometheus has resisted both the temptation to dwell in continuing hatred and the temptation to submit to 'Heaven'. The temptation is a mental one, projected on to mythic figures – Prometheus dismisses Mercury's awed pity with 'Pity the self-despising slaves of Heaven,/Not me', he dismisses the final Fury's call to despair with 'Thy words are like a cloud of winged snakes/And yet I pity those they torture not' (I.429f., 632f.) Only so can he 'Be what it is my destiny to be,/The saviour and the strength of suffering man' (I.816f.) For the Promethean mind's endurance has cosmic and political consequences. The plagues of Jovian tyranny which affect the Earth are removed by the Saviour's resistance, and the celebration of this release is hymned by the Spirit of the Earth and the Spirit of the Hour in language as political as any in *Queen Mab* or *The Mask of Anarchy*.[8]

In Godwinian style, the new society is built by human intelligence, not by revolution or by providence. But in biblical style it is pictured in *Prometheus Unbound* as a new heaven and (more particularly) a new earth. Described in III.iv, the new creation is evoked by the choruses of Act IV as the home of Mind and of Wisdom but also as 'a new earth and sea/And a Heaven where yet Heaven never could be' with the natural elements appearing 'From its chaos made calm by love, not fear' (IV.93–8, 153–8, 164–71). Panthea and Ione celebrate 'Heaven and Earth united now' with several allusions to Daniel's Son of Man and to Ezekiel's vision of the whirling wheels (IV.219–79). Rather than representing the whole of Revelation, as Ferber suggests, this last Act is the equivalent of the two final chapters, using the imagery not only of new creation but of the heavenly marriage of the Lamb and the Bride. As in the Johannine vision 'the Spirit and the Bride say "Come!"', so from Panthea's dreams in Act II the bride Asia hears the call to 'Follow, follow!', leading to the consummation of her love in III.iv and its liturgical celebration (combined with that of the love of earth and moon) in Act IV. Yet in place of the chaste eroticism of the Apocalypse, expelling from the city all that is impure – in place too of the individualistic and escapist eroticism of Shelley's own *Epipsychidion* – this is an inclusive and political eroticism from which tyranny alone is exluded.

The earthly tyranny includes, indeed it is empowered by and epitomised in, the rule of Jupiter. Both in Prometheus's curse and in Jupiter's own speech, Shelley uses language of this god that echoes the praise ascribed in the Bible to Yahweh and to 'the One seated on a throne' in John's vision. Jupiter is presented as a demiurge, though with an 'all-miscreative brain'; yet his strength and wisdom originate from the truly creative Prometheus (I.448, II.iv.43–97). In other words, Jupiter/Yahweh is himself a dark projection of the Promethean mind, and – in a reversal of the biblical cosmology – Prometheus is seen by the falling Jupiter as 'mine enemy above' (III.i.82). The death of God is thus for Shelley an achievement of the Promethean spirit directing the mind to creative Love rather than to enslavement – hard-won, but relatively straightforward when set beside its achievement in Blake and Nietzsche. It is an apocalypse, an unveiling, that reverses the open door into heaven of Rev 4, for it is one in which man is seen in the place of God. And the Promethean or human spirit is not only its seer but its agent:

> … the abyss shouts from her depth laid bare,
> 'Heaven, hast thou secrets? Man unveils me, I have none.'
> (IV.422f.)

The language of secrets and unveiling runs through the first three acts of Shelley's drama, drawing on the Promethean secret of life which the Titan refuses to divulge (I.371–80). The penetration of the secret begins to be accomplished by Asia, the spirit of love, at the end of her journey in Act II: first when 'The veil has fallen' and her vision of Demogorgon enables her to prophesy, and secondly in her own transformation when Panthea sees 'Thy presence thus un-veiled' (II.iv.2; v.20). And when Jupiter is fallen and Prometheus is unbound and reunited with Asia the apocalypse extends through humanity where 'veil by veil evil and terror fall' (III.iii.62). The 'secret' that for Frankenstein had meant destruction is here simply true humanity, and Demogorgon's closing speech celebrating the Promethean spirit is perhaps its complete and definitive revelation.

Prometheus Unbound is far from being Shelley's only apocalyptic poem. There are depictions of unveilings as well as distinct echoes of the Book of Revelation in *Queen Mab, The Revolt of Islam, The Mask of Anarchy, Hellas,* and particularly in Shelley's last uncompleted poem 'The Triumph of Life', with its Dante-esque visions, its imagery of the chariot and the whore, its use of Rousseau as an 'interpreting angel', and its unfolding of history as the incarnation of thought.[9] In each case this might be seen as a less vengeful and more humane apocalypse than that of Patmos, whose spirit the poet contests. Yet, through Shelley's use of myth, his apocalypses are presented with almost equal authority to that of the scriptural one. It was rather disingenuously that he wrote in the Preface to *Prometheus Unbound* that 'Didactic poetry is my abhorrence', for the drama that ensues is actually highly didactic (*SPP*, p. 135). Where all is unveiled there is no room for irony. Unsurprisingly, then, there are many parallels between the mythical language of apocalypse in *Prometheus Unbound* and the didactic prose of *A Defence of Poetry* (1821). Like Prometheus, poetry 'defeats the curse which binds us to be subjected to the accident of surrounding impressions ... creates anew the universe', and 'redeems from decay the visitations of the divinity in man': in contrast to 'Mammon' and 'the owl-winged faculty of calculation', 'Poetry is indeed something divine ... as it were the interpenetration of a diviner nature through our own' (*SPP*, pp. 503–5). As an apocalyptic 'sword of lightning, ever unsheathed, which consumes the scabbard that would contain it', it 'lifts the veil from the hidden beauty of the world ... strips the veil of familiarity from the world, and lays bare the naked and sleeping beauty which is the spirit of its forms' (*SPP*, pp. 491, 487, 505). This is an earthly unveiling, but it can hardly be called a secular one. On the contrary, the works of poets (among whom are included thinkers and 'authors of revolution in opinion' like Plato, Jesus and Bacon) are 'the echo of the eternal music', and 'A poem is the very image of life expressed in its eternal truth' (*SPP*, p. 485). As Bryan Shelley argues, 'the *Defence of Poetry* clearly establishes a theologically oriented poetics'.[10]

In this way Shelley often echoes the language of Coleridge's *Statesman's Manual*, which he had read not long before Peacock's satirical article that led to the *Defence of Poetry*. The difference is of course that what Shelley asserts of 'poetry' – its universality, its inspiration, its 'expression of the Imagination', its religious power, its representation of eternal truth – Coleridge asserts of scripture. The 'sublime IDEAS', 'the Science of Realities', the 'symbol of Eternity' are for the older poet found not in Shelley's infinite 'great poem, which all poets ... have built up since the beginning of the world'.[11] Instead they are contained in one book of Hebrew and Greek writings, and the system of symbols that they constitute stands complete and discrete, a land to be interpreted.

PROPHECY AND STATE RELIGION

For both Coleridge and Shelley, however, the system is a prophetic one. Poets, writes Shelley, 'are the unacknowledged legislators of the world'; he himself prays for the inspiring Wind to be through his lips 'the trumpet of a prophecy' (*SPP*, pp. 508, 223). And for Coleridge the scriptural symbols and narrative are 'the living *educts* of the Imagination' providing 'the best guide to political skill and foresight' (*LS*, p. 29). Coleridge distinguishes 'prophecy' firmly from 'prognostication', while Shelley too insists that he is not speaking of poets as 'prophets in the gross sense of the word' (*SPP*, p. 483). More bluntly still speaks William Blake:

> Prophets in the modern sense of the word have never existed Jonah was no prophet in the modern sense for his prophecy of Nineveh failed   Every honest man is a Prophet   he utters his opinion both of private & public matters   Thus   If you go on So the result is So   He never says such a thing shall happen let you do what you will. A Prophet is a Seer not an Arbitrary Dictator (*BE*, p. 617).

The words were written in 1798 on Blake's copy of *An Apology for the Bible in a Series of Letters addressed to Thomas Paine by R. Watson, DD, FRS*. Watson, the Bishop of Llandaff, had attempted to defend the inspiration and historical accuracy of the Bible against the sceptical deist Paine. But to Blake – who detested deism and had little in common with Paine intellectually – the Doctor of Divinity and Fellow of the Royal Society was just 'a State trickster'. Trying to marshal evidence for the Bible's coherence through rational argument and historical proofs, Watson was actually shoring up the coherence of the whole machinery of the state, which Blake in 1798 and throughout his life saw as one of oppression, falsehood and war. To use the Bible as part of that machinery was a blasphemy far outweighing any blasphemy of Paine's. For Blake inhabited the Bible and believed in its inspiration perhaps more literally than any other English reader has ever done.

   The notion of 'prophecy' can be seen as the nub of the argument between Blake and Watson – and with the latter Blake is in fact arraigning almost the entire tradition of English interpretation of Revelation and other 'prophetic' books. That tradition he sees as a sinister achievement of the Newton–Locke axis, which in its lust for measuring and defining and controlling denied the human imagination. It is the demise of such oppressive 'prophecy' that he celebrates at the exuberant conclusion of his epic *The Four Zoas*:

> Where is the spectre of prophecy? Where the delusive phantom?
> Departed; and Urthona rises from the ruinous walls
> In all his ancient strength to form the golden armour of science
> For intellectual war. The war of swords departed now,
> The dark religions are departed, & sweet science reigns.
>
> (*FZ*, ix.848–52)

This 'sweet science' is as far from Newton's physics as Blake's notion of 'prophecy' was from Newton's lucubrations on the Bible. It is an intuitive, energetic knowledge, the fruit of 'mental fight' responding to divine inspiration, not of analysis of 'vegetative' Nature. It belongs in a cosmos filled not with the carefully calibrated time and space of Newton or Mede but with the superhuman (though often actually fallen and subhuman) mythic creations of Blake's mind. And its spokesman is a London artisan who sees himself as an equal to the prophets Isaiah and Ezekiel, dining with them and discussing the 'Poetic Genius' common to them by which they are to raise others 'into a perception of the infinite' (*MHH*, pl 12f.)

To take the writings of Isaiah, Ezekiel or John of Patmos as coded predictions of the coming of Christ, the history of the Church or the events of the French Revolution is for Blake not the fulfilment but the denial of prophecy, a category mistake as absurd as reading a poem like a railway timetable. T. A. Hoagwood – whose reading of Blake is less convincing than his reading of Shelley – sees *Jerusalem*, like *Prometheus Unbound*, drawing not only on the eighteenth-century 'philosophy of mind' but also on the English tradition of 'prophetic' interpretation. But insofar as this is true, Blake draws on them only in a combative way. Mede's synchronisms, far from encouraging 'multivalency' of reading as Hoagwood suggests, lead more naturally to Newton's 'single vision'.[12] Rather, like Ezekiel and John, Blake saw the reading of prophecy as a kind of sacramental act, as the eating of a scroll, so that the 'consumption' of Blake's works places the reader in the position of an Elisha taking up the prophetic mantle. Blake the prophet wants to put himself out of business by liberating his readers: with prominence in the preface to *Milton* he repeats the prayer of Moses, 'Would to God that all the Lords people were prophets!'[13]

In contrast the unimaginative or Newtonian reading of prophecy actively reinforces the oppressive and inhuman world of 'Religion hid in War'. In Blake's early poems, that world is seen as the creation of the solipsistic demiurge Urizen, crouching in his dens and clutching his books. Urizen's name is probably a cockney-accented pun on 'reason'; his lonely fate a sign of what happens to the reasoning faculty when it is separated from energy and inspiration. In those early poems Urizen's main antagonist is the fiery rebel Orc. But Orc is gradually replaced by the blacksmith Los; and in Los's name there lies perhaps another pun. For Los is the inspired, creative *prophet* with whom Blake identifies himself (and later identifies Jesus). But a true prophet (profit) is actually the opposite of what Newton and Watson take prophets to be, so he is called Los (loss). Urizen wields his compasses and pores over his books, predicting and confining, the master but also the captive of the natural world. Los, in contrast, bears the prophetic hammer with which he is to shape and change humanity into awareness of its divinity and freedom.

The gradual waning of Orc and waxing of Los in Blake's poetry of the 1790s is sometimes seen as a sign of his retreat from politics, or at any rate of his disillusionment with revolutionary France. But to the Blake of every period a prophet is inescapably political, just as a king is inescapably religious. For him, as later for Marx, 'the criticism of religion is the presupposition of all criticism'; but Blake, abjuring any theory/practice distinction, could never have added that 'the criticism of religion is essentially complete'.[14] For there is no point at which religion can be disposed of philosophically: religion permeates human consciousness, and if it is to be abolished that can only be by 'mental fight'. It is certainly true that Blake's political polemic becomes more cryptic from *America* onwards, no doubt partly for reasons of self-preservation: 'To defend the Bible in this year 1798 would cost a man his life', he notes rather dramatically on his copy of Watson's *Apology*, while an aside in Erin's lament in *Jerusalem* regrets that 'deep dissimulation is the only defence an honest man has left'.[15] Los is a bard rather than an Orcian revolutionary; but for Blake as for many of his contemporaries the bard was a public and political figure – indeed Jon Mee argues that Los is in fact more political (because more 'humanised') than Orc.[16] The figure of Albion in Blake's last major poem *Jerusalem* is a political as well as a mystical one, and the connection between forgiveness of sins and the abolition of war is repeatedly emphasised, as in the address 'To the Deists' prefacing the third chapter of that poem, or in the moving address of the Saviour to Albion in chapter II:

> Displaying the eternal vision, the divine similitude,
> In loves & tears of brothers, sisters, sons, fathers & friends
> Which if man ceases to behold, he ceases to exist,
> Saying: 'Albion, our wars are wars of life, & wounds of love,
> With intellectual spears, & long winged arrows of thought.
> Mutual in one another's love & wrath all-renewing
> We live as one man; for contracting our infinite senses
> We behold multitude; or expanding, we behold as one,
> As one man all the universal family: & that one man
> We call Jesus the Christ – & he in us, & we in him,
> Live in perfect harmony in Eden, the land of life,
> Giving, receiving, & forgiving each other's trespasses.
>
> (*J*, 34:11–22)

On the other hand Blake's much earlier *Song of Liberty* (appended to *The Marriage of Heaven and Hell* during the revolutionary wars of 1792) is about religious and moral as much as political and social freedom – to Blake such distinguishing adjectives would seem like allegorising nonsense.

A Song of Liberty culminates in the ecstatic conflict that is shortly to be narrativised as that between 'the gloomy king' Urizen and Orc 'the son of fire'. The former,

> With thunder and fire, leading his starry hosts through the waste wilderness,... promulgates his ten commands, glancing his beamy eyelids over the deep in dark dismay,
>
> Where the son of fire in his eastern cloud, while the morning plumes her golden breast,
>
> Spurning the clouds written with curses, stamps the stony law to dust, loosing the eternal horses from the dens of night, crying:
>
> EMPIRE IS NO MORE! AND NOW THE LION & WOLF SHALL CEASE.[17]

The identification of the gloomy king with Moses is explicit, as later in the Urizen poems, where the thunder, clouds, wilderness and 'stony law' reappear frequently. Less explicit but perhaps as important is the identification of the rebellious son of fire with the Jesus of the Apocalypse 'loosing the eternal horses'. In his 'infernal' reading of the Bible, Blake dispels the traditional typology by which Moses foreshadows Christ in favour of a polemical displacement of Moses by Jesus, Law by Apocalypse, Sinai by Patmos. This is far more than a matter of the relationship between Judaism and Christianity or between past and present. These contraries represent the eternal conflict of law and gospel, though Blake opposes the two far more radically than St Paul or even Luther. As Orc and Los struggle for the genuinely evangelical Divine Humanity expressed perfectly in Jesus, so Moses, Urizen and (in Blake's later poems) Vala and Rahab exude the legalistic Antichrist. But Christendom is aligned with the latter, since for Blake it has become not the religion of Jesus but 'State religion'.

Against such a blasphemous political construct Blake's polemic is constant throughout his career. It appears in the pathetic moral tyranny of the protagonist of *Tiriel* (c. 1789). In his poem with the greatest reference to contemporary politics, *The French Revolution* (c. 1790), it is personified by the reptilian archbishop who arises 'In the rushing of scales and hissing of flames and rolling of sulphurous smoke' and who in the name of cosmic order urges the king to 'let the Bastille devour/These rebellious seditious [and] seal them up ... in everlasting chains' (*FR*, 125–157).[18] *The French Revolution* uses apocalyptic language of living human beings in a rather strained attempt to imbue them with eternal significance in the attack on warmongering State religion; that Blake probably felt that this failed can be seen not only by the fact that he never engraved the poem or wrote the promised six further books of it but also by his change of method in his next major poem, *America* (1791–93), the first to be entitled 'A Prophecy'. *America* is undeniably political and still includes references to contemporaries like Washington, Paine and (thinly disguised) George III; it continues the attack on State religion, but distorts time and space by expressing the conflict not in historical reportage but in apocalyptic myth. As D. Halliburton remarks,

> From a poem in which historical characters dominate the stage, taking upon themselves the difficult task of assuming spiritual, even apocalyptic dimensions, to a work in which this all-important function is assumed by the fictive beings of the poet's own

creation: this is the step Blake took between *The French Revolution* and *America*, and it is a long and decisive one.[19]

The 'Albion's Angel' of *America*, sounding his war-trumpets, is depicted as a priest of Urizenic religion, as in the satirical design of plate 11 of *Europe* (c. 1793), where, over the text describing Albion's Angel's vision of Urizen, an enthroned and bat-winged priest–king with the features of George III wears the papal crown. As part of the tyranny of State religion's moral law is its denial of sexual freedom, so plate 6 of the same prophecy depicts a scaly god of war (the mythical Rintrah or the historical Pitt) above the text of Enitharmon's call to 'tell the human race that Woman's love is Sin ... Forbid all joy'. Blake conducts the same mental fight in more aphoristic form in several of the *Songs of Experience* (1793), such as 'A Little Boy Lost', 'The Chimney-Sweeper' and 'London' – and reading this last song in the context of English radical antinomianism, E. P. Thompson showed how 'the youthful harlot's curse' aligned the poet's home city with the Babylon of the Apocalypse.[20]

Blake's sense that war is the result of sexual and religious perversion is something that recurs in his later writing (for example *FZ*, vii.495–511, viii.82–93), reinforced by his sharp distinction between Innocence (the ground of redemption through Experience) and Virtue or Righteousness (a death-dealing construct of the moral law). The Christian doctrine of atonement, with its stress on sin as the division between God and man, bolsters the tyranny: Fall and redemption are real enough for Blake, but they concern the division *within* humanity (or Albion), which he explores intricately in *The Four Zoas*. Yet State religion is far wider than orthodox Christianity, for among its blind prophets are the unholy trinity of Bacon, Newton and Locke, whom Blake saw as the representatives of Natural Religion and Deism. The whole religion, founded on a grave misreading of Bible and Nature alike, and incorporating priestly, political, military, moral, sexual and artistic tyranny, is attacked by Los's thunderous cry at the climax of *Jerusalem*, when the murderous 'fiends of righteousness' are summoned in the name of Jesus to overthrow their altar and incense, 'Their marriage & their baptism, their burial & consecration', even their God, for 'There is no other/God, than that God who is the intellectual fountain of humanity' (*J*, 91:3–30).

It is this whole artistic–political battle that Blake is joining when he speaks of 'the Net of Religion' or of the 'webs', 'gins' and 'traps' of the Urizenic system. The spider's web fills plate 12 of *Europe,* in the text of which Enitharmon in her dream rejoices at the spreading of the moral law, and monstrous insects also appear in the design of plate 25 of *The Book of Urizen.* This plate describes the web as 'moist, cold, and dim,/Drawing out from his [Urizen's] sorrowing soul', an eery image of the spontaneous generation of the Net of Religion from self-absorption and the lust for power that is developed in *The Four Zoas:*

> ... a white woof covered his cold limbs from head to feet.
> Hair white as snow covered him in flaky locks terrific,
> Overspreading his limbs. In pride he wandered weeping ...
> A living mantle adjoined to his life & growing from his soul,
> And the web of Urizen stretched direful ...[21]

But the primary symbols used to depict the oppressive power of State religion are drawn from Revelation: Babylon, the Whore (Rahab), the dragon and the beast. The dragon is identified with George III in the designs of *America* plate 4 and *Europe* plate 11. Rahab is developed in *The Four Zoas* as the jealous, tyrannous and seductive power of the State: the 'false feminine counterpart lovely, of delusive beauty' conspiring against the Lamb with 'MYSTERY' written on her forehead.[22] And as Rev 17 identifies the Woman with the city, the Whore with Babylon, so, as Blake develops his polemic in *Milton,* Rahab and Babylon become one 'state'. It is seen by Milton and Blake as they stand 'in Satan's bosom & beheld its desolations':

> A ruined man, a ruined building of God not made with hands;
> Its plains of burning sand, its mountains of marble terrible, ...
> Arches & pyramids & porches, colonnades & domes,
> In which dwells Mystery, Babylon; here is her secret place;
> From hence she comes forth on the churches in delight;
> Here is her cup filled with its poisons, in these horrid vales,
> And here her scarlet veil woven in pestilence & war.
> Here is Jerusalem bound in chains, in the dens of Babylon.
>
> (*M*, 38:15–27)

There is, however, a radical displacement of these and other images from Revelation. The Whore and the City are identified with the political and aesthetic state that derives its authority precisely from the Bible and the Apocalypse. The 'righteousness' and chastity of the martyrs of Revelation are not salvific – nor prolific – but devouring; the jealous God and conquering Christ of Revelation belong to Blake's Babylon; Jerusalem and the Divine Humanity of Jesus and potentially of Albion are the enemies of the churches that bear the name of Jesus. From *The Marriage of Heaven and Hell* to his death Blake believed and wrote – sometimes directly, sometimes with tantalising obscurity – what he expressed most aphoristically in the late fragments collected under the title 'The Everlasting Gospel':

> The vision of Christ that thou dost see
> Is my vision's greatest enemy: ...
> Both read the Bible day and night,
> But thou read'st black where I read white.

While adopting the vocabulary and style of the Apocalypse, Blake is violently opposing the Jesus of Patmos to the Jesus of Galilee – not in the name of historical accuracy, which was irrelevant to him, but in the name of freedom. As with his reversal of the canonical roles of Jacob and Esau (Edom) and of angels and devils in *The Marriage of Heaven and Hell*, he here reverses the most central of all identifications in the Christian Bible, that of Father and Son. His method is (in Jon Mee's terminology) one of continually disrupting the biblical paradigms, 'transforming the received language of biblical prophecy into a novel rhetoric which seeks to legitimize revolutionary aspirations and demystify established authority'.[23]

Mee sees this disruption of paradigms as one fundamentally hostile to the Bible as received by the English churches. However, Blake's insistence that he is a Christian and that he holds the Bible to be inspired needs to be taken seriously, as do his clear identification (at any rate in his later poetry) of Jesus as Saviour and above all his inhabiting of the biblical text – dining with Isaiah and Ezekiel and making that imaginative leap in time that Lowth had demanded of his ideal reader of the Bible. One must ask whether this disruption of paradigms, this polemical dialectic relating to contemporary politics, is not *itself* a biblical process.

The criticism of religion which Marx saw as 'essentially complete' in 1844 began at least as early as Isaiah's denunciations of hypocrisy in the eighth century BCE. The elaborate arrangements for the worship of Yahweh laid down earlier in the Torah are ridiculed by the later prophet – yet both are included in the canon. Again, two adjacent chapters (2 Samuel 8 and 9) show Samuel witnessing against the evil of monarchy and anointing the first king of Israel. The Exodus, determining event for Israel, is seen by Jeremiah and second Isaiah as requiring replacement with a new act of God. Examples could be multiplied: the Hebrew Bible as it stands is constantly criticising itself and undermining its canonical authority. It actively demands the luxuriant variety of midrashic interpretation and resists incorporation into a dogmatic system. When the New Testament is added to form the Christian Bible the problem for the canonising impulse becomes more acute still. And although Christians have been more determined and more successful than Jews at interpreting the Bible as purveying a dogmatic and teleological world-view, this is done at a great price – the price of ignoring literal meanings and loose ends, the price of anti-Semitism. Torah is interpreted through the medium of Paul's controversies in the early Church, Jerusalem and the land through the medium of the new Jerusalem of the Apocalypse, and so on. Nor is this simply a matter of smoothing over the dialectic of Old and New Testaments. For within the New Testament canon are huge disparities of viewpoint – Luke's triumphalism against Mark's negative theology, Paul's and James's understandings of faith – and huge disparities in the depiction of the central character: not least the disparity, so clear to Blake, between the Friend of Sinners and the vengeful Conqueror of the Apocalypse. Yet all are bound together in one volume with each other, and with Law, Prophets and Writings, producing a book highly suitable for instigating both vision and controversy but not (one would have supposed) for underwriting a system of 'State religion'.

Blake's 'without contraries is no progression' could almost be used as an epigraph to the Bible. It is the same kind of polemical displacement of types, the same dialectical restlessness, the same resistance to closure, that informs Blake's 'Bible of Hell'. In particular, his combinations of text and design frequently juxtapose mythical, biblical, political and domestic images in ways that demand interpretation that is ethical and pragmatic, not just visionary. As Mee remarks, the pictures in the Lambeth books are rarely 'illustrations' of the words, but instead seek to 'stimulate the imaginative energy of the reader, who is brought in to play as an active intelligence that must strive to make sense of the difference'.[24] One can take *America* as an example. On plate 3, where the text speaks of the oppressive and dragon-like Prince of Albion, the intricate design shows at the bottom people fleeing from flames; but in the centre the flames mingle with those streaming from an Orcian fiery trumpet, and further signs of revolutionary hope are at the top, in the freely floating naked figure and the ears of corn sprouting from the letters of 'A PROPHECY'. The following plate, however, which begins the story of Orc's rising from the Atlantic, shows at the top the dragon form, with people at the bottom crouching among the rocks for safety. The juxtaposition stresses the inescapable conflict of the two states and prevents the reader from simply taking sides and being carried along by narrative or vision towards a happy ending. The irony continues on plate 8, whose text consists entirely of a bold rebellious speech by Orc, alluding to symbols of triumph from biblical accounts of resurrection and apocalypse. Orc is going to 'scatter religion abroad ... renew the fiery joy and burst the stony roof'; but in fact his words are enclosed in a cloud and surmounted by a stony roof on which crouches Urizen, with his arms outstretched over more rocks (*see plate* 2). The outcome of the revolutionary fervour is being questioned by its context, for Urizen presides over this anti-Urizenic speech – or are Urizen's arms actually clutching the stone or cloud for support to prevent him falling into the sea below (the world of Atlantis from which Orc has arisen)? This plate is echoed ironically a little further on, when on plate 10 Orc appears surrounded by flames, with his arms and head in a position identical to Urizen's on plate 8; but the text which the flames threaten to consume is anti-Orcian, the sounding of trumpets across the ocean by Albion's angel (*see plate* 3). The angel's bellicose threats on the text of the previous plate have already been subverted by its design, showing at the bottom the luxuriant harvest of the earth (which, presumably the oppressive angel cannot reap) and hidden beneath its corn a newborn child. The contraries continue: in fact, there are only two plates in *America* (6 and 15) where text and design could be said to correspond, and examples could be taken from other engraved books (for example *BU*, pls 2, 3; *MHH*, pls 1, 2, 24). They urge the energetic, dialectical, ethical kind of reading that is urged also by such juxtapositions in the Bible as Samuel's successively attacking and inaugurating monarchy or the irruptions of praise and peace in the vengeful narrative of Revelation. It is in this sense, perhaps more than any other, that Blake can be called a biblical – possibly a canonical – poet.

Leslie Tannenbaum has gone to great trouble to unearth biblical allusions in the text of the Lambeth books, seeing several of these as actually modelled on biblical books such as Deuteronomy, Canticles and Revelation. In them, he says,

> we see the typological process at work, as Blake seeks to re-create the Bible so as to make it applicable to his own time and thereby redeem the time by re-creating and thus redeeming the paradigmatic events depicted in the Bible from (to repeat Anthony Collins's phrase) 'corrupt glosses, innovations and traditions'.[25]

The process is, Tannenbaum maintains, a 'Christocentric' one, based on traditional Christian typology centred on the Incarnation. But this is questionable. Certainly Blake is concerned with redemption (if not with incarnation in the orthodox sense); but he is more active in disrupting than in redeeming the biblical 'paradigms'. One could say in fact that Blake is both more biblical and less biblical than in Tannenbaum's presentation of him. Less biblical, in that while he is clearly gleaning from biblical narrative and symbol there are nevertheless many other canons for him, or in a sense no canon: his 'Bible of Hell' is an ironic title, for he is not aiming either to supplement, to replace or to 'redeem' the existing Bible with a new authoritative text. But also *more* biblical, in that his method of 'contraries', outlined above, is itself a biblical one, even if it does not lend itself to the construction of a conclusive canon. A 'canon' is a measure, like Urizen's compasses and plummet, and Blake is the enemy of measuring, whether of time or space or righteousness: 'The hours of folly are measured by the clock, but of wisdom no clock can measure' (*MHH*, pl 7). This is the nub of Blake's disillusionment with Swedenborg, who betrayed the energetic biblical vision of contraries by resorting to definitions: a temptation to which Fuzon and sometimes even Los succumb and which Blake clearly experienced himself. For him Swedenborg is (in Harold Bloom's words) 'the eternal type of the prophet who becomes a new kind of priest, and by becoming a church loses his imaginative strength, until he concludes by renewing the religious categories of judgement he came to expose as impostures'.[26]

There are several other features of Blake's poetry that clearly adopt 'biblical' and in particular prophetic style. Tannenbaum draws attention to his episodic narration, use of digressions, chronological disruptions and discursive elaboration.[27] One could add his apocalyptic and Miltonic tendency to dissolve narrative altogether, even – especially – in works considered as 'epics'; the use, like that of Revelation, of grammatical quirks (with this go his idiosyncratic spelling and use of capital letters); his fondness for symbolic numbers, for names, genealogies and lists (such as the listing of the sons and daughters of Albion and of the counties of the British Isles in *Jerusalem*). Yet despite his extensive use of irony Blake is not setting out to parody the Bible in the way that he parodies Swedenborg. His 'prophecies' and 'Bible of Hell' are themselves scriptural writing in the sense that they are deliberately intertextual and are written not just for impact, not even just for conversion, but for *study*. This is the point of another feature that could be seen as biblical and that Blake erects into an aesthetic principle, namely his insistence on attention to what he calls 'Minute Particulars'. Bloom sees the 'frequently homely imagery of the Hebrew prophets' as the precedents for the poet's attention to detail in the account of the building of Los's city in *Jerusalem*.[28] The insistence on Minute Particulars runs through his polemical response to Reynolds's *Discourses*, with its hatred of Venetian painting and its praise of copying (*BE*, pp. 635–62), and it is expressed most authoritatively in the cry of the four living creatures in the third chapter of *Jerusalem*:

Let all indefinites be thrown into demonstrations,
To be pounded to dust & melted in furnaces of affliction.
He who would do good to another must do it in minute particulars;
'General Good' is the plea of the scoundrel, hypocrite & flatterer.
For art & science cannot exist but in minutely organized particulars,
And not in generalizing demonstrations of the rational power.

(*J*, 55:58–63)

This moral and aesthetic insistence on the particular, on close attention and study, might seem to conflict with other principles or characteristics of Blake – his completely sincere claims to direct vision, his support for artisan political radicalism, his persona as a prophet-bard like Isaiah or Los, communicating orally. But these are held in tension with his intellectual restlessness and seriousness. His works are both aristocratic and democratic (and have appealed to readers at extremes of both tendencies); they are, like Revelation, both esoteric and 'unsealed'. To take the question of orality, clearly Blake wants to be heard and heeded, and his gifts for aphorisms and ballad rhythms are used to convey that direct

address; yet it is evident both from the subtlety of their composition and from the great labour involved in their production that the
engraved books are intended to be studied and reread. The importance of the visual and the questioning of verbal rhetoric by juxtaposition of text and design and of text and text mean that a purely
oral (or aural or visual) reading is not possible: Blake's method
faces his readers with the dilemma of the duck/rabbit, which can
be elucidated only by analysis. For instance, the 'Praeludium' of
Europe has a picture vivid enough to make an immediate impact; its
text likewise, if read apart from the design, is rhythmic, alliterative,
evocative (*see plate 4*). But both text and design taken separately
and *a fortiori* taken together raise numerous questions and references that cannot be apprehended simply by verbal or visual
impact. Who is the 'nameless shadowy female'? How is the reader
to visualise the red sun and moon or 'my roots ... brandished in the
heavens, my fruits in earth beneath', and what are the implications
of these images? Or, turning to the design, why does the crouched
assassin have the profile of Edmund Burke and the traveller the
appearance of Bunyan's pilgrim with his burden? Who is the figure
in the bat-winged orb at the bottom, or the slave falling into the
abyss beside it, apparently unrelated structurally to the rest of the
design? To read the plate alertly one needs to follow up political
and literary allusions and to consider the consequences of their juxtaposition, building an interpretation that is, like Blake's vision,
both particular and cosmic. Hence the dictionaries, concordances
and learned elucidations which Blake's critics have both created
and regretted, sensing that beneath all the web of allusions is an
utterly simple vision and message. So there is. But the songs of innocence cannot stand on their own without tarnishing the vision:
experience and therefore digression and transgression are the only
way to its mature communication. Because Blake's vision and
message are as alien today as they were in his lifetime, it is questionable whether there is any way to apprehend them apart from
the imaginative and intellectual labour matching the labour in the
engraver's own workshop; questionable whether Bloom can be
right when he claims of *Milton* that 'the referential scaffolding, once
learned, can be thrown aside'.[29] As with the reading of the Bible,
one must return again and again to the minute particulars.

As we have seen, Blake opposes vision and 'allegory', disdaining
the artificiality of the second for the directness of the first. But the
communication of the vision cannot be direct, whether in writing or

in pictures. So in his notes on 'A Vision of the Last Judgement' he maintains that 'the Greek Fables originated in Spiritual Mystery & Real Visions which are lost & clouded in Fable & Allegory while the Hebrew Bible & the Greek Gospel are Genuine Preserv'd by the Saviour's Mercy', then adds, 'The Nature of my Work is Visionary or Imaginative   it is an Endeavour to Restore what the Ancients calld the Golden Age' (*BE*, p. 555). But the actual endeavour of restoration is laborious, requiring the use of language and art contaminated by traditions of 'Fable & Allegory' and therefore constantly threatened by the occlusion of vision. Before they can read, the visionary needs to teach his adherents to see, and this is a moral not just an aesthetic requirement: 'Every body does not see alike. ... As a man is So he Sees. As the Eye is formed such are its Powers' (*BE*, p. 702). Yet the business of writing and drawing and engraving is inherently artifical, and Blake's chosen method means that while for him vision precedes writing, for his audience reading must precede vision. He is a writing prophet, not an orator or a guru or a demonstrator; his declared aim is to 'rouse the faculties to act', and despite the strength of his feeling and the seriousness of his intent he is usually true to his belief in liberty and uses his techniques of irony and juxtaposition to avoid coercion and closure. Like the highly mysterious but evangelically challenging original ending of St Mark's Gospel, *Europe* ends with visual and verbal images that cannot be pressed into a conclusion either triumphant or conservative (*E*, pl. 15; cf. Mark 16:8; *see plate 5*). Is the saviour of the picture Orc or Los, both of whom are mentioned in the text? Are the flames destructive or purgative? Are the vines and redness signs of hope or of judgement? What is the 'strife of blood' to which Los calls his sons? It may be that the political situation at the time of engraving in 1794 was so uncertain that no 'conclusion' was possible for Blake; but it is likely also that, like St Mark, he is saying to his readers at the end of his 'prophecy', 'Now *you* must judge and act'. All that the artist and prophet of liberty can do is to rouse the faculties.

REVELATION REVERSED

Europe is an apocalyptic book, not only in its use of mythopoeia but also in its aim to unmask (*apokaluptein*) the Empire of the present, just as Revelation aims to unmask the Roman Empire. Yet its avoidance of closure is in marked contrast to the highly authoritative and conclusive end of the Apocalypse, suggesting that Blake's apocalypse, even in *Jerusalem*, is aiming to reverse rather than emulate or supplement John's. As John unmasks the beauty of the eternal city as the sordidness of a painted whore, so Blake unmasks the One seated on a Throne as a jealous tyrant clutching his rock and his ascetic worshippers as frightened insects caught in a web. The descent of the heavenly bride is displaced at the end of *Asia* by a cosmic orgasm (*The Song of Los*, pl. 7). The chaste Enitharmon of *Europe* is actually a domineering whore. In *Jerusalem*, Hoagwood argues, Blake actually 'employs the form of Revelation, presenting one symbolic vision after another' in order to rouse his readers to awareness of their own mental powers.[30] But is he not a poet even more dynamic and more polemical than this implies, concerned not just with perception but with creation and with new creation? What Blake is doing in his prophecies is taking on the mantle of John and entering his world in order to deconstruct it. His systematic use of several of the prominent symbols of the Apocalypse makes this clear.

There are first the images of corruption and oppression, which in Revelation are principally the dragon, the beast, the false prophet, the whore and Babylon. As we have seen, Blake makes extensive use of the image of Babylon as the opposite of Jerusalem and of that of the whore, whom he names Rahab.[31] They are bound together at the climax of the third chapter of *Jerusalem*:

> Thus Rahab is revealed –
> Mystery, Babylon the Great, the Abomination of Desolation,
> Religion hid in war, a dragon red & hidden harlot.
>
> *(J, 75:18–20)*

Similar words appear in *The Four Zoas*, where the clothing of the whore 'MYSTERY' is undertaken by Urizen's 'Synagogue of Satan' (*FZ*, viii.261–75; cf. Rev 2:9), and where Blake writes of Rahab's triumph:

> ... she took Jerusalem
> Captive, a willing captive, by delusive arts impelled
> To worship Urizen's dragon form, to offer her own children
> Upon the bloody altar. John saw these things revealed in heaven
> On Patmos Isle, & heard the souls cry out to be delivered;
> He saw the harlot of the kings of the earth, & saw her cup
> Of fornication, food of Orc & Satan, pressed from the fruit of Mystery.
>
> *(FZ, viii.576–82)*

Yes, that is what John saw, and nowhere else in Blake's writings is his self-identification with the seer of Patmos made so explicit. Yet the context makes clear that in Blake's eyes what John saw he misinterpreted and that the consequences of that misinterpretation are disastrous. The Almighty God of the Apocalypse is actually 'Urizen's dragon form', and the 'harlot of the kings of the earth' is not simply the Roman Empire but the whole apparatus of State religion, founded in its European form on the faith of the vengeful martyrs of John's churches. The verses from *The Four Zoas* are adapted in *Milton* plate 40, where 'Rahab Babylon' is also named 'Moral Virtue', and the images recur at the climax of the fourth chapter of *Jerusalem*, where 'Mystery, Babylon the Great, the druid dragon & hidden harlot' is seen as the incarnation of the 'natural religion' of Bacon, Newton and Locke (*J*, 93:21–6). Jews, Christians and Deists alike have betrayed Jesus' vision of Divine Humanity and created a monstrous seductive machine bowing to the jealous power of the 'Almighty'.

There is also the question of the identification of the dragon and the beast. In *America*, plate 4 (described above) shows Albion's Prince (George III) as a dragon, while on plate 7 Albion's angel addresses the 'serpent form'd' Orc as 'Blasphemous Demon, Antichrist' – though the design surrounding the wrathful words is one of pastoral innocence. There is the clear implication that the beast is the opposite of the Antichrist identified by Burke. And this reversal is given significance reaching beyond contemporary politics when in the conflict of Urizen and Los in the 'second night' of *The Four Zoas* the former is described in language belonging to both the God and the Dragon of the Apocalypse:

'… I am God from eternity to eternity! …
Lo, I am God the terrible destroyer, & not the saviour! …'
So spoke the prince of light, & sat beside the seat of Los.
Upon the sandy shore rested his chariot of fire.
Ten thousand thousand were his hosts of spirits on the wind …
(FZ, ii.76–85; cf. Rev 12:18)

The God of Jesus has been turned into the apocalyptic beast, heaven into hell and hell into heaven. The harvest and the vintage of Rev 14, as rewritten by Blake at the end of *The Four Zoas* and of *Milton*, are the destruction of Mystery, not of the unrighteous. And the lake of fire, stoked by the furnaces of Los, is not for the punishment of souls but for the destruction of the false 'spectre' that lures man away from his true humanity and delight. This is graphically and aphoristically expressed in the reversed writing that the minuscule poet has engraved on the scroll beside the despairing giant Albion in *Jerusalem* plate 37:

> Each Man is in his Spectre's power
> Until the arrival of that hour
> When his Humanity awake
> And cast his Spectre into the Lake.

The same reversal takes place with some of the images of salvation and divinity from Revelation. The perfect number seven, which is so important in the structure of that book, is at the least an ambiguous one for Blake. He does write of the seven angels of the presence and seven eyes of God.[32] But seven is also the number of the deadly sins, of the diseases and of the furnaces of Los, while on plate 10 of *Europe* the serpent of finitude, forming the oppressive druidic temple, is depicted with seven coils. Seven is the number of the days of creation, which for Blake is equivalent to the fall, as in the seven ages 'and a state of dismal woe' that pass over Urizen in the creation of his material body and senses, obliterating his eternal life (*BU*, pls 10–13). And it is the number of the sabbath, which for Blake is not the day of resurrection or liberation or innocence but of their opposites:

> Six days they shrunk up from existence,
> And on the seventh day they rested;
> And they blessed the seventh day, in sick hope –
> And forgot their eternal life.
>
> (*BU*, pl 25)

The seven trumpets of Revelation also face a metamorphosis. Blake usually associates trumpets not with liberation but with Sinai. 'The sound of a trumpet' in *The Book of Urizen* heralds Urizen's speech laying down the stony law, writing it in his book of brass that contains 'Seven deadly sins of the soul' (*BU*, pls 3, 4). On plate 3 of *America* is a picture of the flaming trumpet of (presumably) Orc; but the trumpets that actually sound across the Atlantic are those of Albion's angel, that is, of State religion causing war. The same connection of trumpets and war runs through *The Four Zoas* and *Jerusalem*. And when the seventh trumpet actually sounds at the climax of Enitharmon's dream in *Europe*, there is the supreme irony that the angel who wishes to blow it and destroy Orc is unable to

and that when it is blown by a member of Blake's unholy trinity the
destruction is actually that of the angels:

Furious
The red-limbed angel seized, in horror and torment,
The trump of the last doom; but he could not blow the iron tube!
Thrice he assayed presumptuous to awake the dead to Judgement.
A mighty spirit leaped from the land of Albion
Named Newton; he seized the trump and blowed the enormous blast.
Yellow as leaves of autumn, the myriads of angelic hosts
Fell through the wintry skies seeking their graves,
Rattling their hollow bones in howling and lamentation.

(*E*, pl 13)

The number four is also central to the symbolism of Revelation:
the number of the world, the four winds and the four living creatures, the cherubim seen first in Ezekiel's vision in harmonious conjunction with the four turning wheels. These are of course Blake's
'four zoas'; but the zoas are not superhuman beings but divided
aspects of the one Humanity, and in their fallen state the wheels do
not move in conjunction:

... the four Zoas are Urizen & Luvah & Tharmas & Urthona,
In opposition deadly, and their wheels in poisonous
And deadly stupor turned against each other loud and fierce ...

(*J*, 74:4–6; cf. *FZ*, i.285–9)

This is a development of the 'starry wheels' of Urizen; and again
they are warmongering and death-dealing, elements of Divine
Humanity perverted into cogs of the State. So 'three immense
wheels' are depicted at the foot of plate 22 of *Jerusalem* (*see plate 6*).
Above them are the embracing cherubim, the juxtaposition forming
an image of the heaven and hell that are to be married, and above
them in turn the words of Jerusalem,

Why should punishment weave the veil with iron wheels of war,
When forgiveness might it weave with wings of cherubim?

(*J*, 22:34f.; cf. 18:8–10)

The wheels are three in number, presumably as a sign of their
falling away from the perfection of Divine Humanity; or their

number could also represent Bacon, Newton and Locke, as suggested earlier in the poem, when Blake himself looks up to see 'the fourfold Man, the humanity in deadly sleep' and, in his desire to awaken Albion, the vision continues:

> I turn my eyes to the schools & universities of Europe
> And there behold the loom of Locke whose woof rages dire,
> Washed by the water-wheels of Newton. Black the cloth
> In heavy wreaths folds over every nation; cruel works
> Of many wheels I view, wheel without wheel, with cogs tyrannic
> Moving by compulsion each other: not as those in Eden, which
> Wheel within wheel in freedom revolve, in harmony & peace.
>
> (*J*, 15:14–20)

The circle or orb is usually a symbol of constriction for Blake, as are the wheels hére. But it is possible for the circle to be redeemed, for the wheels and the zoas to be reunited in one Humanity living not in war but in mutual forgiveness. This is a radical humanising and dynamising of the vision of the cherubim, whether in Ezekiel or in Revelation. Rather than evoking an eternal world of heavenly worship and harmony above the human world, they represent the possibility of that harmony through vision and forgiveness in the present.

Another symbol from both Revelation and the Hebrew Bible that Blake uses is that of the Tree of Life, which grows beside the river flowing from the throne of God in the new Jerusalem, its leaves for the healing of the nations (Rev 22:1f.). 'Art is the Tree of Life', says Blake, adding that 'Science is the Tree of Death' and engraving elsewhere on his Laocoon, 'Good & Evil/are Riches & Poverty a Tree of Misery/propagating Generation & Death' (*BE*, p. 273). These aphoristic twists of the biblical symbols are fleshed out in narrative and drawing throughout Blake's career. The bowed Tree of Misery looms menacingly over Los and Enitharmon on plate 1 of *America* and over the instructor of moral virtue in plate 14. It reappears on the haunting title-page of *The Book of Urizen*, combined with the oppressive symbols of stone, books and blindness and perhaps suggesting the Newtonian force of gravity (*see plate 7*).[33] The sequel, *The Book of Ahania*, whose third chapter powerfully tells of the tree's germinating on 'a rock/Barren, a rock which himself [Urizen]/From redounding fancies had petrified':

> Many tears fell on the rock,
> Many sparks of vegetation;

> Soon shot the pained root
> Of mystery under his heel.
> It grew a thick tree; he wrote
> In silence his book of iron. [34]

The tree spreads, roofing over Urizen and rerooting itself 'all around,/An endless labyrinth of woe' – as always for Blake, the forest is a symbol of oppression. And on that tree is nailed the corpse of Urizen's murdered son Fuzon (pl. 4). So Blake subverts the traditional typology of the cross as tree of life and source of atonement. For this tree of the Urizenic religion of sin and law and sacrifice is named 'the accursed TREE OF MYSTERY'. But it is not only an external Urizen who propagates this tree: Urizen is part of all Humanity. In 'The Human Abstract' this tree with its 'dismal shade/Of mystery' is watered by the cruelty that stems from mutual fear, and at the end of the poem,

> The gods of the earth and sea
> Sought through nature to find this tree.
> But their search was all in vain –
> There grows one in the human brain.
> (SE XII)

The flourishing in Eden or Jerusalem of the Tree of Life that is Art depends on humanity's release from the oppressive shade of the Tree of Mystery, the internalised State religion of the externalised jealous God.

This brings us to the most radical deconstruction of the imagery of the Apocalypse, adumbrated in Blake's use of all the symbols surveyed above. That is the symbol of God, the One seated on the Throne, the object of the ceaseless heavenly worship. Whether in his Mosaic, his Johannine, his druidic, his Miltonic or his Newtonian form, this god is for Blake a tyrant. Long before Feuerbach he writes, in conclusion to his brilliantly concise history of world religion on plate 11 of *The Marriage of Heaven and Hell*, that 'all deities reside in the human breast'. It is a theme reiterated in the *Marriage*, where to the angel's fury the poet insists that 'the worship of God is honouring his gifts in other men.... Those who envy or calumniate great men hate God, for there is no other God.' The theology of these aphorisms is given extensive narrative form in *The Four Zoas, Milton* and *Jerusalem*. Here the delusive and oppressive religion requiring systems of law, punishment, atonement

and theodicy is contrasted with the innocent delight of mutual forgiveness in the 'Divine Humanity', 'the universal man, to whom be
glory ever more. Amen'.[35] The Divine Humanity is identified with
Jesus – and 'God is Jesus' (*BE*, p. 274). But it cannot be restricted to
his body in either its historical or its ecclesial form, since it compre-
hends each and every human being as one man or Albion.[36] To
Blake all other gods are false and all worship pathological; only
with the death of 'God' is the apocalyptic reconciliation that ends
Jerusalem possible.[37]

THE BOOKS OF FIRE

This persistent and polemical transvaluation of images is of course
something that Revelation itself does with equal dedication within
the context of the Roman Empire's version of State religion. Blake is
engaged in a sustained, serious but ironic attempt to rewrite and
redraw the Apocalypse in words and visual images similar to its
own and adopting both John's visionary particularity and his 'infernal' and 'corrosive' method of contraries. There was in the 1790s a
growing awareness of the constitutive, rather than simply descrip-
tive, powers of language – an awareness owing much to Lowth's
sensitivity to *dabar* and *mashal* in the Hebrew Bible. Like Tom Paine,
Blake rejects the authority of Church and State to name and define
and curse, arrogating such performative authority to his own words
from the time of 'A Song of Liberty'.[38] 'Fourfold vision' is to be
restored by his own apocalyptic art,

Driving outward the body of death in an eternal death and
    resurrection,
Awaking it to life among the flowers of Beulah, rejoicing in unity
In the four senses, in the outline, the circumference & form, for ever
In forgiveness of sins which is self-annihilation. It is the Covenant
    of Jehovah.
The four living creatures, chariots of Humanity Divine
    incomprehensible,
In beautiful paradises expand. These are the four rivers of paradise
And the four faces of humanity fronting the four cardinal points
Of heaven, going forward, forward – irresistible from eternity to
    eternity.

                                                    (*J*, 98:20–27)

In contrast, 'May God us keep/From Single vision and Newton's sleep!' Only with the restored fourfold vision can humanity discover the true and particular outline of eternal reality, undistorted by 'Venetian' colorist blurring. What is heard, seen, written and drawn by the new John is the Infinite shattering reason, religion and empire – Newton, the Pope and George III, or Urizen, Vala and Hand. So Blake's Jerusalem relates to the city and bride of Rev 21, where there is no temple or sun or moon, no time and no death, no division between God and humanity; but while John only hints that this involves the dissolution of his previous scenes of heavenly worship, Blake abolishes such imperial projections from the start, replacing eternal worship with 'eternal delight'. The new heaven and new earth 'will come to pass by an improvement of sensual enjoyment', though first the 'doors of perception' must be cleansed (*MHH*, pl. 14). This requires the actual destruction of the cloudy empire of reason and religion that is historically built upon Revelation's own displacement of the Roman Empire; hence the need for strenuous 'mental fight' and the dedicated study of vision and prophecy such as Blake himself publishes.

Does such vision therefore constitute a new scripture and its reading a new hermeneutics? Since Blake is often seen as creating a new 'canon' out of fragments of biblical and hermetic tradition, it is worth examining what he actually writes and draws of another image frequent in Revelation, that of the book or scroll (cf. Rev 1:11, 5:1, 10:8–10, 20:12). The title-page of *The Book of Urizen* (1794) shows the bearded creator crouching beneath a tree in front of two tables of stone; his eyes are shut and his foot rests on an open book covered with meaningless hieroglyphs, while both hands reach out inscribing more letters on stone (*see plate 7*). The picture is a wry comment on the Mosaic religion of moral law whose stone tablets Blake saw re-erected in both the orthodox Christianity and the 'natural religion' of his own day, and it satirically undermines the picture on plate 5 of the same book, where Urizen, now with his eyes blazing and halo above him, holds up the book for obedient reading. But on that book are still the same hieroglyphs that forbid understanding and imagination. Far from wishing to revive a hermetic or mystical scripture from scraps of Neoplatonism or Behmenism, Blake is the declared enemy of 'Mystery' and secrecy. The text of the previous plate sees the writings of this blind law-giver as harder even than stone, for they form 'the book/Of eternal brass':

> Here alone I, in books formed of metals,
> Have written the secrets of wisdom,
> The secrets of dark contemplation
> By fightings and conflicts dire
> With terrible monsters sin-bred,
> Which the bosoms of all inhabit –
> Seven deadly sins of the soul.
>
> (*BU*, pl. 4)

But as the sight appears of 'his hand/On the Rock of Eternity unclasping/The book of brass', those deadly sins erupt to force Urizen to run, delving furiously among 'deserts and rocks' for a cave to hide in, fleeing from the vengeance he himself has caused, like the kings of the earth after the opening of the sixth seal (Rev 6:15–17). The fall of Urizen recurs as vigorously in the 'sixth night' of *The Four Zoas*, where he collapses and dies 'in the bosom of slime'; but his hardness recovers, and as his flight continues

> ... still his books he bore in his strong hands, & his iron pen;
> For when he died they lay beside his grave, & when he rose
> He seized them with a gloomy smile.
>
> (*FZ*, vi.164–6)

The book of brass and iron pen are weapons more destructive than any swords or spears, since their hieroglyphs underwrite the whole life-denying system of what Paine called 'the manuscript assumed authority of the dead'; its author Urizen combines the oppressive features of Yahweh, Moses, Bacon, Newton, Locke and George III. Insofar as this book is identified with the Bible, it is with Watson's Bible; and insofar as Blake wears the mantle of Urizen's enemies Orc and Los, he is an anti-canonical poet, the hater of books and laws and predictions.

Yet the irony (of which Blake himself was supremely conscious) is that he himself is a maker of books – in fact a maker of books in a more literal sense and in a more laborious way than any other poet in history. Moreover his books are filled with obscurity, encouraging a hieroglyphical hermeneutic and leading into a referential maze as intricate as Urizen's 'net of religion'. Blake is too serious a prophet to remain content with satire or parody. He is obscure and ironic only because he can find no other way of writing and drawing, since – as he sees it – language and consciousness have been so corrupted by centuries of the 'State religion' of Urizen's followers. Vala – whose name is presumably a pun on 'veil' and who largely inherits the oppressive power of Urizen in Blake's later poetry – has cast her veil of mystery over the powers of human expression, seducing even genuine prophets like Milton into apostasy. Like Ezekiel eating dung and lying on his right side and then on his left, Blake must write in parables and myths if he is to 'cleanse the doors of perception' (*MHH*, pl. 13f). But he will do so, he claims, not in books of brass but in books of fire.

Two of the 'memorable fancies' of *The Marriage of Heaven and Hell* comment ironically on the fall and the redemption of writing. In the third (plate 15) the poet enters in turn the six chambers of 'a printing-house in Hell', where he sees the infernal (that is, right) 'method in which knowledge is transmitted from generation to generation' – the hollowing of the cave of knowledge by dragons, its adornment by vipers, its expansion by eagles, the liquefying of metal by 'lions of flaming fire' and their being cast into the expanse by 'unnamed forms', only after which are they 'received by men' as books and 'arranged in libraries'. This beautiful, energetic, liquid and scorching process is the opposite of the formulation by synods or law-makers of a 'book of brass'. But such a book of metal has the Bible become, as it is presented in the next 'memorable fancy' (plates 17–20). After an angel has taken the poet to see a vision of his fate in hell, the poet escapes by the power of his imagination and takes the angel in turn to see his fate, returning to the stable and the church, where 'I took him to the altar and opened the Bible, and lo! it was a deep pit, into which I descended, driving the angel before me'. Inside are 'seven houses of brick' (the seven churches of Asia?), and the one they enter contains a gathering of warring 'monkeys, baboons, and all of that species, chained by the middle, grinning and snatching at one another'. The stench of this hermeneutical pit overpowers poet and angel, so that 'we went into the mill, and in my hand I brought the skeleton of a body, which in the mill was Aristotle's *Analytics*'. Such is the stinking corruption of writing and the Bible as they have been solidified by 'angelic' churches and philosophers.

So if the corruptions of religion are to be overcome and the prophetic inspiration of 'Poetic Genius' is to be recovered, a redemption of reading and writing is necessary. The metal of an authoritative canon must be melted by 'hellish' fire, a new hermeneutic must be forged. In plate 24, accordingly, poet and converted angel 'often read the Bible together in its infernal or diabolical sense'. But there is a hint that this does not go far enough, that interpretation is still a subsidiary activity liable to Urizenic corruption; for, Blake adds cryptically, 'I have also the Bible of Hell'. That is, not just a new hermeneutic but a new poetic: the companion of Isaiah and Ezekiel is, it seems, to create a new inspired canon which will do battle with the religion founded on the solidification of the old. So Northrop Frye infers from the great effort Blake put into his work that 'the engraved poems were intended to form an exclusive and definitive canon' and that his 'poetic testament or "Bible of Hell" was ready for the world, apart from engraving, by about the end of 1808', while less sweepingly Leslie Tannenbaum describes the Lambeth books as Blake's 'attempt to emulate the biblical canon by combining a number of disparate books into a coherent and unified vision of human life from the Creation to the Apocalypse'.[39]

Such claims need considerable qualification, however. It is not just that Blake's 'Bible of Hell' – say, the engraved books that succeed that promise in *The Marriage of Heaven and Hell*, from *America* to *Jerusalem* – is filled with reference to the old biblical canon, which the poet continually (perhaps increasingly) sees as inspired. That fact in itself could lead one to view the works of Blake as intended as a kind of third Testament. But affording any kind of canonical status to Blake's works runs counter also to two of the poet's most consistent principles as well as to his highly deliberate method of book production. The principle that 'without contraries is no progression' (*MHH*, pl. 3) undermines any achievement of closure, any production that is 'exclusive and definitive': none of the constant objects of Blake's belief – the experience of 'sweet delight', the necessity of 'mental fight', the exercise of forgiveness – is such as to encourage a state of stasis. That would in any case be suspected by a second principle, namely Blake's consistently antinomian attitude to all authority, whether of church or state or classical tradition. In Blake's riposte to Watson's defence of the historical authority of the book which he (Blake) undoubtedly read as inspired there is a radical protestantism:

> The Bible or Peculiar Word of God, Exclusive of Conscience or the Word of God Universal, is that Abomination which like the Jewish ceremonies is for ever removed & henceforth every man may converse with God & be a King & Priest in his own house (*BE*, p. 615).

Of course anybody can betray his or her principles. But in Blake's case there is less cause for suspecting this because of the variety of versions of the supposedly 'canonical' books produced by his method of engraving. To hunt down a Blakean *Urtext* takes us straight into the vision of the bestial biblical scholars in their deep pit, for the production of his books was more erratic even than the transmission of the biblical ones: as S. L. Carr suggests, there is a 'radical variability' among the few surviving copies of Blake's engraved plates (particularly in their colouring) which militates against any notion of a final or authoritative text.[40] Nor is there any definitive order of the plates of *Europe, Milton* or *Jerusalem*, let alone *The Four Zoas*.

I would suggest then that Blake is aiming neither to create a new canon nor simply to interpret an old one. He wants to say something that to him is utterly self-evident but which he believes has been tragically veiled by the vegetative delusion of State religion, under which term he undiscriminatingly subsumes natural religion, moral law, deism, priestcraft and kingship. The veiling is all the more tragic because more than anywhere else Blake recognises kindred spirits in the biblical writers and in Jesus, whose vision has been canonically distorted to bolster the *status quo*. So he writes in their style and using many of their symbols, but systematically displaces those symbols and scatters them within a non-biblical mythopoeia, in order to 'rouse the faculties to act': the reading of both his own poetry and the Bible's is to lead into the perception of the infinite, of the Divine Humanity rather than its natural spectre, into the world redeemed by forgiveness that the poet already inhabits. But even in the work which seems closest to a programme or *ars poetica, The Marriage of Heaven and Hell* – perhaps most of all there – Blake refuses a 'straight-talking' or 'objective' stance. As Dan Miller notes, 'this is an apocalypse of, not beyond, contrariety'.[41] Only by rewriting the Bible can Blake make it readable; only by poiesis can he redeem the satanic work of hermeneutics. And it is evident in his depiction of Los and Urizen, as well as in some of his personal letters, that for all his belief in the reality of his vision the actual material of words and figures was constantly threatening to lure him back into the web of the natural world and tempting him to deny imagination (that is, to sin against the Holy Spirit). This is the meaning of the conflicts between Los and his spectre in *The Four Zoas* and between Milton and his spectre in *Milton*. And since the gloomy Urizen is also a creator, Blake is in him too. As David Erdman comments on the frontispiece to *Europe* ('The Ancient of Days'), 'the power of this emblem is beyond satire because the artist is not outside the picture but in its core'; while from *The Book of Urizen* Harold Bloom draws

> a strong sense of the internal menace embodied in that fallen angel of thought. Urizen is within us as he was within Blake, and there is even a self-mocking aspect of his poem, demonstrating how uncomfortable Blake was in trying to keep the compass-wielding categorizer in his place. Even a parody of an orthodox cosmology begins to be overly involved in the Urizenic spirit, and Blake may have begun to worry that as a true poet he might be of Jehovah's party without knowing it.[42]

The struggle to be faithful to prophetic vision is one with that of Jeremiah or Ezekiel or of Jesus in Gethsemane. It requires the utmost attention to 'the Minute Particulars' if the prophet is not to relapse into the conventional perception inculcated by State religion, into secrecy or into 'allegory'. To read prophecy as prediction or to write it as an 'Arbitrary Dictator' is to attempt to bind the eternal in chains and nets of religion, and

> He who binds to himself a joy
> Does the winged life destroy;
> But he who kisses the joy as it flies
> Lives in eternity's sunrise.
> *(PN XXXIX)*

So in the 'seventh night' of *The Four Zoas* Orc, who is bound in chains against his will, mocks Urizen, who is bound in snow and cloud of his own devising:

> … still thy pen obdurate
> Traces the wonders of futurity, in horrible fear of the future.
> *(FZ, vii.85f.)*

The phrase of Orc–Blake is acute. The self-absorption of Urizen–Newton is an obsession with measuring, even the measuring of futurity, that actually derives from fear, the refusal to kiss the joy as it flies and to discover the delight of forgiveness. So – more frequently in fact than he is shown in control with his compasses –

Blake depicts Urizen as one who is bound: under rocks (*BU*, pl. 9), in water (*BU*, pl. 12) or in chains (*BU*, pl. 22). It is the ironic consequence of his own relentless binding, numbering, measuring and dividing, his chronologer's lust for 'futurity':

> Times on times he divided and measured
> Space by space in his ninefold darkness,
> Unseen, unknown...
>
> (*BU*, pl. 3; cf. pl. 20)

This is the same fear as that which makes biblical interpreters huddle in their bookish dens with their 'prophetic' calculations of futurity; and, Blake implies, it actually forbids entry into futurity just as into eternity. Far from being eschatological, it is cyclical, a binding to the menacing wheels that churn at the bottom of plate 22 of *Jerusalem*, 'three immense wheels, turning upon one another, Into non-entity' (*J* 18:8f.; *see plate 6*). The prophet's task is not to calculate the movements of the stars or the decrees of an alien god for the future but to liberate humanity from the grinding revolutions of this meaningless cycle. So in his direct address 'To the Christians' that opens the final chapter of *Jerusalem*, Blake interprets the vision of Ezekiel 1 through his own vision of a devouring fiery wheel. He asks a 'watcher' what it is called:

> He answered, 'It is the wheel of religion.'
> I wept and said, 'Is this the law of Jesus,
> This terrible devouring sword turning every way?'
> He answered, 'Jesus died because he strove
> Against the current of this wheel: its name
> Is Caiaphas, the dark preacher of death,
> Of sin, of sorrow, and of punishment,
> Opposing nature! It is Natural Religion:
> But Jesus is the bright preacher of life...'
>
> (*J*, 77:58–66)

The irony here is not only that 'Natural Religion' is against nature. It is compounded when the manifestation of Natural Religion (the Babylon-worshipping 'Bacon, Newton, Locke') becomes at the climax of the poem a 'signal of the morning' (*J*, 93:20–26). But above all there is the irony that the apocalyptic unveiling comes by a denial of the 'apocalyptic' mentality. The Lamb is no longer wrathful, no sword comes from the mouth of Jesus; no angel measures the temple, and no god decrees the destruction of the earth or the punishment of the wicked. Rather the destruction comes from the dissolution of humanity itself, and the Divine Humanity embodied in this 'bright preacher of life' is concerned only to forgive and to create. The rewriting of Apocalypse by Blake's Jesus is as radical as the rewriting of Genesis by his Urizen.

To say that glory is due not to an objective God but to the Divine Humanity or that 'all deities reside in the human breast' is not so much a mystical as an apocalyptic assertion, built upon the conviction of visionary power that stemmed from the poet's identification of himself with the seer and prophet and bard and political witness of Patmos. It is perhaps to John that he alludes when in *The French Revolution* the inhabitant of one of the seven towers of the Bastille is a man 'confined for a writing prophetic' (*FR*, 29). There is certainly allusion to John's own model Ezekiel when Blake writes of himself in *Jerusalem*:

> Trembling I sit day and night; my friends are astonished at me.
> Yet they forgive my wanderings, I rest not from my great task –
> To open the eternal worlds, to open the immortal eyes
> Of man inwards into the worlds of thought – into Eternity
> Ever expanding in the bosom of God, the human imagination.
>
> (*J*, 5:16–20)

And the domestic and angelic imagery of plates 36 and 42 of *Milton* show that for Blake, Felpham (the village where he lived under William Hayley's patronage from 1800 to 1803 and where it seems that the form of both *Milton* and *Jerusalem* was conceived) *was* Patmos; just as Tyburn (the place of executions in London) was Golgotha. In his picture of 'The Angel of the Revelation' (c. 1805), Blake shows the seer–scribe writing below the gigantic figure of the revealing angel; shows himself, that is, for like John, like the tiny poet engraving his mirror-writing on plate 37 of *Jerusalem*, Blake is actually inside the biblical canon (*see plate 1*). Though an astute and persistent reader of the Bible, as of Milton, he is a poet, a maker, working creatively and polemically from within; not an interpreter standing outside, like Newton with his measuring instruments or the young Coleridge with his 'religious musings'. It is that stance that gives him – more prophetically still than Shelley – the authority to unveil the 'Unveiling' of John and the Veil of State religion stemming from it.

7

The Half-Unravelled Web

The survey above, which ends rather abruptly at 1834 (the death of Coleridge), shows the prominent place Revelation maintained in English self-understanding and religious thought well after the seventeenth century. The story could be continued, but I hope that enough has been said to indicate the persistent appeal of the book to people of a very wide range of temperaments and its initial affinity to their systems. It served as far more than a reservoir of vivid images. The Apocalypse buttressed theological doctrines of the providence and justice of God and historical outlines of world chronology. It provided rhetorical frameworks for political arguments both radical and conservative and for evangelical appeals for religious conversion. It supported plans for a return to primitive Christianity; it predicted the dissolution of Church and world in the near future. It verified science; it overturned human reason. It represented metaphysical realities; it described earthly events. It epitomised a passing stage of first-century religious imagination; it was an authoritative vision for all ages. It was exalted as the key to scripture; it was dismissed as an embarrassing appendix to it.

All of these contradictory interpretations brought the book alive and enabled it to speak to different constituencies. Yet none of them can provide *the* meaning of the text. For while the Apocalypse of John constantly invites interpretation by its vividness, its obscurity and its authority, it actively resists the search for meaning. It is not just that the images and narrative of Revelation are multivalent: they seem to constitute a book that is multi-veiled. For John claims to unveil a reality beyond the text, and indeed the text itself can be unveiled so far; but then its structure or its imagery veils the reader's mind again, and any historical or spiritual reality that they might reveal recedes. Eichhorn with his historical knowledge, Irving with his religious zeal, Faber with his political seriousness: each failed to provide a convincing interpretation of the text after all his massive labour. Even so astute a reader as Coleridge, who combined the qualities of all these three and also brought to the text

209

poetic sensibility and metaphysical yearning, failed as an interpreter of the Apocalypse.

Yet where Coleridge failed it could be argued that Shelley and
even more Blake succeeded and that they did so by leaping over
the hermeneutical endeavour in order to rewrite Revelation. They
relativise the canon by ceasing to treat it as an object for interpretation. Instead they wrestle and create *within* the text, becoming or at
any rate presenting themselves as prophets or visionaries just as
John himself was. Their stance distances them both from orthodox
Christianity with its concern for authoritative text and from
Newtonian principles of perception and investigation; it achieves
what Coleridge had adumbrated in his theories of symbol and
imagination and in the vision of *Kubla Khan* but had skirted when
it came to involvement with the biblical text. While Coleridge
resented the intrusion of Eichhorn's historical investigations as he
resented that of the person on business from Porlock, perhaps for
his sanity he actually needed both objectivising forces. For exposure to the world of authoritative vision means the risk of madness,
which perhaps only one who seriously believes that 'all deities
reside in the human breast' is prepared to run.

In the opening of *The Fall of Hyperion*, Keats promised to rehearse
a dream that he hoped would prove to be a poet's rather than a
fanatic's.[1] As it proceeds, Keats's dream contains a further vision,
which Moneta, like the angel of the Apocalypse, unveils and interprets to the poet,

> Whereon there grew
> A power within me of enormous ken
> To see as a God sees, and take the depth
> Of things as nimbly as the outward eye
> Can size and shape pervade. The lofty theme
> At those few words hung vast before my mind,
> With half-unravelled web. I set myself
> Upon an eagle's watch, that I might see,
> And seeing ne'er forget.
>
> (I.302–10)

In the Romantic period, the word 'unravel' retained its older sense
of 'reveal or expose'.[2] But significantly, despite this heady aim, *The
Fall of Hyperion* remained unfinished – like its predecessor and like
the vision of *Kubla Khan*. The transcription and the interpretation of

vision are fraught with difficulty, since the verbal unravelling threatens to dissolve them or to entangle them in a web more complex still. If people have visions – as Keats and Blake and Coleridge all firmly believed they did – then the institutionalisation of them in what Blake called 'the Net of religion' is almost inevitable.

It was ironically in the age of Constantine and Christian Empire that the vision of Patmos was finally institutionalised within the biblical canon. So begins the hermeneutical trail that leads in our own century to D. H. Lawrence's obsession with and vituperations against the 'book of thwarted power-worship'.[3] There are two religions in the New Testament, claims Lawrence: 'the Christianity of tenderness' focused on Jesus and 'the Christianity of self-glorification' focused on the Apocalypse. And although the latter really rules only one book, its appeal has outweighed that of Jesus, Peter, Paul and John the evangelist put together.[4] Lawrence mocks the priggish, virginal, 'bourgeois' New Jerusalem and the mean-spirited 'Patmossers' gloating over their enemies' torment in the lake of fire. And he mocks the tortured attempts of Christian interpreters like his contemporary the erudite Archdeacon Charles to draw from this violent text a lesson of Christian love and orthodoxy. Yet from Charles's massive commentary Lawrence himself draws a theory of the Apocalypse as a book dismembered and divided against itself. Charles saw the original book of John of Patmos as a Christian apocalypse drawing on both Jewish and pagan imagery; but an ignorant Christian editor, whom Charles castigates in the most scornful terms, had hacked it about and overlaid it with glosses, so that the interpreter now has to be an archaeologist delving for the real gold of inspiration. In a less meticulous but more passionate way, Lawrence the poet and ideologist postulates a book that has not only a sevenfold seal but also a fourfold palimpsest, so to speak: a vital pagan original, a scribal Jewish adaptation, the semi-Christian adaptation by John, and the final redaction by Charles's ignorant Christian editor. The last three he sees as increasingly mean-spirited lapses from the glory of the first, from the vision of sun and moon and stars, of dragon and woman and *kosmokrator*; but it is a vision that even through the grimy filter of John's envy, of chapels and archdeacons and a petty religion of sin and personal salvation, can still thrill the decayed heart of modern man (Lawrence is less hopeful about modern woman) to luxuriate in a religion of pagan sensual intuition. In place of the vulgar collectivism of the age of Lenin man can live once more in the joyful collectivism of the cosmos. So Lawrence ends his satirical but serious tract with a call to worship the sun. His attack on the Apocalypse is itself an apocalyptic one. For the evil dragon of Logos and mind and linear history can be conquered – and ironically the good dragon of the new era still crouches below the vulgar 'Christian' imagery of the last and most destructive book of the Bible.[5]

Lawrence's exorcising commentary has hardly been noticed by Christian exegetes, even in his own country, since its publication in 1931. But in its cavalier way it raises three points that have troubled the Church from the beginning of its wrestling with Revelation, three modes of *displacement* that unsettle the pattern of orthodox belief and devotion, even when as in the eighteenth century the book is apparently domesticated. First is the Apocalypse's Iscariot role and the apparent incompatibility of its spirit with that of the neighbourly love hymned in the rest of the New Testament: does the book pervert the gospel of love, as numerous uneasy Christians suspect, or does it actually complete it, as subtle Christian interpreters have tried to demonstrate? Secondly, the book seems to be at odds not only with the New Testament but with itself: whether or not one believes with Lawrence and Charles in various layers of editing, there are aporias and changes of strata in the book that make it almost impossible to draw from it a coherent 'message' or even a coherent spirit. The book, says Lawrence, shows 'the things that the human heart secretly yearns after'; but it does so 'by its very resistance'.[6] Apocalypse by its very nature scorns the restraints of earthbound logic. And thirdly, in this engagement with the inevitable and divided Judas, the reader is likely to undergo apocalyptic tendencies herself, to find her criteria of sanity being undermined. Its rhetoric is in a literal sense amazing, luring the reader into a maze. Turnings purport to lead to a hermeneutical centre, but in reality they become either cul-de-sacs or openings into a different world where new bearings must be sought. But could it be that, by dismissing the rhetoric of apocalypse and retreating into the doctrinal core of the New Testament, those interpreters of the New Testament who stopped at the end of the letter of Jude were also dismissing the archetypes that originate and invigorate the Christian and any other religion?[7]

There is an interesting parallel here between D. H. Lawrence and his contemporary C. G. Jung. Jung was much more sympathetic to Christianity than Lawrence, however idiosyncratic his interpretation of it; but he too saw the Book of Revelation as both inimical to the conscious spirit of the gospel of love and inevitable as the cry of a deeper unconscious religion against the impossibility of that spirit.[8] Unlike Lawrence and Charles, Jung supposes that the John who wrote the vengeful Apocalypse is the same as the John who wrote the first Epistle, with its reiteration of the command to selfless love: this, he suggests, is not illogical but psychologically appropriate, since the human impossibility of practising his perfectionist teaching was likely to lead such a person to revelations expressing the repressed negative and dark feelings.[9] Jung's argument does not depend on the identification of the two authors, however, since what is repressed in the gospel of love is the *collective* unconscious's need for a gospel of fear. For Jung this need is fulfilled by the resurgence of the brutal Yahweh despite the greater intelligence of his son Satan and the greater purity of his new son Jesus. John the apostle of love – and the Christian ego since his time – fail to see that 'the power of destruction and vengeance is that very darkness from which God had split himself off when he became man'.[10] In the collective Christian psyche, as in individual psychoanalysis, the archetypes that the conscious or doctrinal mind has repressed will reassert themselves. Jung sees the epitome of this in the vision of the woman in Rev 12, where 'heathen' vital forces for which the Jewish and Christian cosmos has no official place are resurgent: John's unconscious turns to the humane myths of Leto and Apollo and of Tammuz or Adonis, while his conscious mind tries unsuccessfully to assimilate this to the scheme of the war of the Lamb and the army of martyrs. And the wrathful Lamb itself (really an 'aggressive and irascible ram', as Jung remarks) is in turn the resurgence of an archetype repressed by the unbearable light of the teaching of divine love. This psychoanalytical deconstruction of the Book of Revelation is for Jung the partial unveiling of the conflicts of the gods, that is, of the deep and necessary conflicts of human religion. Partial, because the conflict is too complex for any complete representation and because the conscious mind cannot in reality separate itself from the unconscious; but an unveiling nevertheless – that is, an 'apocalypse'.

The role of this Judas, then, would seem to be a religiously vital one, instilling scepticism about the orthodox system to which its authoritative place in the canon would suggest it belongs, while at the same time affirming the possibility of faith that is socially and psychologically transformative. Like twentieth-century surrealist

and apocalyptic writing, the Book of Revelation is constantly trans-
gressing the boundaries of the 'real'. It is not just that many of the
images are in fact unimaginable. The transgressions seem to have a
polemical point, a determination to subvert the political, cosmolo-
gical and philosophical categories by which the book's readers
place themselves in the world. So the glory of the imperial power
becomes a tawdry harlot, the sky is rolled up like a scroll, and the
dwelling of God is with humanity. Though it remains in the canon,
the Apocalypse cannot be subsumed in a logical (or theological)
system. Noting that 'Revelation's theological and historical location
is in the margins of the Christian canon and of mainline theology',
Elisabeth Schüssler Fiorenza sees it as speaking particularly today
on three 'margins' of society: those of fundamentalist literalism, of
revolutionary utopianism, and of feminist criticism.[11] But in fact all
these are movements that generate their own sub-systems which
may in turn veil the archetypes of raw religion and arrest the
dynamic of apocalyptic reading. If the reader in a pluralist world is
to persist with the unveiling of Unveiling, to work from within the
text and not to rest in any 'interpretation' that makes the text an
object and places it among other objects, then she becomes aware of
the infinite recession of veils, the relentless transgression of further
boundaries.

It seems that John himself sensed the deconstructive power of his
own vision and was alarmed by it. He, or the Christ who unveils
reality to him, tears the imperial mask from Rome. The centre of
the earth is swallowed up, God comes to dwell with humanity,
and, fittingly in the face of such inversion, the language of the
Greek world has its grammar made chaotic. But if Rome is relativised, if even the boundary of heaven and earth is relativised,
where is the process to stop? There is no temple in the new
Jerusalem, though the throne of God and the worship of him continue (Rev 22:3). Here is a process of decentring that is not fully
carried through. Thomas Altizer, who sees the apocalyptic Blake
and Hegel, preachers of the death of God, as inaugurators of the
modern world, proclaims that with the advances since their time in
philosophy, physics and psychology, 'the very possibility of centre
as such has ended' and that 'now chaos and cosmos are indistin-
guishable'.[12] But, as Altizer argues, the roots of this crisis lie in biblical dialectic and apocalyptic religion, and the fear of it goes back
far before the nineteenth century. The chaos threatens John's own
book and the canon that it closes; perhaps the 'great high wall'

around the new Jerusalem that excludes the unclean and the curses hanging over those who alter the book are desperate attempts to repair the dike that has been breached by vision.

This is partly why it is hard to take the book as it stands – rather than the apocalyptic spirit that initiates it and bursts beyond its narrative – as (in Edward Schillebeeckx's words) 'a real basis for a *Christian* theology of liberation'.[13] Such statements need qualification – and often receive them. Schillebeeckx himself notes that John is not interested in the liberation of those other than Christians, while Fiorenza, in her liberationist reading of the Apocalypse, is very aware of the other uses to which the book is put in twentieth-century America and stresses that 'Revelation will elicit a fitting theo-ethical response only in those sociopolitical situations that cry out for justice'.[14] So Allan Boesak, writing in 1987 from such a situation, can say with some authority that those 'who do not struggle together with God's people for the sake of the gospel, and who do not feel in their own bodies the meaning of oppression and the freedom and joy of fighting against it shall have grave difficulty understanding this letter from Patmos'.[15] Christopher Rowland and Mark Corner, who see apocalyptic as providing 'a discourse for social criticism', recognise that its outlook can nevertheless be 'appropriated and neutralized by its incorporation into the dominant ideology', but put their hope in the radical dualism of such literature as the power to unmask injustice.[16] Yet the dualism is double- or treble-edged. As well as Rowland's ethical dualism, the Apocalypse can speak as a metaphysical dualism, which by stressing the transcendent and futuristic realm is actually (according to Jack Sanders) a 'retreat from the ethical dimension' that makes the book's 'existence and its place in the canon..., in the fullest sense of the word, evil'.[17] Or, through its apparent exclusion of women from the new Jerusalem and its stereotyping of female roles, it can speak as a dualism of gender which – in Tina Pippin's words – means that 'the transformation of society in the Apocalypse is only partial transformation ... gender oppression is left untouched by the sword of God'.[18] The diversity of 'rhetorical situations' for the reading of the book make a definition of *the* response or *the* meaning impossible, the hermeneutical quest doomed to frustration. It seems that the process of unravelling begun in the vision and writing of Patmos has opened a canon of worms.

The question remains whether this tendency simultaneously to invite and to resist interpretation is a particular feature of this book or whether it is bound to occur with all apocalyptic writing – or indeed with all canonical or all religious writing. Is there a wild and visionary element in religion which cannot be tamed by canon or doctrine or church? Does the recovery by twentieth-century scholarship of the apocalyptic origins of Christianity mean that this is especially true of a religion that can justly be called biblical? And if so, were men as diverse as Joachim of Fiore, Isaac Newton, William Blake, Edward Irving and D. H. Lawrence right to treat Revelation as the key to unlock scripture? Is the polemical anti-nomian rewriting of scripture by Blake a more authentic response to the Bible than the reams of hermeneutical labours?

Speaking in 1980, Jacques Derrida approached the question of apocalypse by working with and against Kant's lampoon of 1796 *Von einem neuerdings erhobenen vornehmen Ton in der Philosophie*, the other text to which he mainly refers being the Book of Revelation.[19] Derrida sketches the oppositions that Kant draws out in his defence of thought that aims to be both rational and transcendental: poets and 'mystagogues' *versus* real philosophers, aristocracy *versus* democracy, vision *versus* hearing, Plato's letters *versus* his dialectic, and esotericism, numerology, apocalypse and oracle *versus* reason. Kant had no doubt which side he stood on. Derrida is characteristically more elliptical, claiming 'not to take sides ... between metaphor and concept, literary mystagogy and true philosophy, but for a start to recognize the ancient interdependence of these antagonists or protagonists'.[20] In fact the modern philosopher cannot go back behind Kant and the Enlightenment, Derrida maintains; but what is this 'light' for? 'Mystagogy' and apocalypse also claim to bring light, vision, demystification and unveiling (here he quotes Rev 22:5). Bringing the two 'tones' into action on each other, he looks for an apocalypse of apocalypse, that is, an unveiling of unveiling. This actually begins to unravel the finality and authority of the original apocalypse: the opening verses of Revelation suggest a multiplicity or interlacing of messages or sendings (*envois*), so that far from containing oracular presence the apocalyptic tone leads into ever greater indeterminacy. Reflecting on the repeated 'Come!' of the Apocalypse, Derrida says that again this

> does not address itself, does not appeal, to an identity determinable in advance. It is a drift [*une dérive*] underivable from the identity of a determination. 'Come' is *only* derivable, absolutely derivable, but only from the other, from nothing that

may be an origin or a verifiable, decidable, presentable, appropriable identity.[21]

This demystification of the apocalypse that claims to unveil is however an instance of what Derrida maintains is true of *all* texts, including those of Kant's 'real philosophy':

> if the dispatches [*envois*] always refer to other dispatches without decidable destination, the destination remaining to come, then isn't this completely angelic structure, that of the Johannine Apocalypse, isn't it also the structure of every scene of writing in general? ... wouldn't the apocalyptic be a transcendental condition of all discourse, of all experience itself, or every mark or every trace?[22]

The supreme unveiling that the apocalyptic tone achieves, then, is that of the 'apocalyptic' or metaphorical or fictional nature of all writing; but because 'apocalypses' in the narrow sense show this so blatantly they are particularly effective, Derrida suggests, in challenging cultural or philosophical assumptions and helping to 'dismantle the dominant contract or concordat'. Thus, it is implied, the Apocalypse unveils not the reality that it claims is its origin but rather the indeterminacy of all 'reality'. There is no 'great voice', only textual echoing.

These readings of the Apocalypse from our own century by Lawrence, Jung and Derrida suggest – as does Blake's earlier response to it – that the summons from this book is to out-Judas Judas, to enter the vortex of Unveiling and to follow its dynamic, despite the curse with which it closes both its own text and the Christian canon. Is there even an invitation to this in John's title to his book, which is not in fact '*the* revelation of Jesus Christ' (as it is usually translated) but simply 'revelation', without the definite article – *an* unveiling that leads into further unveilings, an unravelling that will never be completed, so that neither the visions of the book nor the Christ who gives them are as final as they appear to be? There is not just one Judas, even in the canon.

In a plainer narrative than that of the Apocalypse, the kiss of Judas is in fact a salutary one, the catalyst of resurrection and of meaning. In Gethsemane or on Patmos, the Judas is handing over (*paradidonai*) the body – or the text – to be stripped and abused 'outside the camp' of orthodox religion or literary practice. Without those treacherous but redemptive kisses, is any unveiling, any revelation possible? Without people prepared to move to the margins of the canonical system, even to step off its edge, even to push its god from his throne, all remains veiled in interpretation, while the supposed object of interpretation recedes ever further from the boundaries of the worlds we inhabit.

Notes and References

(The abbreviations used below are listed on pages xiii–xiv.)

Introduction

1. *The Fall of Hyperion*, I. 1–18, in John Keats, *The Complete Poems*, ed. John Barnard, 2nd edn (Harmondsworth 1977), p. 435.
2. Moses Stuart, *Commentary on the Apocalypse* (London 1845); E. B. Elliott, *Horae Apocalypticae* (London 1846), vol. IV, pp. 297–476; Willhelm Bousset, *Die Offenbarung Johannes* (Göttingen 1896), pp. 51–141; R. H. Charles, *Studies in the Apocalypse* (Edinburgh 1913), pp. 1–78; Isbon T. Beckwith, *The Apocalypse of John: Studies in Introduction* (New York 1919), pp. 318–36; Otto Böcher, *Die Johannesapokalypse* (Darmstadt 1980), pp. 123–54; C. A. Patrides and J. Wittreich (eds), *AERTL*, pp. 369–440.
3. Frederick van der Meer, *Apocalypse: Visions from the Book of Revelation in Western Art* (London 1978); Arthur W. Wainwright, *Mysterious Apocalypse: Interpreting the Book of Revelation* (Nashville, TE 1993).
4. Richard Bauckham, *Tudor Apocalypse: Sixteenth-Century Apocalypticism, Millenarianism and the English Reformation* (Sutton Courtenay 1978); Katharine Firth, *The Apocalyptic Tradition in Reformation Britain 1530–1645* (Oxford 1979); David Brady, *The Contribution of British Writers between 1560 and 1830 to the Interpretation of Rev 13:16–18* (Tübingen 1983); cf. Christopher Hill, *The English Bible and the Seventeenth-Century Revolution* (Harmondsworth 1993).
5. Clarke Garrett, *Respectable Folly: Millenarians and the French Revolution in France and England* (Baltimore 1975); J. F. C. Harrison, *The Second Coming: Popular Millenarianism 1780–1850* (London 1979).
6. E. L. Tuveson, *Millennium and Utopia: A Study in the Background of the Idea of Progress* (Berkeley, CA 1949); E. S. Shaffer, *'Kubla Khan' and The Fall of Jerusalem: The Mythological School in Biblical Criticism and Secular Literature 1770–1880* (Cambridge 1975); W. H. Oliver, *Prophets and Millennialists: The Uses of Biblical Prophecy in England from the 1790s to the 1840s* (Auckland, NZ 1978).
7. Cf. especially M. H. Abrams, 'Apocalypse: Theme and Variations', *AERTL*, pp. 342–68; Anthony John Harding, *Coleridge and the Inspired Word* (Montreal 1985); Terence Allan Hoagwood, *Prophecy and the Philosophy of Mind: Traditions of Blake and Shelley* (Alabama 1985); Bryan Shelley, *Shelley and Scripture: the Interpreting Angel* (Oxford 1994); Leslie Tannenbaum, *Biblical Tradition in Blake's Early Prophecies: The Great Code of Art* (Princeton, NJ 1982); Michael Yogers, 'Covenant

of the Word: the Bible in William Blake's late prophetic poems' (unpublished doctoral dissertation, University of Washington, 1991).

1   A Book Resisting Interpretation

1. D. H. Lawrence, *Apocalypse* (Harmondsworth 1974), p. 18. The book was first published in 1931.
2. Cf. Milan Kundera, *The Unbearable Lightness of Being* (ET London 1984), pp. 248–56.
3. Frank Kermode, *The Sense of an Ending: Studies in the Theory of Fiction* (Oxford 1967), p. 112.
4. Norman Cohn, *The Pursuit of the Millennium: Revolutionary Messianism in the Middle Ages…* (London 1957).
5. Hal Lindsey, *The Late Great Planet Earth* (New York 1973). Cf. Paul Boyer, *When Time Shall Be No More: Prophecy Belief in Modern American Culture* (Cambridge, Mass. 1992).
6. *Luther's Works* (Philadelphia 1960), xxxv, p. 398f. On his change of mind, cf. Firth, pp. 10–13.
7. Ulrich Zwingli, *Sämmtliche Werke* (Zürich 1982), ii, p. 208f. On Calvin, cf. T. H. L. Parker, *Calvin's New Testament Commentaries* (London 1971), pp. 75–8.
8. Rudolf Bultmann, *Theology of the New Testament* (ET London 1955), ii, p. 175.
9. Daniel Whitby, *Paraphrase and Commentary on the NT* (London 1700); Samuel Clarke, *Paraphrase with Critical Notes* (London 1738); Samuel Bloomfield, *Critical Digest* (London 1826–8); William Trollope, *Analecta Theologica* (London 1830–35).
10. Whitby, ii, p. 688.
11. Cf. Klaus Koch, *The Rediscovery of Apocalyptic* (ET London 1972; published in German as *Ratlos vor der Apokalyptik)*; Gerhard von Rad, *Old Testament Theology* (ET Edinburgh 1965), ii, p. 301–8.
12. J. J. Collins, 'Towards the Morphology of a Genre', *Semeia* 14 (1979), p. 9. Collins adds that 'the key word in the definition is transcendence'.
13. Cf. P. D. Hanson, *The Dawn of Apocalyptic: The Historical and Sociological Roots of Jewish Apocalyptic Eschatology*, rev. edn (Philadelphia 1979); also the critiques of Hanson's argument by R. P. Carroll, 'Twilight of Prophecy or Dawn of Apocalyptic?', *JSOT* 14 (1979), pp. 3–35, and by C. Rowland, *The Open Heaven: a Study of Apocalyptic in Judaism and Early Christianity* (London 1982), pp. 194–202.
14. *Open Heaven*, esp. pp. 70–2. Cf. M. E. Stone, 'Lists of Revealed things in the Apocalyptic Literature', in F. M. Cross (ed.), *Magnalia Dei* (New York 1976), pp. 414–52.
15. F. D. Mazzaferri, *The Genre of the Book of Revelation from a Source-critical Perspective*, BZNW 54 (Berlin 1989), pp. 223–58.
16. Austin Farrer, *A Rebirth of Images: the Making of St John's Apocalypse* (London 1949).
17. David Lawton, *Faith, Text and History: the Bible in English* (London 1990), p. 187.

18. Cf. Rev 1:5,10ff.; 5:5,9,13; 19:10f.; 21:9,22; 22:16. See also M. E. Boring, 'The Voice of Jesus in the Apocalypse of John', *Nov T* 34 (1992), pp. 334–59, esp. pp. 351–6.
19. Rev 1:3; 22:18f.; cf. Rev 10:7–11; 11:3–13.
20. Cf. Richard Bauckham, *The Theology of the Book of Revelation* (Cambridge 1993), pp. 2–5; Mazzaferri, pp. 264–96.
21. Cf. Justin, *Dialogue with Trypho* 80–81 (*ANCL* II. 199–201); Irenaeus, *Adv. Haer.* v.25–30 (*ANCL* v.ii.121–39); 35 (*ANCL* v.ii.154f.); Tertullian, *Adv. Marc.*, III. 24; 13; *Scorpiace* XII; *De Corona* XIII (*ANCL* VII).
22. Origen, *Comm. in Joh.* II. 42–63. Cf. *Comm. in Joh.* I. 40; *Comm. in Rom.* I. 4; *De Principiis* III. vi.8,9; IV.13; Jerome, *Ep. ad Avitum* 12. See further H. de Lubac, *Histoire et Esprit* (Paris 1950), p. 229; R. P. C. Hanson, *Allegory and Event* (London 1959), pp. 351–6; Jean Pépin, 'L'absurdité, signe de l'allégorie', in *La Tradition de l'allégorie de Philon d'Alexandrie à Dante* (Paris: Etudes Augustiniennes, 1987), pp. 167–86. An interesting comparison of the early Christian tension between literal and allegorical readings with that in the modern USA is made by A. Y. Collins, 'Reading the Book of Revelation in the Twentieth Century', *Int.* 40 (1986), pp. 229–42.
23. Eusebius, *H.E.* X.
24. *H.E.* VII.24;25. For a thorough survey of Eusebius's attitude to Revelation, questioning the common assumption of his hostility towards it, see Clementina Mazzucco, 'Eusèbe de Césarée et l'Apocalypse de Jean', *Studia Patristica* XVII. 1, pp. 317–24.
25. Paula Fredriksen, 'Tyconius and Augustine on the Apocalypse', in R. K. Emmerson and B. McGinn (eds), *The Apocalypse in the Middle Ages* (Ithaca 1992), p. 29. Kenneth Steinhauser (*The Apocalypse Commentary of Tyconius: A History of its Reception and Influence*, Frankfurt 1987) has made a thorough attempt to reconstruct Tyconius's commentary.
26. W. S. Babcock (ed.), *Tyconius: the Book of Rules* (Atlanta 1989), p. 111. Cf. Paula Fredriksen, 'Apocalypse and Redemption in Early Christianity', *Vig. Chr.* 45 (1991), pp. 157–60.
27. Augustine, *The City of God* xx.7–17. Literal and allegorical readings coexist happily in the third-century commentary of Victorinus (*ANCL* XVIII, pp. 394–433) and in Hippolytus's treatise *De Antichristo.*
28. Origen, *Comm. in Joh.* v.2.
29. Origen, *De Principiis* IV.3.
30. Babcock, pp. 2f. Augustine quotes the *Liber regularum* extensively in *De Doctrina Christiana* III. 30, 42–37, 56, but expresses some reservations about Tyconius's confidence in resolving obscurities.
31. Gerald Bruns, 'Midrash and Allegory: The Beginnings of Scriptural Interpretation', in R. Alter and F. Kermode (eds), *A Literary Guide to the Bible* (London 1987), p. 640. For other recent theological defences of allegorical readings, see Frances Young, 'Allegory and the Ethics of Reading', in Francis Watson (ed.), *The Open Text: New Directions for Biblical Studies?* (London 1993), pp. 103–20; Christopher Burdon, 'The Fathers and the Birds: Allegorical Reading of the Bible', in *Theology* XCIX (1996), pp. 442–51.

32. J. Whitman, *Allegory: the Dynamics of an Ancient and Medieval Technique* (Oxford 1987), p. 58. Cf. ibid., p. 80; L. M. Poland, 'Augustine, Allegory, and Conversion', *L&T* II.1 (1988), pp. 37–48.

33. Daniel Boyarin, *Intertextuality and the Reading of Midrash* (Indianapolis 1990), p. 110. Cf. Susan Handelman, '*Emunah*: the Craft of Faith', in *Cross Currents*, Fall 1992, p. 304.

34. Austin Farrer, *The Revelation of St John the Divine* (Oxford 1964), pp. 4, 88, 30.

35. Cf. Bruns, 'Midrash and Allegory', pp. 628f.

36. G. G. Porton, *Understanding Rabbinic Midrash* (Hoboken, NJ: Library of Judaic Learning V, 1985), pp. 5f.; cf. Boyarin, p. 26.

37. But contrast the argument of Steve Moyise that 'John does not define how the new [scripture] relates to the old but forces the reader/hearer to think it out for themselves', in 'Intertextuality and the Book of Revelation', *Exp T* 104 (1993), pp. 295–8. On the dancing flames, cf. *Song of Songs Rabba* 42.

38. Ernst Lohmeyer, *Die Offenbarung des Johannes*, 3rd edn (Tübingen 1970), p. 200; Farrer, *Revelation*, p. 29.

39. The narrative complexity of the book is analysed by E. Schüssler Fiorenza, suggesting that it cannot be divided into segments on a linear pattern (*The Book of Revelation: Justice and Judgement*, Philadelphia 1985, pp. 159–80), and by M. Eugene Boring, delineating its different 'narrative levels' ('The Theology of Revelation', *Int.* 40 [1986], pp. 257–69, and 'Narrative Christology in the Apocalypse', *CBQ* 54 [1992], p. 721); but Boring fails to convince that the whole work is narrative, with the meaning 'in' rather than 'beyond' the story.

40. *Offenbarung*, p. 157; cf. pp. 199f.

41. John Sweet, *Revelation* (London: SCM Pelican Commentaries, 1979), p. 17.

42. Karl Schellenberg, *Dürers Apokalypse* (Munich 1923), pp. 18, 28. Cf. van der Meer, pp. 163, 283–313.

43. Martin Butlin, *William Blake* (London 1978), p. 95. See, for instance, 'Death on a pale horse' or 'The Angel of Revelation'. On West, see Morton D. Paley, *The Apocalyptic Sublime* (New Haven, CT 1986), pp. 19–50.

44. On Martin's 'curious mixture of scientific thought with religious fervour', see Ruthven Todd, *Tracks in the Snow: Studies in English Science and Art* (London 1946), pp. 94–122. Cf. Paley, *Apocalyptic Sublime*, pp. 122–54.

45. Walter Ong has argued for the importance of sound, hearing and therefore 'orality' as being the most effective way of registering interiority (*Orality and Literacy: The Technologizing of the Word*, London 1982, pp. 71–4). Cf. Ernst Bloch, *Essays on the Philosophy of Music* (Cambridge: ET 1985), p. 197.

46. Cf. D. L. Barr, 'The Apocalypse of John as Oral Enactment', *Int.* 40 (1986), pp. 243–56, esp. pp. 244–9.

47. John Banville, *Doctor Copernicus* (London 1976), p. 49.

48. *NB* 52 fol. 5ᵛ. See pp. 160–71 below.

49. George Steiner, *Real Presences* (London 1989), p. 217f. Cf. Hans Küng, *Mozart: Traces of Transcendence* (London: ET 1993).

50. G. B. Caird, *The Revelation of St John the Divine*, 2nd edn, (London: Blacks NT Commentaries, 1984), p. 106.
51. There are examples in the ancient and modern phenomenon of speaking in tongues; in Augustine's remarks on psalm-singing in *Confessions* x.49; and in Origen's discussion of some biblical language as incantation *(epodē)* in *Philokalia* xii, xvii, xxii. See further in Hanson, *Allegory*, pp. 205–8.
52. *Essays*, p. 194.
53. If anywhere in modern music, Bloch's 'utopian yearning' can be found in two innovative works written as interpretations of Revelation, Olivier Messiaen's 'Quatuor pour la fin du temps' (1941) and John Taverner's choral work 'The Apocalypse' (1993). But Messiaen's evocation of 'the harmonious silence of heaven', like Tavener's attempt at 'timeless' sound, misses the specificity of the text's symbols and their context in the macronarratives of the Bible and human history.
54. Paul de Man, *Allegories of Reading* (New Haven, CT 1979), p. 10.
55. Amos Wilder, *Jesus' Parables and the War of Myths* (London 1982), p. 157.
56. Cf. Farrer, *Revelation*, p. 58.
57. Cf. Barr, 'Oral Enactment', pp. 252–6. On *apokalypsis* as part of early Christian worship, cf. 1 Cor 14:26.
58. Cf. respectively Massey H. Shepherd, *The Paschal Liturgy and the Apocalypse* (London 1960), part 2; Pierre Prigent, *Apocalypse et Liturgie* (Neuchatel 1964); Farrer, *Revelation*, p. 23; M. D. Goulder, 'The Apocalypse as an Annual Cycle of Prophecies', *NTS* 27 (1981), pp. 342–67, and Ugo Vanni, 'Liturgical Dialogue as a Literary Form in the Book of Revelation', *NTS* 37 (1991), pp. 348–72.
59. J. E. Hurtgen, *Anti-Language in the Apocalypse of John* (Lewiston, NY 1993), p. 141.
60. *Justice and Judgement*, pp. 196–8. Cf. her *Revelation: Vision of a Just World* (Minneapolis 1991), pp. 5–15; Christopher Rowland, 'The Apocalypse: Hope, Resistance and the Revelation of Reality', *Ex Auditu* 6 (1990), pp. 129–44.
61. D. L. Barr, 'The Apocalypse as a Symbolic Transformation of the World: A Literary Analysis', *Int.* 38 (1984), pp. 47, 49f. In denying that the experience is ephemeral, Barr is contesting the similar use of Lévi-Strauss's theories to interpret Revelation by John Gager, *Kingdom and Community* (Englewood Cliffs, NJ 1975), pp. 49–57.
62. J. Sys, 'L'espace Apocalyptique', *Graphè* 1 (1992), p. 79.
63. See David Jasper, *Rhetoric, Power and Community* (London 1993), pp. 72–88.
64. *Sense of Ending*, p. 8. In the same work Kermode writes of the persistence of the 'apocalyptic types' of interpretation of history (p. 29).
65. *Justice and Judgement*, p. 199.

2. Apocalypse and Reason

1. See p. 8 above.
2. See Wainwright, pp. 49–61.
3. *Tudor Apocalypse*, pp. 29, 61. Cf. Firth, pp. 38–68; Tuveson, pp. 34–6.

4. Bauckham, *Tudor Apocalypse*, p. 87. Cf. Firth, pp. 76–110.
5. Firth, p. 166. Cf. Bauckham, *Tudor Apocalypse*, pp. 223f.
6. *Apocalyptic Tradition*, p. 179.
7. *English Bible*, pp. 298–323.
8. Ibid,. ch. 19, especially pp. 428, 431.
9. *Apocalyptic Tradition*, p. 228. Cf. ibid., pp. 229–41; Hill, *English Bible*, p. 304; Tuveson, p. 76 (though Tuveson overestimates Mede's 'progressivism').
10. R. B. Cooper, *A Translation of Mede's Clavis Apocalyptica* (London 1833), p. 22.
11. *Clavis*, p. 1. On Mede, see further, Firth, pp. 213–28; Tuveson, pp. 76–85; Brady, p. 97; Michael Murrin, 'Revelation and Two Seventeenth-century Commentators', in *AERTL*, pp. 125–46. On his influence in the tradition of 'physico-theology', cf. Tuveson, pp. 92–152 *passim*.
12. For example Christopher Hill, *Antichrist in Seventeenth-century England* (London 1971), pp. 154–77, and *English Bible*, pp. 322f.; P. J. Korshin, 'Queuing and Waiting: the Apocalypse in England, 1660–1750', in *AERTL*, pp. 240–65; M. H. Abrams, 'Apocalypse: Theme and Variations', in *AERTL*, pp. 342–68.
13. (Daniel Mace), *The New Testament in Greek and English … with Notes and Various Readings* (London 1729), II. pp. 944–1022.
14. *Contribution of British Writers*, p. 164.
15. Edmund Gosse, *Father and Son* (Harmondsworth 1949), pp. 50f. Gosse's autobiography was first published in 1907.
16. For example E. P. Thompson, *The Making of the English Working Class* (Harmondsworth 1963); J. F. C. Harrison, *The Second Coming: Popular Millenarianism 1780–1850* (London 1979). See further Clarke Garrett, *Respectable Folly: Millenarians and the French Revolution in France and England* (Baltimore, MD 1975), pp. 1–15; Hill, *English Bible*, pp. 196–250.
17. Sir Isaac Newton, *Observations upon the Prophecies of Daniel and the Apocalypse of St John* (London 1733), p. 251.
18. Moses Lowman, *A Paraphrase and Notes on the Revelation of St John* (London 1737), p. 257.
19. *Millennium and Utopia*, p. 152.
20. Richard Hurd, *An Introduction to the Study of the Prophecies Concerning the Christian Church, and, in particular, Concerning the Church of papal Rome* (London 1776), I, p. 118; II, p. 67.
21. The phrase is Lowman's, *Paraphrase*, p. vi.
22. Thomas Pyle, *A Paraphrase, with Notes, on the Revelation of St John*, rev. edn (London 1795), pp. vii, x.
23. Thomas Newton, *Dissertations on the Prophecies, which have remarkable been fulfilled and at this time are fulfilling in the World* (London 1826), pp. 3, 714.
24. Ibid., pp. 493–681, 703.
25. On the important exceptions of Jonathan Swift and (to a lesser extent) Joseph Butler, see pp. 67–71 below.
26. *The Works of John Locke* (London 1823), VII, p. 128.
27. Sir Leslie Stephen, *English Thought in the Eighteenth Century* (London 1876), I, p. 100.

28. John Toland, *Christianity not Mysterious*, 2nd edn (London 1702), pp. 44, 31.
29. Samuel Clarke, *Works*, ed. Hoadly (London 1738), ii.532, 550f.
30. *Works*, ii, p. 675. For an assessment of Clarke's teaching see J. F. Ferguson, *An Eighteenth-Century Heretic, Dr Samuel Clarke* (Kineton 1976).
31. Matthew Tindal, *Christianity as Old as the Creation* ... (London 1731), pp. 50, 60, 159.
32. Ibid., p. 93; cf. p. 115.
33. On the physico-theologians and Shaftesbury, see Tuveson, pp. 93–108; Basil Willey, *The Eighteenth-Century Background* (London 1940), chs 2, 4.
34. 'Autumn', 1352–58. Quotations of Thomson are from the edition by James Sambrook (2 vols, Oxford 1981, 1986).
35. 'Summer', 1531–79. These verses are followed by eulogy of 'wild Shakespeare', Milton and 'the gentle Spenser'.
36. F. E. Manuel, *The Religion of Isaac Newton* (Oxford 1974), p. 20.
37. Sir Isaac Newton, Yahuda MS 1.1, fols 8, 12 (printed in Manuel, Appendix A, pp. 114–18).
38. Yahuda MS 1.1, fol. 16 (Manuel, p. 122).
39. Yahuda MS 1.1, fol. 15 (Manuel, p. 121).
40. Keynes MS 5, fols 1–6. The opening parts of this MS are printed in H. McLachlan (ed.), *Sir Isaac Newton: Theological Manuscripts* (Liverpool 1950), pp. 119–26.
41. Cf. P. J. Korshin, *Typologies in England 1650–1820* (Princeton, NJ 1982), esp. pp. 36f, 86–91, 165–72, 374. On Newton's interpretation of prophecy, see further G. E. Christianson, *In the Presence of the Creator: Isaac Newton and his Times* (New York 1984), pp. 259–65.
42. Sir Isaac Newton, *The Chronology of Ancient Kingdoms Amended* (Dublin 1728), p. 8. Cf. R. S. Westfall, *Never at Rest: A Biography of Isaac Newton* (Cambridge 1980), pp. 808–15.
43. Keynes MS 1, fols 1–18.
44. Manuel, p. 78. Cf. Maurice Wiles, 'Newton and the Bible', in *A Shared Search* (London 1994), pp. 46–59.
45. William Whiston, *An Essay on the Revelation of St John, So far as concerns the Past and Present Times* (Cambridge 1706), pp. 270–2.
46. John Wesley, *Explanatory Notes upon the New Testament*, 2nd edn (London 1757), p. 678. On Bengel, see further Stuart, i, p. 469f.; Hans Frei, *The Eclipse of Biblical Narrative: A Study in Eighteenth and Nineteenth Century Hermeneutics* (New Haven, CT 1974), pp. 175–9. On Wesley's use of him, see Wainwright, p. 79; Brady, pp. 218–24.
47. James Kershaw, *An Essay on the Principal Parts of the Book of the Revelations* ... (Stockton, 1780), ii, p. 274.
48. Thomas Reader, *Remarks on the Prophetic Part of the Revelation* ... (London 1778), pp. 39–44, 305–12.
49. *Essay*, pp. 176–93. An interesting personal application of this kind of numerological ingenuity can be seen in the diaries of the contemporary Welsh Methodist Howel Harris, of whom Derec Llwyd Morgan remarks that 'his Book of Chronicles and his Book of Revelation were to him one and the same' (D. L. Morgan, *The Great Awakening in Wales*, London ET, 1988, p. 74).

50.	*Memoirs of the Life and Writings of Mr William Whiston, containing Memoirs of Several of his Friends also*, 2nd edn (London 1753), III, pp. 46–141.
51.	Ibid., I, p. 201.
52.	Anthony Collins, *A Discourse of the Grounds and Reasons of the Christian Religion* (London 1724). For an account of the Whiston/Collins debate, cf. Henning Graf Reventlow, *The Authority of the Bible and the Rise of the Modern World* (ET, London 1984), pp. 362–9.
53.	*Paraphrase*, p. iv.
54.	Ibid., pp. 2f., 81, 183.
55.	(E. S. Bowdler), *Practical Observations on the Revelation of St John written in the year 1775 by the late Mrs Bowdler* (Bath 1800), p. 150f.
56.	*Works*, I, p. 422; II, p. 122; I, p. 410f.
57.	Cf. Locke's discussion of 'natural Revelation' in *Essay Concerning Human Understanding*, IV.19.4. Had this vocabulary taken root the Deistic disputes might have taken a very different turn, for fundamentally all its protagonists believed in some form of natural revelation.
58.	*Religion*, p. 3.
59.	Charles Blount, *Oracles of Reason*, in *Miscellaneous Works* (London 1693), I, p. 89; quoted in Reventlow, p. 293).
60.	Tindal, p. 13; cf. p. 254.
61.	Cf. Ibid., pp. 137–9; Pyle, p. xvii; Thomson, 'Liberty', IV.1135–91.
62.	Cf. Reventlow, pp. 303–5.
63.	Ibid., p. 341.
64.	For example Keynes MS 3, fols 39–42. Several of the manuscripts in which Newton worked out this reductionist creed are transcribed by McLachlan, including seven drafts of his 'Irenicum', his 'Short Scheme of the True Religion', twelve articles of belief, 'seven statements on religion' and the fruits of some anti-Athanasian researches.
65.	*Religion*, p. 103.
66.	For example Keynes MS 3, fol. 35; MS 8, articles 1–6.
67.	*Memoirs*, I, pp. 34–6, 250f.
68.	Ibid., I, p. 326f.
69.	Collins, *Grounds and Reasons*, pp. 273–84.
70.	Edward Evanson, *A Letter to the Bishop of Litchfield and Coventry…* (London 1777), pp. 36–50.
71.	*Memoirs*, I, p. 325. The *Apostolical Constitutions*, a lengthy collection of canons relating mainly to liturgy and church order, do purport to have such an origin, but in fact probably date from the early fourth century – ironically, they do not recognise the canonicity of the Apocalypse.
72.	Ibid., I, p. 121. On Whiston's Arianism, cf. Maurice Wiles, *Archetypal Heresy: Arianism through the Centuries* (Oxford 1996), pp. 93–110.

3   Prophecy and Poetry

1.	Samuel Johnson, *The History of Rasselas, Prince of Abyssinia*, ed. R. W. Chapman (Oxford 1927), p. 189 (chapter 42).
2.	Jonathan Swift, *Prose Works*, ed. H. Davis (Oxford 1939–68), XI, p. 182 (*Gulliver's Travels*, III, 8).

3. Ibid., xi, p. 116 (*Gulliver*, ii, 6).
4. Alexander Pope, *Works*, ed. P. Rogers (Oxford 1993), pp. 514–6 (*The Dunciad* iv, 1–16).
5. *Dunciad* IV.627–56; cf. iii, 235–48.
6. Joseph Butler, *The Analogy of Religion Natural and Revealed to the Constitution and Course of Nature*, ed. Steere (London 1857), ii, 6.
7. Willey, p. 82.
8. *Analogy*, ii, 5. The talk of the earth as a 'ruin' echoes the pre-Newtonian cosmology of Thomas Burnet's *Sacred Theory of the Earth* (1684).
9. William Law, *A Serious Call to a Devout and Holy Life Adapted to the State and Condition of all Orders of Christians*, ed. J. H. Overton (London 1898), pp. 57, 99.
10. Ibid., pp. 107, 117, 127.
11. See Gordon Rupp, *Religion in England 1688–1791* (Oxford 1986), pp. 290–5.
12. John Wesley, *Sermons on Several Occasions* (London 1825), i, pp. 1–10.
13. Ibid., I, pp. 31–46.
14. Ibid., I, pp. 167–81.
15. Ibid., ii, pp. 168–75. For parallels with the redemptive cosmology of Burnet and Worthington, see Tuveson, pp. 117–22, 142–5. But in contrast to Burnet's progressivism, see Wesley's sermon on 'The Cause and Cure of Earthquakes' (ii, pp. 35–47), delivered after the London earthquakes of 1750, which contains much detailed reporting of recent earthquakes in Sicily, Jamaica and Peru: these are God's warning to flee from wrath and lead to an evangelical plea for individual faith and repentance.
16. *Sermons*, i, pp. vii.
17. Charles Wesley, MS Richmond 105f., printed in Frank Baker (ed.), *Representative Verse of Charles Wesley* (London 1962), p. 184f. Compare the birthday hymn no. 491 in the 1876 collection.
18. See also the extensive use of apocalyptic imagery in hymns 47, 56, 57, 61-64, 67, 73, 75, 333, 343, 454, 749, 926; *Scripture Hymns* (1762) II.410, 426, 430 (in Baker, pp. 234f.)
19. *Hymns on God's Everlasting Love* (1741; in Baker, pp. 158–61). Cf. 'Universal Redemption' (ibid., p. 167), and hymns 2 and 39 in the 1876 collection.
20. William Williams, *Aleluja* (London 1758), 11; quoted and translated by Dyfnallt Morgan in Morgan, *Great Awakening*, p. 288. Pantycelyn wrote a mere thousand hymns beside Charles Wesley's nine thousand, but unfortunately very few have been translated.
21. William Williams, *Ffarwel Weledig*, 4; quoted and translated by J. Gwilym Jones, *William Williams Pantycelyn* (Cardiff 1969), p. 41.
22. Morgan, pp. 200–17.
23. Quoted and translated by Morgan, pp. 255f.
24. William Cowper, *The Task*, vi, 729–822.
25. Robert Lowth, *Lectures on the Sacred Poetry of the Hebrews*, trans. R. Gregory, 4th edn (London 1839), lectures i, xiv. On Lowth's poetics, see further Stephen Prickett, *Words and the Word: Language, Poetics and Biblical Interpretation* (Cambridge 1986), pp. 105–23.

26. Richard Hurd, *Letters on Chivalry and Romance with the Third Elizabethan Dialogue*, ed. Edith Morley (London 1911), p. 139.
27. Ibid., p. 154. On Hurd, see further M. H. Abrams, *The Mirror and the Lamp: Romantic Theory and the Critical Tradition* (Oxford 1953), pp. 18f., 279.
28. Hurd, *Introduction*, I, pp. 84, 47f.
29. Bryce Johnston, *A Commentary on the Revelation of St John* ... (Edinburgh 1794), I, pp. iiif, 36–42.
30. William Cooke, *The Revelations Translated and Explained Throughout* (Yarmouth 1789), pp. xiii, 175.
31. On Eichhorn, see further pp. 144–8 below.
32. See R. T. Clark, *Herder: His Life and Thought* (Berkeley, CA 1955), pp. 268–72. Clark is not really fair, however, in describing the 1779 book as 'a hodge-podge of contradictory statements ... a horrible example of the committee principle in literary composition'.
33. Stuart, II, pp. 491–504.
34. References are to Herder, *Sämmtliche Werke*, ed. Sulphan (Berlin 1893), vol. 9.
35. *Eclipse*, p. 185.
36. Ibid., p. 199.

4 Revelation and Revolution

1. See Oscar Cullmann, *Christ and Time: The Primitive Christian Conception of Time and History* (ET, London 1951), part I, esp. pp. 37–50.
2. William Wordsworth, *The Prelude* (1805), x, 855f.
3. *Justice and Judgement*, ch. 7, esp. p. 199.
4. *Respectable Folly*, pp. 225, 227.
5. Ibid., pp. 165–71. Cf. Oliver, p. 39f.
6. Sayer Rudd, *An Essay towards a New Explication* ... (London 1734), p. 25.
7. Thomas Vivian, *The Book of the Revelation of St John the Divine Explained* (Plymouth 1785), pp. 50–7, 158–63.
8. Ibid., pp. 169–74.
9. Jack Fruchtman, 'The Apocalyptic Politics of Richard Price and Joseph Priestley: A Study in Late Eighteenth-Century English Republican Millennialism', *Transactions of the American Philosophical Society* 73.4 (1983), p. 49.
10. Marilyn Butler, 'Revolving in Deep Time; the French Revolution as Narrative', in *RER*, p. 12. Butler distinguishes such responses from the more explicit (but also apocalyptic) responses to revolution by Burke and Wordsworth.
11. Garrett, *Respectable Folly*, p. 133.
12. *CP* , p. 75 (ll. 387–94).
13. Increase Mather, *Exhortations to Faith* (1710), p. 97; quoted by James Bicheno in *A Word in Season* (London 1795), p. 19. The claim made during the 1989 bicentennial celebrations that before 1789 the word 'revolution' did not have its modern meaning but refers only to

360-degree revolutions is disproved by this and several other eighteenth-century references to 'revolutions' as earthquakes and apocalyptic upheavals; cf. Mather, *Exhortations*, p. 87; Pyle, p. 60; Hurd, *Introduction*, II, p. 100. See Butler, 'Revolving in Deep Time', pp. 3f.

14. James Bicheno, *The Fulfilment of Prophecy farther illustrated by the Signs of the Times* (London 1817), p. 41. On Bicheno, see further Oliver, p. 46–50.

15. Bicheno, *Word in Season*, p. 18.

16. On Towers, see F. K. Donnelly, 'Joseph Towers and the Collapse of Rational Dissent', *E&D* 6 (1987), pp. 31–9; J. T. Boulton, *The Language of Politics in the Age of Wilkes and Burke* (London 1963), p. 89; Harrison, p. 76.

17. J. L. Towers, *Illustration of Prophecy*, ed. W. Vint (Airedale 1828), II, pp. 206, 238.

18. Harrison, pp. 25–38. Cf. E. P. Thompson, *Witness against the Beast: William Blake and the Moral Law* (Cambridge 1993), esp. chapters 3, 5, & 6.

19. Harrison, p. 54. Cf. Garrett, *Respectable Folly*, ch. 7, and for some parallels in contemporary France, chs 1–5.

20. Iain McCalman, *Radical Underworld: Prophets, Revolutionaries and Pornographers in London, 1795–1840* (Cambridge 1988).

21. On Brothers, see Harrison, pp. 57–85; Garrett, *Respectable Folly*, pp. 209–16. On Southcott, see Harrison, pp. 86–134; Garrett, ibid., pp. , 216–23. On both, see Morton D. Paley, 'William Blake, The Prince of the Hebrews, and the Woman Clothed with the Sun', in *WBK*, pp. 260–93.

22. Robert Hole, *Pulpits, Politics and Public Order in England 1760–1832* (Cambridge 1989), pp. 170–2. See further Oliver, pp. 51–4.

23. Henry Kett, *History the Interpreter of Prophecy*, 5th edn (London 1805), I, p. 301.

24. Ibid., I, pp. 377–408; II, pp. 113–286.

25. Joseph Galloway, *Brief Commentaries* (London 1802), pp. 223–306.

26. Lewis Mayer, *A Hint to England* … (London 1803), p. 35f.

27. See Hill, *English Bible*, pp. 264–70.

28. Frederic Thruston, *England Safe and Triumphant* … (Coventry 1812), I, pp. x, xviii.

29. Garrett, *Respectable Folly*, p. 211f. On different ways of forming Napoleon/Bonaparte from 666, see Brady, pp. 242–6.

30. J. E. Clarke, *Dissertation on the Dragon, Beast and False Prophet, of the Apocalypse* … (London 1814), pp. 5–122.

31. R. B. Cooper, *Commentary on the Revelation of St John … by an Humble Follower of the Pious and Profoundly Learned Joseph Mede* (London 1833), p. 182f.

32. G. S. Faber, *A Dissertation on the Prophecies* …, 5th edn (London 1814), II, pp. 113–485. His final work in 1853 was *The Predicted Downfall of the Turkish Power, the Preparation for the Return of the Ten Tribes*.

33. *Dissertation on Prophecies*, II.168.

34. *Prophets and Millennialists*, p. 63. Cf. the sceptical comments on Faber by Coleridge (*CM*, II.573–85; *CN*, III.3793).

35. George Croly, *The Apocalypse of St John, or Prophecy of the Rise, Progress and Fall of the Church of Rome* (London 1827).
36. M. H. Abrams, 'Apocalypse: Theme and Variations', in *AERTL*, pp. 342–68.
37. *Word in Season*, pp. 50f.
38. David Hartley, *Observations on Man*, 5th edn (Bath 1810), I, pp. 513, 518. On Hartley's belief in progress and his millennialism, see further Willey, pp. 133–49; Fruchtman, 'Apocalyptic Politics', pp. 16–20.
39. For a useful summary of Unitarian ethos and belief, see H. L. Short, 'Presbyterians under a New Name', in C. G. Bolam *et al.*, *The English Presbyterians, from English Puritanism to Modern Unitarianism* (London 1968), pp. 219–86.
40. On Price, see the full critical biography by D. O. Thomas, *The Honest Mind: The Thought and Work of Richard Price* (Oxford 1977); Fruchtman, 'Apocalyptic Politics'; Henri Laboucheix, *Richard Price* (Paris 1970; parts of this work are translated as 'Richard Price as Moral Philosopher and Political Theorist', *Studies on Voltaire and the Eighteenth Century* 207 [Oxford 1982]).
41. Edmund Burke, *Reflections on the Revolution in France*, ed. Conor Cruise O'Brien (Harmondsworth 1968), pp. 94, 101, 159. Burke's ironic point, though, is that the rationalism of thinkers such as Price is in fact a kind of idolatry.
42. See Thomas, *Honest Mind*, p. 127.
43. Richard Price, *Political Writings*, ed. D. O. Thomas (Cambridge 1991), p. 5. Subsequent references are to this edition.
44. Ibid., pp. 195f.; cf. Laboucheix, pp. 221–3.
45. Thomas, *Honest Mind*, pp. 302–8.
46. See Oliver, pp. 43–6. For a biographical survey of Priestley's consistent millennialism, see Clarke Garrett, 'Joseph Priestley, the Millennium and the French Revolution', *JHI* XXXIV.1 (1973), pp. 51–66. Fruchtman's fuller treatment of Price's and Priestley's 'republican millennialism' does not really bring out this contrast.
47. John Money, 'Joseph Priestley in Cultural Context', *E&D* 7 (1988), p. 60. Cf. Priestley's sermon of 5 November 1785 'on the importance and extent of free inquiry in matters of religion', in *Tracts printed and published by the Unitarian Society for Promoting Christian Knowledge and the Practice of Virtue* (London 1791), III, pp. 73–94.
48. *The Theological and Miscellaneous Works of Joseph Priestley*, ed. J. T. Rutt (Hackney 1816–31), I.i, p. 146. Subsequent references to Priestley are to this edition.
49. Ibid., II, pp. 348–67. Cf. J. Fruchtman, 'Joseph Priestley and Early English Zionism', *E&D* 2 (1983), pp. 39–46.
50. Cf. Fruchtman, 'Apocalyptic Politics', pp. 49, 59–61.
51. Cf. Garrett, 'Joseph Priestley', pp. 51f., 62–64.
52. Richard Holmes, *Coleridge: Early Visions* (Harmondsworth 1990), p. 97.
53. *CL*, I, pp. 145f. 163–73, 158.
54. To Benjamin Flower (*CL* I.197). Cf. similar phrases to Thelwall (*CL*, I, p. 205).

55. *CP*, pp. 64–76: ll. 100–13; 416–19. Cf. ll. 120, 268, 403, 435.
56. References to Burke's *Reflections* are to the Penguin edition (n. 41 above). For a survey of the resulting controversy, see Marilyn Butler, *Burke, Paine, Godwin, and the Revolution Controversy* (Cambridge 1984), pp. 1–17. For a rhetorical analysis of much of the writing concerned, see Boulton, part 2.
57. Edmund Burke, *A Philosophical Inquiry into the Origin of our Ideas of the Sublime and Beautiful*, ed. J. T. Boulton, rev. edn (Oxford 1987), p. 86.
58. Thomas Paine, *Rights of Man*, ed. Eric Foner (Harmondsworth 1984), pp. 116, 64, 73f.
59. *Reflections*, pp. 169–71. Cf. Tom Furniss, 'Gender in Revolution: Edmund Burke and Mary Wollstonecraft', in *RIW*, pp. 65–100.
60. *The Writings and Speeches of Edmund Burke*, ed. Paul Langford (Oxford 1981–), IX, p. 156.
61. Laboucheix, p. 235.
62. References are to the Penguin edition cited above (n. 58). On the disputed circulation figures for *Rights of Man*, see Olivia Smith, *The Politics of Language 1791–1819* (Oxford 1984), pp. 57f.
63. *Language of Politics*, pp. 137, 146, 149. A careful analysis of the different notions and uses of 'vulgarity' by Paine and Burke is made by Olivia Smith, pp. 35–57, 77.
64. Thomas Paine, *Common Sense*, ed. I Kramnick (Harmondsworth 1976), pp. 100, 120.
65. McCalman, ch. 3, esp. pp. 63–6. See also Olivia Smith, pp. 96–109; T. R. Knox, 'Thomas Spence: the Trumpet of Jubilee', *Past and Present* 76 (1977), p. 98.
66. Mary Wollstonecraft, *Political Writings*, ed. Janet Todd (Oxford 1994), p. 60.
67. Ibid., p. 295.
68. Harriet Devine Jump, '"The Cool Eye of Observation": Mary Wollstonecraft and the French Revolution', in *RIW*, p. 107.
69. *Prophets and Millennialists*, p. 11; cf. pp. 22f., 40f., 68–79, 84–98.
70. *Fulfilment of Prophecy*, pp. 243–7.
71. Morton D. Paley, '"These Promised Years": Coleridge's "Religious Musings" and the Millenarianism of the 1790s', in *RER*, pp. 49–65.
72. M. H. Abrams, *Natural Supernaturalism: Tradition and Revolution in Romantic Literature* (New York 1971), p. 334.

5 Coleridge and the Limits of Interpretation

1. *AR*, p. 181. Cf. Kiyoshi Tsuchiya, 'Coleridge's Phantom and Fact: Two Natures, Trinitarian Resolution, and the Formation of the Pentad to 1825' (unpublished PhD thesis, University of Glasgow, 1994), pp. 275–7.
2. Cf. Shaffer, '*Kubla Khan*', ch. 1.
3. Ibid., pp. 74, 81.
4. Ibid., p. 18.

5. Ibid., p. 152f.
6. M. H. Abrams, *Natural Supernaturalism: Tradition and Revolution in Romantic Literature* (New York 1973), p. 47.
7. Cf. Abrams, Ibid., p. 267.
8. Wordsworth, *The Prelude* (1805), III.82–94. Subsequent references are all to the 1805 version.
9. Ibid., X.409f.
10. Ibid., I.428–31, VI.564–72.
11. Ibid., X.855f; cf. X.474–83, 539–52, 931–40.
12. David Jasper, *Coleridge as Poet and Religious Thinker* (Alison Park 1985), p. 43.
13. J. D. Michaelis, *Introduction to the New Testament ... translated from the Fourth Edition of the German ... by Herbert Marsh* (Cambridge 1801), IV, pp. 457, 460, 487.
14. *CL* I, p. 494; *BL* x. Cf. Holmes, *Coleridge*, pp. 220–9.
15. J. G. Eichhorn, *Commentarius in Apocalypsin Johannis* (Göttingen 1791), I, p. liv.
16. *CM* ii, pp. 410. Cf. *CM* ii, pp. 401–3; *LS*, pp. 29–31.
17. *CM* ii, pp. 516f. Cf. *CN* IV.4912, IV.5406, fols 93ᵛ–94ᵛ.
18. *CN* IV.5382. Cf. IV.5421.
19. *LS*, pp. 123f. Cf. Carlyle's essay 'On History', in G. B. Tennyson (ed.), *A Carlyle Reader* (Cambridge 1984), pp. 55–66.
20. On Coleridge's understanding of 'symbol', see further his comments on Herder (*CM* ii, p. 1062); Mary Rahme, 'Coleridge's Concept of Symbolism', *SEL* 9 (1969), pp. 619–32; L. C. Knights, *Further Explorations* (London 1965), pp. 155–68; M. Jadwiga Swiatecka OP, *The Idea of Symbol: Some Nineteenth-Century Comparisons with Coleridge* (Cambridge 1980), pp. 44–66.
21. Quoted by A. L. Drummond in *Edward Irving and his Circle* (London 1937), p. 50.
22. M. O. W. Oliphant, *The Life of Edward Irving* (London 1862), p. 428. On Irving's 'God-centredness' and incarnationalism, cf. the appreciative remarks of F. D. Maurice in *The Doctrine of Sacrifice* (rev. edn, London, 1879), p. xiiif., and *The Kingdom of Christ*, 1842 edn, ed. Vidler (London 1958), p. 154f. On his character and leading ideas, especially the relationship of 'sovereign God' and 'purified earth', cf. Oliver, pp. 99–107.
23. Cf. Gordon Strachan, *The Pentecostal Theology of Edward Irving* (London 1973), pp. 56, 98, 106–8; Oliphant, p. 102. Contrary to Oliver (p. 106), Irving's 'high-church' tendencies predate his meeting with Coleridge.
24. Oliphant, pp. 299f.
25. *CL* VI, p. 474; *CM* iii, pp. 431, 11.
26. *Life of Irving*, p. 105f.
27. On the Albury Group and the emergence of the Catholic Apostolic Church, cf. Oliver, pp. 113–49; Oliphant, ch. 12. Oliver notes interesting parallels with the slightly later Tractarians.
28. *The Morning Watch* (1829–33), VII, pp. 399–402.
29. Edward Irving, *Babylon and Infidelity Foredoomed of God* (Glasgow 1826), I, pp. 247–55.

30. *CL* vi, pp. 683–5. For other expressions of doubts about the canonicity of Daniel and Revelation, cf. *CM* iii, p. 418, 421; *CN* iv.4755; *NB* 35, fol. 38ᵛ.
31. *The Prophetical Works of Edward Irving* (London 1867), i, pp. 63, 25, 84f., 19.
32. Ibid., i, pp. 238–41, ii, p. 291f.
33. Ibid., i, p. 230.
34. *The Morning Watch*, v, p. 441, vi, p. 228.
35. Cf. *TT* i, p. 127, n.11, i, p. 422f., i, p. 567f., ii, p. 430.
36. *AR*, p. 322f.; *CIS*, p. 40. Cf. the references in Beer's excursus on 'Coleridge and the Abyss of Being' in *AR*, p. 563f., which underscores Coleridge's debt to Boehme; Anne Marie Perkins, *Coleridge's Philosophy: The Logos as Unifying Theme* (Oxford 1994), pp. 96–8; John Beer, *Coleridge the Visionary* (London 1959), pp. 59–62.
37. *NB* 54, fol. 13; *NB* 35, fol. 30.
38. For example *NB* 41, fols 10ᵛ, 65ᵛ, 86. Cf. *CN* iv.5249; *AR*, pp. 257–64.
39. Cf. Coleridge's Brabant manuscript, published in *Westminster Review* 37 (1870), pp. 351–4; *NB* 49, fol. 21.
40. *NB* 55, fol. 20ᵛ. Cf. *NB* 33, fols 11–17.
41. For example *NB* 44, fols 42–44; *NB* 45, fols 2–10.
42. *NB* 36, fols 19ᵛ, 20ʳ. Cf. (on Acts) *NB* 38, fols 10–18.
43. Cf. Tim Fulford, 'Coleridge, Kabbalah and the Book of Daniel', in P. J. Kitson and T. N. Corns (eds), *Coleridge and the Armoury of the Human Mind* (London 1991), pp. 63–77. For notes on *kabbalah*, cf. *NB* 53, fol. 6.
44. S. T. Coleridge, 'On the Prometheus of Aeschylus', *Transactions of the Royal Society of Literature* 2 (1834), pp. 391, 397. On the lecture, cf. Beer's bibliographical note in *AR*, p. 561f.; Nigel Leask, *The Politics of Imagination in Coleridge's Critical Thought* (London 1988), pp. 200–9.

6 Rewriting Apocalypse: Shelley and Blake

1. See Michael Ferber, *The Poetry of Shelley* (Harmondsworth 1993), p. 66.
2. Mary Shelley, *Frankenstein* (Harmondsworth 1992), p. 9. Cf. P. B. Shelley, 'The Triumph of Life' ll. 40–2 (*SPP*, p. 456).
3. *Natural Supernaturalism*, p. 300.
4. Ibid., p. 306; Ferber, p. 82. Cf. Earl R. Wassermann, *Shelley's 'Prometheus Unbound': A Critical Reading* (Baltimore, MD 1965), p. 182.
5. Bryan Shelley, *Shelley and Scripture: the Interpreting Angel* (Oxford 1994), p. 184f.
6. *PU* i.158, 658f., 690f., 706f., 799f. Cf. Terence Allan Hoagwood, *Prophecy and the Philosophy of Mind: Traditions of Blake and Shelley* (Alabama 1985), pp. 152–4.
7. For example *PU* i.20, 31–38, 546–65, 598–615, ii.iv.126f. Cf. Bryan Shelley, pp. 106–8; Wassermann, pp. 92–107. But Prometheus is also to be 'loosed' like the Satan of Rev 20:7 (*PU* ii.ii.93–5, iii.96f.)
8. Cf. *PU* i.152–86, iii.iii.84–107, iii.iv.131–41, 173–97.
9. See Bryan Shelley, pp. 38, 63–6, 89, 162–72.

10. Ibid., p. 132.
11. *LS*, pp. 24, 49, 29; *SPP*, p. 493.
12. Cf. Hoagwood, pp. 5, 36–58.
13. Num 11:29; *M*, pl i. I owe the observations in this and the previous sentence to an unpublished paper by Stephen Behrendt, 'Something in my Eye: Irritants in Blake's Illuminated Texts'.
14. Karl Marx, 'Towards a Critique of Hegel's *Philosophy of Right*', in D. McLellan (ed.), *Karl Marx: Selected Writings* (Oxford 1977), p. 63.
15. *BE*, p. 611; *J* 49:23. See further David Erdman, *Blake: Prophet Against Empire* (Princeton 1954), p. 138f.
16. Jon Mee, *Dangerous Enthusiasm: William Blake and the Culture of Radicalism in the 1790s* (Oxford 1992), p. 184f.
17. *MHH*, pl 27; the verses are adapted in Orc's speech in *A*, pl 8.
18. W. F. Halloran ('*The French Revolution:* Revelation's New Form', in D. V. Erdman and J. E. Grant, eds, *Blake's Visionary Forms Dramatic*, Princeton, NJ 1970, pp. 30–56) maintains that the 'main source' of the poem is the Book of Revelation, though his argument from structure is weaker than that from the use of symbols (harvest, vintage, white cloud and so on); the source is used dialectically, to celebrate the dissolution of the court of heavenly worship of Rev 4.
19. D. Halliburton, 'Blake's *French Revolution:* The *Figura* and Yesterday's News', *S in R* 5 (1966), p. 168.
20. E. P. Thompson, *Witness Against the Beast: William Blake and the Moral Law* (Cambridge 1993), pp. 191–3. On Blake's affinity to the antinomian and Muggletonian traditions, cf. ibid., pp. 91–114.
21. *FZ* vi.237–45. Cf. *FZ* ii.355–74; Rev 1:14.
22. *FZ* viii.266–75. Cf. Rev 17:4f.
23. Mee, p. 70.
24. Ibid., p. 17.
25. Leslie Tannenbaum, *Biblical Tradition in Blake's Early Prophecies: The Great Code of Art* (Princeton, NJ 1982), p. 123. Cf. ibid., pp. 102–5.
26. Harold Bloom, *Blake's Apocalypse: A Study in Poetic Argument* (London 1963), p. 71.
27. *Biblical Tradition*, pp. 43–8.
28. *Blake's Apocalypse*, p. 378f.
29. Ibid., p. 329.
30. *Prophecy and Philosophy*, p. 81.
31. The adoption of this name (from the Babylonian sea-monster) is probably itself a deliberate reversal of Christian typology, in which Rahab is the faithful prostitute of Jericho whose action is a type of Christ's salvation; cf. Bloom, pp. 259f.
32. For example *FZ* i.267f.; *M* 14:42. Cf. Rev 1:20, 5:6.
33. On this plate, see further Morris Eaves, 'The Title-Page of *The Book of Urizen*', in *WBK*, pp. 225–30.
34. *The Book of Ahania*, pl 3. Cf. *FZ* vii.627; *J* 28:13–19.
35. *FZ* i.6; beside these words is written in Greek John 1:14 ('and he dwelt among us'), as in the similar passage about universal love in *FZ* ix.634–6, there is a marginal reference to Eph 3:10. Cf. *M* 14:1–3.

36. For this reason it is unhelpful to speak with Tannenbaum (*Biblical Tradition*, pp. 74–85) of Blake's art as 'centred on the Incarnation' and even built on Augustinian theology; the traditional dualistic doctrine of Incarnation is something Blake rejects and mocks, for example *E*, pls 2 and 3.

37. Cf. Thompson, *Witness*, pp. 153–160; T. J. J. Altizer, *History as Apocalypse* (Albany 1985), pp. 184–207.

38. I owe the observations in these two sentences to an unpublished paper by Angela Esterhammer, 'Calling into Existence: *The Book of Urizen*'.

39. Northrop Frye, *Fearful Symmetry: A Study of William Blake* (Princeton, NJ 1947), pp. 6, 104; Tannenbaum, p. 7.

40. S. L. Carr, 'Illuminated Printing: Toward a Logic of Difference', in Nelson Hilton and T. A. Vogler (eds), *Unnam'd Forms: Blake and Textuality* (Berkeley, CA 1986), p. 182f.

41. Dan Miller, 'Contrary Revelation: *The Marriage of Heaven and Hell*', *S in R* 24 (1985), p. 506.

42. David Erdman, *The Illuminated Blake*, 2nd edn (New York 1992), p. 156; Bloom, p. 175.

7   The Half-Unravelled Web

1. *The Fall of Hyperion*, I.1–18. See p. 1 above.

2. See *Oxford English Dictionary*.

3. See pp. 5–7 above.

4. *Apocalypse*, p. 11.

5. Ibid., pp. 90–8.

6. Ibid., p. 125.

7. See p. 7f. above.

8. C. G. Jung, *Answer to Job* (ET, London 1965), esp. pp. 120–146. *Antwort auf Hiob* was first published in 1952, soon after the papal proclamation of the dogma of the Assumption of the Blessed Virgin Mary, to which much of the book's argument relates.

9. *Answer to Job*, pp. 125, 145.

10. Ibid., p. 135.

11. *Vision of a Just World*, pp. 5–15.

12. Thomas J. J. Altizer, *Genesis and Apocalypse: A Theological Voyage toward Authentic Christianity* (Louisville 1990), p. 176.

13. *Christ: the Christian Experience in the Modern World* (London ET 1980), p. 461.

14. Ibid., p. 462; Schüssler Fiorenza, *Vision of a Just World*, p. 139.

15. Allan Boesak, *Comfort and Protest: Reflections on the Apocalypse of John of Patmos* (Edinburgh 1987), p. 38.

16. Christopher Rowland and Mark Corner, *Liberating Exegesis: The Challenge of Liberation Theology to Biblical Studies* (London 1990), pp. 133, 152f. Cf. Christopher Rowland, *Radical Christianity* (Oxford 1988), p. 80f.

17. Jack T. Sanders, *Ethics in the New Testament* (London 1975), pp. 112–15.

18. Tina Pippin, *Death and Desire: The Rhetoric of Gender in the Apocalypse of John* (Louisville 1992), pp. 98, 105. See also her 'Eros and the End: Reading for Gender in the Apocalypse of John', *Semeia* 59 (1992), pp. 193–209.
19. Jacques Derrida, 'Of an Apocalyptic Tone Recently Adopted in Philosophy', *Semeia* 23 (1982), pp. 63–97.
20. Ibid., p. 76.
21. Ibid., pp. 86, 94.
22. Ibid., p. 87.

Select Bibliography

Manuscripts

British Library, Coleridge Notebooks (1827–34): Add. MSS 47,528 (*NB* 33), 47,529 (*NB* 34), 47,530 (*NB* 35), 47,531 (*NB* 36), 47,532 (*NB* 37), 47,533 (*NB* 38), 47,534 (*NB* 39), 47,535 (*NB* 40), 47,536 (*NB* 41), 47,537 (*NB* 42), 47,538 (*NB* 43), 47,539 (*NB* 44), 47,540 (*NB* 45), 47,541 (*NB* 46), 47,542 (*NB* 47), 47,543 (*NB* 48), 47,544 (*NB* 49), 47,545 (*NB* 50), 47,546 (*NB* 51), 47,547 (*NB* 52), 47,548 (*NB* 53), 47,549 (*NB* 54), 47,550 (*NB* 55).

Glasgow University Library: MS Hunter 398 (16th-cent. French Apocalypse).

King's College Library, Cambridge, Keynes MSS (microfilm copies at Cambridge University Library): MS 1 (Newton: *Tuba Quarta*), MS 3 (Newton: *Irenicum*), MS 5 (Newton: *The Language of the Prophets*), MS 8 (Newton: Articles of Religion)

Unpublished Theses

Buzard, Ina Lipkowitz, 'Romanticism and Biblical Poetics', doctoral dissertation, Columbia University (1991).

Tsuchiya, Kiyoshi, 'Coleridge's Phantom and Fact: Two Natures, Trinitarian Resolution, and the Formation of the Pentad to 1825', doctoral thesis, University of Glasgow (1994).

Yogers, Michael, 'Covenant of the Word: the Bible in William Blake's late Prophetic Poems', doctoral dissertation, University of Washington (1991).

Published Books, Journals and Articles

1. *Works Written Between 1700 and 1834*

Bengel, Johann Albrecht, *Exposition of the Revelation of St John* (ET London 1757; first published 1740).

Allwood, Philip, *A Key to the Revelation of St John the Divine...*, 2 vols (London 1829).

Bicheno, James, *A Word in Season; or, A Call to the Inhabitants of Great Britain, to stand prepared for the Consequences of the Present War* (London 1795).

Bicheno, James, *The Fulfilment of Prophecy farther illustrated by The Signs of the times...* (London 1817).

Bingham, George, *Dissertations, Essays, and Sermons*, 2 vols (London 1804)

(Blake, William,) *The Complete Poetry and Prose of William Blake*, ed. David V. Erdman, rev. edn (New York 1988).

Bloomfield, Samuel, *Critical Digest*, 4 vols (London 1826–28).

(Bowdler, Elizabeth Stuart,) *Practical Observations on the Revelation of St John Written in the Year 1775 by the late Mrs Bowdler* (Bath 1800).

Burke, Edmund, *Reflections on the Revolution in France and on the Proceedings in Certain Societies in London Relative to that Event*, ed. C. C. O'Brien (Harmondsworth 1968; first published 1790).

(Burke, Edmund,) *Writings and Speeches of Edmund Burke*, ed. Paul Langford (Oxford 1981–).

Burke, Edmund, *A Philosophical Inquiry into the Origins of our Ideas of the Sublime and Beautiful*, ed. J. T. Boulton, rev. edn (Oxford 1987).

Butler, Joseph, *The Analogy of Religion Natural and Revealed to the Constitution and Course of Nature*, ed. Steere (London 1857; first published 1736).

Carlyle, Thomas, 'Signs of the Times', in G. B. Tennyson (ed.), *A Carlyle Reader* (Cambridge 1984), pp. 31–54; first published 1829.

Carlyle, Thomas, 'On History', in G. B. Tennyson (ed.), *A Carlyle Reader* (Cambridge 1984), pp. 55–66; first published 1830.

Clarke, J. E., *Dissertation on the Dragon, Beast, and False Prophet, of the Apocalypse...* (London 1814).

Clarke, Samuel, *Paraphrase with Critical Notes* (London 1738).

Clarke, Samuel, *Works*, ed. Hoadly, 4 vols (London 1738).

Coleridge, S. T., *Collected Letters of Samuel Taylor Coleridge*, ed. E. L. Griggs, 6 vols (Oxford 1956-71).

Coleridge, S. T., *Collected Notebooks of Samuel Taylor Coleridge*, ed. Kathleen Coburn, 4 vols (London 1957–).

Coleridge, S. T., *Collected Works of Samuel Taylor Coleridge*, 14 vols (Princeton, NJ: Bollingen Series LXXV 1971–).

Coleridge, S. T., *Confessions of an Enquiring Spirit*, ed. H. St J. Hart (London 1956, first published 1840).

(Coleridge, S. T.,) 'On the Prometheus of Aeschylus', *Transactions of the Royal Society of Literature* 2 (1834), pp. 384–404.

Coleridge, S. T., *Poems*, ed. John Beer (London 1986).

Collins, Anthony, *A Discourse of Free-Thinking, Occasion'd by The Rise and Growth of a Sect call'd Free-Thinkers* (London 1713).

Collins, Anthony, *A Discourse of the Grounds and Reasons of the Christian Religion* (London 1724).

Cooke, William, *The Revelations Translated, and Explained Throughout ... A Copious Introduction, Argument and Conclusion* (Great Yarmouth 1789).

(Cooper, R. Bransby,) *Commentary on the Revelation of St John ... by an Humble Follower of the Pious and Profoundly Learned Joseph Mede B. D.* (London 1833).

Cooper, R. Bransby, *A Translation of Mede's 'Clavis Apocalyptica'* (London 1833).

(Cowper, William,) *The Poems of William Cowper*, ed. J. D. Baird and C. Ryskamp (Oxford 1980–).

Croly, George, *The Apocalypse of St John, or Prophecy of the Rise, Progress and Fall of the Church of Rome; the Inquisition; the Revolution of France; the Universal War; and the Final Triumph of Christianity* (London 1827).

Eichhorn, Johann Gottfried, *Commentarius in Apocalypsin Johannis* (Göttingen 1791).

Evanson, Edward, *A Letter to the Right Reverend the Lord Bishop of Litchfield and Coventry* ... (London 1777).

Faber, George Stanley, *A Dissertation on the Prophecies that have been fulfilled and are now fulfilling, or will hereafter be fulfilled...* (London 1814).

Faber, George Stanley, *The Sacred Calendar of Prophecy...* (London 1828).

Galloway, Joseph, *Brief Commentaries upon such Parts of The Revelation and other Prophecies, as immediately refer to the Present Times...* (London 1802).

Godwin, William, *An Enquiry Concerning Political Justice and its Influence on Morals and Happiness* (Harmondsworth 1976; first published 1793).

Habershon, M., *A Dissertation on the Prophetic Scriptures...* (London 1834).

Hartley, David, *Observations on Man, his Frame, his Duty, and his Expectations,* 5th edn (Bath 1810; 1st edn 1749).

Herder, J. G. von, *Sämmtliche Werke,* ed. Suphan (Berlin 1893).

Hurd, Richard, *An Introduction to the Study of the Prophecies Concerning the Christian Church, and, in particular, Concerning the Church of Papal Rome,* 4 vols, 4th edn (London 1776; delivered as Warburton Lectures 1772).

Hurd, Richard, *Letters on Chivalry and Romance with the Third Elizabethan Dialogue,* ed. E. Morley (London 1911; first published 1759).

Irving, Edward, *Babylon and Infidelity Foredoomed of God: A Discourse on the Prophecies of Daniel and the Apocalypse which relate to these Latter times, and until the Second Advent,* 2 vols (Glasgow 1826).

Irving, Edward, *The Prophetical Works of Edward Irving,* 2 vols (London 1867).

Irving, Edward, *The Signs of the Times* (London 1829).

Johnson, Samuel, *The History of Rasselas, Prince of Abyssinia,* ed. R. W. Chapman (Oxford 1927; first published 1759).

Johnston, Bryce, *A Commentary on the Revelation of St John...,* 2 vols (Edinburgh 1794).

Keats, John, *The Complete Poems,* ed. John Barnard, rev. edn (Harmondsworth 1977).

Kershaw, James, *An Essay on the Principal Parts of the Book of the Revelations; in a Series of Dialogues between Didascalos and Phylotheos,* 2 vols (Stockton 1780).

Kett, Henry, *History the Interpreter of Prophecy,* 3 vols (London 1799).

Law, William, *A Serious Call to a Devout and Holy Life Adapted to the State and Condition of all Orders of Christians,* ed. J. H. Overton (London 1898; first published 1728).

Lewelyn, William, *An Exposition of the Revelation* (Gloucester 1792).

(Locke, John,) *The Works of John Locke* (London 1823).

Lowman, Moses, *A Paraphrase and Notes on the Revelation of St John* (London 1737).

Lowth, Robert, *Lectures on the Sacred Poetry of the Hebrews,* trans. G. Gregory, 4th edn (London, 1839; first published 1753).

(Mace, Daniel,) *The New Testament in Greek and English, Containing the Original Text Corrected from the Authority of the Most Authentic Manuscripts: and a New Version ... with Notes and Various Readings* (London 1729).

Mackintosh, Sir James, *Vindiciae Gallicae* (London 1791).

Mayer, Lewis, *A Hint to England; or, A Prophetic Mirror ... proving Bonaparte to be the Beast that arose out of the Earth* (London 1803).

Michaelis, Johann David, *Introduction to the New Testament ... translated from the Fourth Edition of the German ... by Herbert Marsh* (Cambridge 1801).

The Morning Watch, or Quarterly Journal on Prophecy, and Theological Review, 7 vols (London 1829–33).

Murray, Richard, *An Introduction to the Study of the Apocalypse ... Selected chiefly from the best and most approved writers on the subject* (Dublin 1826).

Newton, Sir Isaac, *The Chronology of Ancient Kingdoms Amended* (Dublin 1728).

Newton, Sir Isaac, *Observations upon the Prophecies of Daniel and the Apocalypse of St John* (London 1733).

(Newton, Sir Isaac,) *Sir Isaac Newton: Theological Manuscripts*, ed. H. McLachlan (Liverpool 1950).

Newton, Thomas, *Dissertations on the Prophecies, which have remarkably been fulfilled and at this time are fulfilling in the World*, 3 vols (London 1826; first published 1754–8).

Paine, Thomas, *Common Sense*, ed. I. Kramnick (Harmondsworth 1976; first published 1776).

Paine, Thomas, *Rights of Man*, ed. Eric Foner (Harmondsworth 1984; first published 1791–2).

Pope, Alexander, *Works*, ed. P. Rogers (Oxford 1983).

Price, Richard, *Political Writings*, ed. D. O. Thomas (Cambridge 1991).

(Priestley, Joseph,) *The Theological and Miscellaneous Works of Joseph Priestley*, ed. J. T. Rutt, 12 vols (Hackney 1816–31).

Pyle, Thomas, *Paraphrase, with Notes, on the Revelation of St John* (London 1795; first published 1735).

Reader, Thomas, *An Inquiry, whether Popery is a proper Subject of Toleration, in Protestant States* (London 1783?).

Reader, Thomas, *Israel's Salvation: or, An Account from the Prophecies of Scripture of the Grand Events which await the Jews, to the End of Time* (Taunton 1788).

Reader, Thomas, *Of the Time of the General Judgment* (Taunton 1785).

Reader, Thomas, *Remarks on the Prophetic Parts of the Revelation of St John; especially the Three Last Trumpets* (London 1778).

Reader, Thomas, *Remarks on the Three First Chapters of the Revelation of St John...* (Taunton 1785).

Rudd, Sayer, *An Essay towards a New Explication of the Doctrines of the Resurrection, Millennium, and Judgment, being the Substance of several Discourses on the Twentieth Chapter of the Revelation of St John* (London 1734).

Shelley, Mary, *Frankenstein or the Modern Prometheus*, ed. M. Hindle (Harmondsworth 1992; first published 1818).

(Shelley, Percy Bysshe), *Shelley's Poetry and Prose*, ed. D. H. Reiman and S. B. Powers (New York 1977).

Simpson, David, *A Plea for Religion and the Sacred Writings; Addressed to the Disciples of Thomas Paine, and to Wavering Christians of every Persuasion...* (Liverpool 1812; first published in 1797).

Swedenborg, Emanuel, *The Apocalypse Revealed*, 3 vols (Boston 1907; first published 1766).

Swedenborg, Emanuel, *The True Christian Religion*, 3 vols (Boston 1907; first published 1771).

Swift, Jonathan, *Prose Works*, ed. H. Davis (Oxford 1939–68).

Thomson, James, *Poems*, ed. James Sambrook, 2 vols (Oxford 1981–86).

Thruston, Frederic, *England Safe and Triumphant; Or, Researches into the Apocalyptic Little Book and Prophecies, Connected and Synchronical* (Coventry 1812).

Tindal, Matthew, *Christianity as old as the Creation, or, The Gospel a Republication of the Religion of Nature* (London 1731).

Toland, John, *Christianity Not Mysterious; Or, a Treatise Shewing, That there is nothing in the GOSPEL Contrary to REASON, Nor Above it: And that no Christian Doctrine can be properly call'd A MYSTERY* (London 1702).

Towers, J. L., *Illustrations of Prophecy...* ed. W. Vint (Airedale 1828; first published 1796).

Tracts printed and published by the United Society for Promoting Christian Knowledge and the Practice of Virtue (1791).

Trollope, William, *Analecta Theologica*, 6 vols (London 1830–35).

Vivian, Thomas, *The Book of the Revelation of St John the Divine Explained...* (Plymouth 1785).

(Walmesley, Charles,) *The General History of the Christian Church, from her Birth to her final triumphant state in Heaven, chiefly deduced from the Apocalypse of St John...* by Sig. Pastorini (Cork 1820; first published in 1771).

(Wesley, Charles,) *Representative Verse of Charles Wesley*, ed. F. Baker (London 1962).

Wesley, John, *A Collection of Hymns for the Use of the People called Methodists*, rev. edn (London 1876).

Wesley, John, *Explanatory Notes upon the New Testament*, 2nd edn (London 1757)

Wesley, John, *Sermons on Several Occasions*, 2 vols (London 1825; first published 1771).

Whiston, William, *An Essay on the Revelation of Saint John, So far as concerns the Past and Present Times...* (Cambridge 1706).

(Whiston, William,) *Memoirs of the Life and Writings of Mr William Whiston, Containing Memoirs of Several of his Friends also. Written by Himself*, 2nd edn (London 1753; first edn published 1749).

Whitby, Daniel, *A Paraphrase and Commentary on the New Testament in Two Volumes*, 7th edn (London 1760; first edn published 1700).

Wollstonecraft, Mary, *Political Writings*, ed. Janet Todd (Oxford 1994).

Wollstonecraft, Mary, *A Wollstonecraft Anthology*, ed. Janet Todd (Cambridge 1989).

Woodhouse, J. C., *Annotations on the Apocalypse ... for the Use of Students in Prophetical Scripture* (London 1828).

Woodhouse, J. C., *The Apocalypse ... with Notes, Critical and Explanatory* (London 1805).

Wordsworth, William, *Poetical Works* ed. E. de Selincourt and Helen Darbishire, 5 vols (Oxford 1940–49).

Wordsworth, William, *The Prelude: 1799, 1805, 1850*, ed. Jonathan Wordsworth, M. H. Abrams and Stephen Gill (New York 1979).

2. *Other Published Works*

Abrams, M. H., 'Apocalypse: theme and variations', in *AERTL*, pp. 342–68.
Abrams, M. H., *The Mirror and the Lamp: Romantic Theory and the Critical Tradition* (Oxford 1953).
Abrams, M. H., *Natural Supernaturalism: Tradition and Revolution in Romantic Literature* (New York 1971).
Altizer, Thomas J. J., *Genesis and Apocalypse* (Louisville 1990).
Altizer, Thomas J. J., *History as Apocalypse* (Albany 1985).
Bauckham, Richard, *The Theology of the Book of Revelation* (Cambridge 1993).
Bauckham, Richard, *Tudor Apocalypse: Sixteenth-Century Apocalypticism, Millenarianism and the English Reformation* (Sutton Courtenay 1978).
Bloom, Harold, *Blake's Apocalypse: A Study in Poetic Argument* (London 1963).
Boesak, Allan, *Comfort and Protest: Reflections on the Apocalypse of John of Patmos* (Edinburgh 1987).
Boulton, J. T., *The Language of Politics in the Age of Wilkes and Burke* (London 1963).
Brady, David, *The Contribution of British Writers between 1560 and 1830 to the Interpretation of Rev 13:16–18 (Beiträge zur Geschichte der biblischen Exegese* 27: Tübingen 1983).
Butler, Marilyn, *Burke, Paine, Godwin and the Revolution Controversy* (Cambridge 1984).
Charles, R. H., *A Critical and Exegetical Commentary on the Revelation of St John*, 2 vols (Edinburgh 1920).
Charles, R. H., *Studies in the Apocalypse* (Edinburgh 1913).
Cohn, Norman, *The Pursuit of the Millennium: Revolutionary Messianism in the Middle Ages and its Bearing on Modern Totalitarian Movements* (London 1957).
De Man, Paul, *Allegories of Reading* (New Haven, CT 1979).
Derrida, Jacques, 'Of an Apocalyptic Tone Recently Adopted in Philosophy', *Semeia* 23 (1982) pp. 63–97.
Elliott, E. B., *Horae Apocalypticae*, 4 vols (London 1847).
Erdman, David V., *Blake, Prophet Against Empire* (Princeton, NJ 1954).
Erdman, David V., *The Illuminated Blake*, 2nd edn (New York 1992).
Farrer, Austin, *A Rebirth of Images: The Making of St John's Apocalypse* (London 1949).
Farrer, Austin, *The Revelation of St John the Divine* (Oxford 1964).
Firth, Katharine, *The Apocalyptic Tradition in Reformation Britain 1530–1645* (Oxford 1979).
Frei, Hans, *The Eclipse of Biblical Narrative: A Study in Eighteenth and Nineteenth Century Hermeneutics* (New Haven, CT 1974).
Fruchtman, Jack, 'The Apocalyptic Politics of Richard Price and Joseph Priestley: A Study in Late Eighteenth-Century English Republican Millenarianism', *Transactions of the American Philosophical Society* LXXIII.4 (1983).
Garrett, Clarke, *Respectable Folly: Millenarians and the French Revolution in France and England* (Baltimore, MD 1975).
Harding, Anthony John, *Coleridge and the Inspired Word* (Montreal 1985).

Harrison, J. F. C., *The Second Coming: Popular Millenarianism 1780–1850* (London 1979).

Hill, Christopher, *The English Bible and the Seventeenth-Century Revolution* (Harmondsworth 1993).

Hoagwood, Terence Allan, *Prophecy and the Philosophy of Mind: Traditions of Blake and Shelley* (Alabama 1985).

Hole, Robert, *Pulpits, Politics and Public Order in England 1760–1832* (Cambridge 1989).

Jones, J. Gwilym, *William Williams Pantycelyn* (Cardiff 1969).

Jung, C. G., *Answer to Job* (ET, London 1965; first published 1952).

Kermode, Frank, *The Sense of an Ending: Studies in the Theory of Fiction* (Oxford 1967).

Korshin, P. J., 'Queuing and Waiting: the Apocalypse in England, 1660–1750', in *AERTL*, pp. 240–65

Korshin, P. J., *Typologies in England 1650–1820* (Princeton, NJ 1982).

Kucich, Greg, 'Ironic Apocalypse in Romanticism and the French Revolution', in *RER*, pp. 67–88.

Laboucheix, Henri, *Richard Price, théoricien de la révolution américaine, le philosophe et le sociologue, le pamphlétaire et l'orateur* (Paris 1970).

Lawrence, D. H., *Apocalypse* (Harmondsworth 1974; first published 1931).

Leask, Nigel, *The Politics of Imagination in Coleridge's Critical Thought* (London 1988).

Lohmeyer, Ernst, *Die Offenbarung des Johannes*, 3rd edn, *Handbuch zum N.T.* (Tübingen 1970; first edn 1926).

Lohse, Eduard, *Die Offenbarung des Johannes (Das N.T. Deutsch)* (Göttingen 1979).

Manuel, F. E., *The Religion of Isaac Newton* (Oxford 1974).

Maurice, F. D., *Lectures on the Apocalypse* (Cambridge 1861).

McCalman, Iain, *Radical Underworld: Prophets, Revolutionaries and Pornographers in London 1795–1840* (Cambridge 1988).

Mee, Jon, *Dangerous Enthusiasm: William Blake and the Culture of Radicalism in the 1790s* (Oxford 1992).

Morgan, Derec Llwyd, *The Great Awakening in Wales* (ET, London 1988).

Oliphant, M. O. W., *The Life of Edward Irving* (London 1862).

Oliver, W. H., *Prophets and Millennialists: The Uses of Biblical Prophecy in England from the 1790s to the 1840s* (Auckland 1978).

Paley, Morton D., *The Apocalyptic Sublime* (New Haven, CT 1986).

Paley, Morton D., 'William Blake, The Prince of the Hebrews, and the Woman Clothed with the Sun', in *WBK*, pp. 260–93

Pattison, Mark, 'Tendencies of Religious Thought in England, 1688–1750', in *Essays and Reviews* (London 1860).

Perkins, Anne Marie, *Coleridge's Philosophy: The Logos as Unifying Theme* (Oxford 1994).

Pippin, Tina, *Death and Desire: The Rhetoric of Gender in the Apocalypse of John* (Louisville 1992).

Prickett, Stephen, *Words and* The Word: *Language, Poetics and Biblical Interpretation* (Cambridge 1986).

Reventlow, Henning Graf, *The Authority of the Bible and the Rise of the Modern World* (ET, London 1984).

Rowland, Christopher, *The Open Heaven: A Study of Apocalyptic in Judaism and Early Christianity* (London 1982).

Rupp, Gordon, *Religion in England 1688–1791* (Oxford 1986).

Schüssler Fiorenza, Elisabeth, *The Book of Revelation: Justice and Judgement* (Philadelphia 1985).

Schüssler Fiorenza, Elisabeth, *Revelation: Vision of a Just World* (Proclamation Commentaries: Minneapolis 1991).

Shaffer, E. S., *'Kubla Khan' and* The Fall of Jerusalem: *The Mythological School in Biblical Criticism and Secular Literature 1770–1880* (Cambridge 1975).

Shelley, Bryan, *Shelley and Scripture: The Interpreting Angel* (Oxford 1994).

Smith, Olivia, *The Politics of Language 1791–1819* (Oxford 1984).

Stephen, Sir Leslie, *English Thought in the Eighteenth Century*, 2 vols (London 1876).

Strachan, Gordon, *The Pentecostal Theology of Edward Irving* (London 1973).

Stuart, Moses, *Commentary on the Apocalypse*, 2 vols (London 1845).

Sweet, John, *Revelation* (London: SCM Pelican Commentaries 1979).

Swete, H. B., *The Apocalypse of St John*, 2nd edn (London 1907).

Sys, Jacques, 'L'espace apocalyptique', *Graphè* 1 (1992), pp. 79–104.

Tannenbaum, Leslie, *Biblical Tradition in Blake's Early Prophecies: The Great Code of Art* (Princeton, NJ 1982).

Thomas, D. O., *The Honest Mind: The Thought and Work of Richard Price* (Oxford 1977).

Thompson, E. P., *Witness Against the Beast: William Blake and the Moral Law* (Cambridge 1993).

Tuveson, Ernest Lee, *Millennium and Utopia: A Study in the Background of the Idea of Progress* (Berkeley, CA 1949).

Wainwright, Arthur, *Mysterious Apocalpse: Interpreting the Book of Revelation* (Nashville, TE 1993).

Wasserman, Earl R., *Shelley's 'Prometheus Unbound': A Critical Reading* (Baltimore, MD 1965).

Index

Note: principal references are indicated in *italics*.

Abrams, M. H.   36, 105, 132, 138–9,
    174–5, 219 n7, 228 n27
Addison, Joseph   58
Aeschylus   172–3, 174, 175
Albury House group   154
allegory   11–14
Allwood, Philip   105
Altizer, Thomas   214, 235 n37
American Revolution   109–10, 125
apocalypse, genre of   8–10
Apostolical Constitutions   64
Arianism   61–5
Augustine, St   12, 31, 76, 139, 221
    n30, 223 n51

Babcock, W. S.   221 n26
Babylon, identity of   119, 129, 155,
    185–7, 194–5
Bacon, Francis   46, 105, 179, 185,
    198
Baker, Frank   227 n17
Bale, John   31–2
Banville, John   22
Barbauld, Mrs   98
Barr, David   27–8, 222 n46,
    223 n57
Bauckham, Richard   3, 32, 221 n20,
    224 n4
Beast, identity of   32, 78, 92–3, 98,
    100–3, 195
Beckwith, Isbon T.   2
Beer, John   233 n36
Beethoven, Ludwig van   23
Behrendt, Stephen   234 n13
Bengel, Johann Albrecht   51, 76
Bicheno, James   95–7, 98, 105–6,
    119–20, 128–9, 133

Blake, William   132, 143, 151,
    180–208, 210, 214, 216, 217
    America   184–5, 188–9
    and Bible   180, 187–91, 204–5
    and death of God   175, 199–200
    and deconstruction of Revelation
        193–200
    and Jesus   187, 188, 206
    and 'Minute Particulars'   191–2,
        206
    and 'State religion'   115, 184–7,
        205
    'The Angel of the Revelation'
        21, 208
    The Book of Urizen   186, 196, 198,
        201, 207
    Europe   185, 186, 192, 193, 196–7
    'The Everlasting Gospel'   187
    The French Revolution   184, 208
    Jerusalem   182, 185, 191, 197–8,
        207–8
    The Marriage of Heaven and Hell
        182, 199, 203–4, 205
    Milton   181, 186, 208
    on Newton   47, 85, 181, 198
    on nature of prophecy   180–2,
        193
    on Swedenborg   190
    Songs of Experience   185, 199
    Tiriel   184
    Vala or *The Four Zoas*   181, 185,
        186, 202, 206
Bloch, Ernst   24, 222 n45
Bloom, Harold   29, 190–1, 192, 206,
    234 n31
Bloomfield, Samuel   220 n9
Blount, Charles   59

Böcher, Otto 2
Boehme, Jakob 72, 162, 169, 233 n36
Boesak, Allan 215
book, symbol of 25–6, 201–5
Boring, M. Eugene 221 n18, 222 n39
Boulton, J. T. 125, 229 n16
Bousset, Willhelm 2
Bowdler, Elizabeth Stuart 56
Boyarin, Daniel 14, 222 n36
Boyer, Paul 220 n5
Boyle, Robert 46
Brady, David 3, 36, 225 n46, 229 n29
Brightman, Thomas 32–4, 68, 102
Brothers, Richard 94–5, 99–100, 133
Bruns, Gerald 13, 222 n35
Buchan, Mrs 99
Bultmann, Rudolf 7–8
Bunyan, John 33, 192
Burdon, Christopher 221 n31
Burke, Edmund 81, 101, 108, 111, 121–5, 126, 192, 195
Burnet, Thomas 227 n8
Butler, Joseph 60, 69–71, 72, 90
Butler, Marilyn 93, 228 n13
Butlin, Martin 222 n43

Caird, George 23
Calvin, Jean 7–8, 31, 39, 78
Cambrai Apocalypse 20
Carlyle, Thomas 232 n19
Carr, S. L. 205
Carroll, R. P. 220 n13
Catholic Apostolic Church 64, 153–4, 158
Charles, R. H. 2, 211
Christianson, G. E. 225 n41
chronology, Revelation as key to 48–54, 90–1
chronometer, British naval 38, 50, 90
Church of England, depicted in Revelation 102–3
'church-historical' interpretation 31–7
Clark, R. T. 228 n32

Clarke, J. E. 103
Clarke, Samuel 44, 47, 53, 57, 59, 61, 72, 220 n9
Cohn, Norman 6
Coleridge, Edward 155
Coleridge, Hartley 172, 174
Coleridge, S. T. 22–3, 65, 73, 88, 114–19, 126, 128, 129–33, 134–73, 175, 180, 208, 209–11, 229 n34
Aids to Reflection 134, 149, 155, 159, 161
and Bible 134–5, 160–73
and Eichhorn 143–52, 158, 169–70
and hell 160–8
and Irving 152–61, 166
and Wordsworth 136–43, 151
as millennialist 114–19
as preacher 115–17, 161
Confessions of an Enquiring Spirit 134–5, 150, 157, 161, 168, 171
conversation poems 130–2
'Dejection: An Ode' 136, 139–40, 142–3
'France: An Ode' 130
'Kubla Khan' 1, 136–40, 142–3, 173, 210
Lay Sermons 145–6, 149–51, 160, 179
Lectures on Revealed Religion 116
'Ode to the Departing Year' 131
on symbol and allegory 149–52
On the Constitution of the Church and State 158–9
'On the Prometheus of Aeschylus' 172–3, 174
'Religious Musings' 94, 114, 115–19, 130–1, 138, 167
'The Rime of the Ancient Mariner' 138, 142–3
scientific interests 85, 114–15
'To William Wordsworth' 140–2
unitarianism 61, 114
The Watchman 117–9, 130, 136
Collins, Adela Yarbro 221 n22
Collins, Anthony 39, 54, 60, 63
Collins, J. J. 220 n12

Cooke, William   84–5, 86
Cooper, R. Bransby   34–5, 103–4
Corner, Mark   215
Cowper, William   80
Croly, George   104–5, 151, 157, 171
Cullmann, Oscar   228 n1

Daniel   48, 50, 91, 135, 155–6
Dante   25
de Lubac, H.   221 n22
de Man, Paul   24
Deism   42–5, 60
Derrida, Jacques   4, 216–17
Descartes, René   42
Dionysius of Alexandria   11, 36
Doddridge, Philip   57
Donnelly, F. K.   229 n16
drama, Revelation as   84, 86, 144–6, 157–8
Drummond, A. L.   232 n21
Dürer, Albrecht   19–21

Eaves, Morris   234 n33
Eichhorn, J. G.   86, 137, *144–52*, 156, 169–70, 209
Elliott, E. B.   2, 36–7, 104
England (as subject of Revelation)   32, 101–3
English Revolution   33, 37, 99, 102
Erdman, David   206, 234 n15
Esterhammer, Angela   235 n38
Eusebius of Caesarea   12, 221 n23
Evans, Mary   99
Evanson, Edward   61, 63–4
Eyre, Mrs   99
Ezekiel   150–1, 160, 181, 197–8

Faber, G. S.   36, *104–5*, 151, 209
Farrer, Austin   10, 15, 16, 18, 23, 223 n56
Fast sermons   93–5, 113–14
Ferber, Michael   175, 177, 233 n1
Ferguson, J. F.   225 n30
Firth, Katharine   3, 32–3, 34, 220 n6, 223 n3, 224 n4
Flaubert, Gustave   22
Flaxmer, Sarah   99
Flower, Benjamin   230 n54

Foxe, John   31–2
Frederick II, Emperor   37
Fredriksen, Paula   12, 221 n26
Frei, Hans   61, 85–6, 88, 225 n46
French Revolution   *91–133*
   and apocalyptic rhetoric   119–28
   and British government   94–5, 98
   and fragmentation of interpretation   132–3
   as evidence of progress   110–12, 127
   as experience of immediacy   89, 99
   as rhetorical situation   30, 91–2, 123
   as sign of the end   100–3
Frere, Hatley   154
Fruchtman, Jack   109, 228 n9, 230 n38
Frye, Northrop   204
Fulford, Tim   233 n43
Furniss, Tom   231 n59

Gager, John   223 n61
Galloway, Joseph   101
Garrett, Clarke   3, 91–2, 224 n16, 228 n11, 229 n19, 230 n46
George III   184
Gilfillan, George   152
'Glorious Revolution' (1688)   60, 67, 97
Godwin, William   115, 117, *128*, 129
Goethe, J. W. von   85
Gosse, Edmund   224 n15
Gosse, Mrs   37
Gothicism   82, 85
Goulder, M. D.   223 n58
grammar of Revelation   18, 24
Gregory IX, Pope   37
Grotius, Hugo   36

Hades   160–8
Halhed, Richard   99
Halliburton, D.   184–5
Halloran, W. F.   234 n18
Hamburg Apocalypse   20
Händel, G. F.   80–1

Handelman, Susan 222 n33
Hanson, P. D. 220 n13
Hanson, R. P. C. 221 n22, 223 n51
Harding, Anthony John 219 n7
Harris, Howel 225 n49
Harrison, J. F. C. 3, 99, 224 n16, 229 n16
Hartley, David 31, 58, *106–8*, 112–13, 118, 119, 126
'heart-religion' 72–80
Hegel, G. W. F. 214
Herder, J. G. von 81, 85, *86–9*, 90–1, 137, 169
'higher criticism' 85–6, 143–51
Hill, Christopher 33, 36, 219 n4, 224 n9, 229 n27
Hippolytus of Rome 221 n27
Hoagwood, T. A. 181, 194, 219 n7, 233 n6
Hobbes, Thomas 44
Hole, Robert 229 n22
Holmes, Richard 115, 232 n14
Horsley, Samuel 100
Hume, David 70
Hurd, Richard 38, 63, *81–3*, 85, 86, 228 n13
Hurtgen, John 26

Irenaeus 11
Irving, Edward 65, *152–60*, 166, 209, 216

Jasper, David 142–3, 223 n63
Joachim of Fiore 31–2, 216
John of Patmos
  and monstrous imagery 122
  as bard 137–9
  as prophet 9–11, 181
  as scribe 25
  as seer 135, 214
Johnson, Samuel 67, 85
Johnston, Bryce 83–4
Jones, J. Gwilym 227 n21
Jones, Sir William 85
Josephus 89
Judas Iscariot 5–7, 213, 217–18
Jump, Harriet Devine 127
Jung, C. G. 212–13, 217
Justin Martyr 11

kabbalah, kabbalists 162, 169, 172–3
kairos 91
Kant, Immanuel 73, 85, 135, 169, 216–17
Keach, Benjamin 49
Keats, John 1, 210
Kermode, Frank 5–6, 29
Kershaw, James 51–2
Kett, Henry 100–1
Knights, L. C. 232 n20
Knox, T. R. 231 n65
Koch, Klaus 220 n11
Korshin, P. J. 36, 225 n41
Kundera, Milan 220 n2
Küng, Hans 222 n49

Laboucheix, Henri 111, 125
Lacunza, Manuel 157–8
lake of fire 163–7, 195–6
landscape gardening 45
Law, William 65, 72–4
Lawrence, D. H. 5–6, 25, *211–13*, 216, 217
Lawton, David 10
Leask, Nigel 233 n44
Leibniz 42, 50
Lessing, Gottfried 136
Lévi-Strauss, Claude 27
liberation theology 215
Lindsey, Hal 6
Lindsey, Theophilus 112
liturgy 26–9
Locke, John *42–3*, 46, 57, 58, 60, 67, 112, 185, 198, 226 n57
Lohmeyer, Ernst 16, 19
Louis XVI 98, 101
Lowman, Moses 37–8, *54–7*, 69, 77
Lowth, Robert *81*, 85, 86, 124, 169, 187
Luther, Martin 7, 31, 32, 33, 75, 76, 88, 135, 143, 147, 153, 159, 184

Mace, Daniel 36
Mahler, Gustav 23
Manuel, F. E. 47, 50, 58, 61
Martin, John 21
Marx, Karl 105, 182, 187
Mather, Increase 95, 228 n13
Maurice, F. D. 232 n22

Mayer, Lewis   101–2
Mazzaferri, F. D.   9–10
Mazzucco, Clementina   221 n24
McCalman, Iain   99, 126–7
McLachlan, H.   225 n40, 226 n64
Mede, Joseph   34–5, 39, 53, 56, 68,
    71, 84, 181
Mee, Jon   182, 187, 188
Memling, Hans   21
Messiaen, Olivier   223 n53
Methodism   72, 74–80, 85, 99, 100,
    108
Michaelis, J. D.   86, 116, 143–4, 169
midrash   14–16
millenarianism   99
Millennium
    as culmination of progress
        105–19
    as era of liberty   98
    date of   51–2
    in early Christianity   11–12
    length of   75, 113
Miller, Dan   205
Milton, John   33–4, 82, 119, 122,
    162
Money, John   112
Montagu, Basil   153, 156
morality, usefulness of Revelation
    for   54–60
More, Henry   49, 147
Morgan, Derec Llwyd   225 n49,
    227 n20
Morning Watch   154
Moses   184
Moyise, Steve   222 n37
Muggletonians   99
Murrin, Michael   224 n11
music   22–4
myth, Revelation as   16–18

Napoleon Bonaparte   95, 102–3
narrative, Revelation as   16–18
necessitarianism   106–8, 116–17,
    119
new heaven/new earth   177
Newton, Sir Isaac   31, 36, 37–9, 41,
    42, 46–51, 58, 61–2, 65, 67, 71,
    85, 90, 110, 112, 119, 208, 216
Newton, John   80

Newton, Thomas   40–1

Oliphant, Margaret   153–4
Oliver, W. H.   3, 104, 129, 228 n5,
    229 n14, 230 n46, 232 n22
Ong, Walter   222 n45
oral enactment, Revelation as   22,
    25
Origen   11–14, 139, 171, 223 n51
Ossian   86
Owen, Robert   105

Paine, Thomas   115, 116, 122–3,
    125–7, 129, 180, 184
Paley, Morton D.   130, 222 n43,
    229 n21
Paley, William   116
Pantycelyn, William Williams
    79–80
Parker, T. H. L.   220 n7
Pascal, Blaise   67, 73, 74
Pastorini, Signor   see Walmesley
Patrides, C. A.   2
Pattison, Mark   41, 43
Paul, St   139, 148, 159, 163, 184
Peacock, Thomas Love   179
Pépin, Jean   221 n22
Perkins, Anne Marie   233 n36
'physico-theology'   45–7, 57–9
Piozzi, Hester Thrale   103
Pippin, Tina   215
Pitt, William   98
Plato   179
poetry, Bible as   80–9
Poland, L. M.   222 n32
Pope, Alexander   47, 68–9
Porton, G. G.   222 n36
Price, Richard   93, 94, 97, 108–12,
    121, 123–5, 126
Prickett, Stephen   227 n25
Priestley, Joseph   31, 58, 61, 62, 65,
    93, 94–5, 106, 112–14, 119, 126,
    128, 129, 133
Prigent, Pierre   223 n58
Prometheus   172–3, 174–9
prophecy, definitions of   10–14,
    90–1
providence, Revelation as evidence
    of   39–47, 96–7

purity, Revelation as call to   60–5
Pyle, Thomas   39–41, 51, 57, 60, 77,
    228 n13

Rad, Gerhard von   220 n11
Rahme, Mary   232 n20
Ray, John   45, 58
Ranters   99
Reader, Thomas   52
realised eschatology   27–8, 77
Reformation   31–3, 60–1, 67, 112
Reventlow, Henning Graf
    226 n52
Reynolds, Sir Joshua   191
rhetoric, Revelation as   24–9,
    119–28
Rousseau, Jean-Jacques   85
Rowland, Christopher   9, 215, 220
    n13, 223 n60
Rudd, Sayer   92
Rupp, Gordon   227 n11

Sanders, Jack   215
Schellenberg, Karl   20
Schelling, F. W. J. von   169
Schillebeeckx, Edward   215
Schleiermacher, Friedrich   7–8, 31
Schüssler Fiorenza, Elisabeth
    27–8, 30, 91, 214, 215, 222 n39
Shaffer, E. S.   3, 137–8
Shaftesbury, 2nd Earl of   45
Shakers   99
Shakespeare, William   82, 122
Shelley, Bryan   175, 179, 219 n7,
    233 n9
Shelley, Mary   174
Shelley, Percy Bysshe   143, 174–9,
    180, 208
    and death of God   178
    and Jesus   176–7, 179
    A Defence of Poetry   179
    Epipsychidion   177
    Hellas   178
    The Mask of Anarchy   177, 178
    'Ode to the West Wind'   180
    Prometheus Unbound   174–9, 181
    Queen Mab   177, 178
    respect for Bible   174–5
    scientific interests   85

'The Triumph of Life'   178–9,
    233 n2
Shepherd, Massey H.   223 n58
Short, H. L.   230 n39
Smith, Olivia   231 n62
South, Robert   2
Southcott, Joanna   100
Southey, Robert   115–17
Spence, Thomas, and Spenceans
    100, 127
Spenser, Edmund   82
Spinoza, Baruch   39, 44, 136
Steiner, George   23
Steinhauser, Kenneth   221 n25
Stephen, Sir Leslie   42
Stone, M. E.   220 n14
Strachan, Gordon   232 n23
Stuart, Moses   2, 87, 225 n46
Swedenborg, Emanuel   170, 172,
    190–1
Sweet, John   20
Swiatecka, M. Jadwiga   232 n20
Swift, Jonathan   67–8, 72
Sys, Jacques   28

Tannenbaum, Leslie   189–90, 204,
    219 n7, 235 n36
Taverner, John   223 n53
Tertullian   11
Thelwall, John   116, 117
Thomas, D. O.   230 n40
Thompson, E. P.   185, 224 n16, 229
    n18, 235 n37
Thomson, James   45–7, 58–9, 60,
    67, 109
Thruston, Frederic   102
Tindal, Matthew   44–5, 59–60
Todd, Ruthven   222 n44
Toland, John   43, 60
Towers, Joseph   97–9
Tree of Life   198–9
Trollope, William   220 n9
trumpets (of Revelation)   175–6,
    196–7
Tsuchiya, Kyoshi   231 n1
Tudor, John   154
Turner, J. M. W.   21
Tuveson, Ernest Lee   3, 38, 223 n3,
    224 n9, 225 n33, 227 n15

Tyconius 12–13, 31

Unitarianism 108

van der Meer, Frederick 3, 222 n42
Vanni, Ugo 223 n58
Vico, Giambattista 85
Victorinus of Pettau 221 n27
Vivian, Thomas 92–3
vision, Revelation as 18–21

Wainwright, Arthur 3, 223 n2, 225
    n46
Walmesley, Bishop (Signor
    Pastorini) 36
Washington, George 184
Wassermann, Earl R. 233 n3
Watson, Richard 180, 204
Wesley, Charles 74, 77–9, 91
Wesley, John 51, 65, 74–7, 90, 113

West, Benjamin 21
Westfall, R. S. 225 n42
Whiston, William 37–9, 51, 52–5,
    58, 61–5, 67, 69, 86
Whitby, Daniel 8, 31, 220 n9
Whitefield, George 74
Whitman, Jon 14
Wilder, Amos 25
Wiles, Maurice 225 n44, 226 n72
Willey, Basil 70, 225 n33, 230 n38
Williams, William *see* Pantycelyn
Wittreich, Joseph 3
Wollstonecraft, Mary 127–8, 129
Wordsworth, William 47, 132,
    136–43, 151, 228 n2

Yogers, Michael 219 n7
Young, Frances 221 n31

Zwingli, Huldrych 7